ANGER, AND BEYOND

ANGER,

NEW YORK

AND BEYOND

THE NEGRO WRITER
IN THE UNITED STATES

Edited and with an Introduction

by HERBERT HILL

HARPER & ROW, PUBLISHERS

Grateful acknowledgment is extended to the following for permission to reprint material:

Lines from "To Midnight Nan at Leroy's" in *The Weary Blues* by Langston Hughes, copyright 1926 by Alfred A. Knopf, Inc., and renewed 1954 by Langston Hughes; reprinted by permission of the publisher. "Lift Ev'ry Voice and Sing" used by permission of Edward B. Marks Music Corporation. Eight lines of verse from "Fifty Years" in *St. Peter Relates an Incident* by James Weldon Johnson, copyright 1917, 1921, 1935 by James Weldon Johnson, 1962 by Grace Nail Johnson; reprinted by permission of The Viking Press, Inc. The sonnet "If We Must Die" by Claude McKay reprinted by permission of the publisher, Bookman Associates, Inc. "The Poet" by Melvin B. Tolson, copyright 1944 by Dodd, Mead & Company, Inc.; reprinted by permission of the publisher. Scene from the play *Purlie Victorious* reprinted by permission of Ossie Davis and Samuel French, Inc. Excerpt from *12 Million Black Voices* by Richard Wright, published by Viking Press, copyright 1941 by Richard Wright; reprinted by permission of Paul R. Reynolds, Inc. Excerpts from *Shadow and Act* by Ralph Ellison, copyright © 1964 by Ralph Ellison; reprinted by permission of Random House, Inc.

FIRST EDITION

LIBRARY OF CONGRESS CATALOG CARD NUMBER: 65-14654

M-P

TO THE MEMORY
OF
ALAIN LOCKE

Contents

Acknowledgments

The editor wishes to express his gratitude to the University of California (Berkeley) Extension Program for its sponsorship of the seminar on "The Negro Writer in the United States" during the summer of 1964. Several of the essays appearing in this book were originally presented, although in different form, on that occasion. The seminar was of great importance in giving a long-delayed recognition to the literary creativity of American Negroes. Both as director of the seminar and as editor of this volume I wish to express my personal appreciation to Dr. Morton Gordon and Mrs. Alice Kermeen, director and assistant head, respectively, of the Extension Program.

I should like to express my appreciation to Miss Jeannette Hopkins of the editorial staff of Harper & Row, not only for her professional assistance throughout this project but for her special insights and interest in the subject of this volume.

I wish to acknowledge my thanks to Mrs. Muriel S. Outlaw, who conscientiously typed these essays in their various drafts and revisions.

Above all I wish to express my appreciation for the assistance given to me by my wife, Carol, at every stage in the preparation of this book and also for her warm encouragement and love.

It is a peculiar sensation, this double-
consciousness, this sense of always looking
at one's self through the eyes of others, of
measuring one's soul by the tape of a world that
looks on in amused contempt and pity. One ever
feels his two-ness—an American, a Negro—two
souls, two thoughts, two unreconciled strivings; two
warring ideals in one dark body, whose dogged
strength alone keeps it from being torn asunder.

The history of the American Negro is the
history of this strife . . . this longing to
attain self-conscious manhood, to merge his
double self into a better and truer self.

W. E. B. Du Bois (1897)

Whoever wishes to see the Negro in his essential
traits, in the full perspective of his achievement
and possibilities, must seek the enlightenment of
that self-portraiture which the present developments
of Negro culture are offering. . . . So far as he is
culturally articulate, we shall let the Negro speak
for himself.

Alain Locke (1925)

Herbert Hill

Introduction

The American Negro literary tradition is a complex one because it is many things. It is the literature of the Negro community, but also the assertion of a universal humanity. It is an important part of American literature, and it is also implicitly an attack upon the racist assumptions of American society. Although it has been for the most part a non-ideological literature it has been infused and informed by writers greatly concerned with ideology.

From a historical point of view one may detect several major tendencies in Negro literature. There is the early folk tradition based mainly upon Southern rural material that has been richly exploited by several generations of Negro writers such as Daniel Webster Davis, Paul Laurence Dunbar and James Weldon Johnson. Langston Hughes has used the same folk material but in relation to the rural Negro now living in the big cities of the North. There is the important tradition of racial protest; first expressed during the antislavery struggle, including the slave narratives, many of which have genuine literary value. There are the novels of caste and color that began with J. McHenry Jones' *Hearts of Gold* in 1896 to the novels of Jessie Fauset and Nella Larsen in the 1930's and then the Harlem School and the Negro Renaissance whose gifted writers derided the pretensions and genteel style of the older group. Later there were those involved with the naturalist tradition and the "proletarian literature" school. Among the young writers working in the 1950's and 1960's there were those, such as the gifted William Demby, who were influenced by existentialism, while others were influenced by the concepts and emotions of *Négritude* and the French African literary tradition. But in each generation the work of the Negro writer was the response of the creative imagination as an individual reaction to the Negro's social experience. Today the essential characteristic of that response is an intense concern with literary discipline and technique *together* with a profound social commitment.

Thus, the perennial debate about the conflict between art and ideology has become an exercise in futility. For the serious writer there must be a fundamental connection between artistic means, that is, technique and discipline, with social and moral conviction, and a recognition of the significant relationship between individual freedom and social necessity, between form and content.

A major example of a writer deeply concerned with literary technique and with social commitment is the brilliant novelist Ralph Ellison, who denies a distinction between "a purely literary work" and a work in the "tradition of social protest." In his collection of essays, *Shadow and Act,* Mr. Ellison states:

I recognize no dichotomy between art and protest. Dostoevski's *Notes from the Underground* is, among other things, a protest against the limitations of nineteenth-century rationalism; *Don Quixote, Man's Fate, Oedipus Rex, The Trial*—all these embody protest even against the limitation of human life itself. If social protest is antithetical to art, what then shall we make of Goya, Dickens and Twain? One hears a lot of complaints about the so-called Protest Novel, especially when written by Negroes, but it seems to me that the critics could more accurately complain about their lack of craftsmanship and their provincialism.*

* Ralph Ellison, *Shadow and Act.* New York: Random House, 1964.

The urgencies of social protest cannot be invoked, as they have been in the past, as an excuse for shoddy undisciplined writing. For writing without artistic quality can only lead to dull and ineffective protest literature. Such writing is in fact neither protest nor literature, it is only an act of self-indulgence, an expression of rage and little else. It makes no impact on the real world and is of doubtful value as a cathartic. Indeed, for the writer, a serious and purposeful commitment to racial justice and social action requires the most intense devotion to literary technique and artistic discipline.

As the race question emerges as the major issue confronting American society there is occurring a remarkable burst of literary creativity among Negroes. One is immediately reminded of the similar development at the turn of the century in Ireland, where the revolutionary movement of the Irish people was accompanied by a literary renaissance that has given us many of the great names in modern literature.

The literature created by Negroes is not only a protest against the irrational racial situation, not only an attempt to explain the unique status of American Negroes to white society and to the world, but, most significantly, the literature of American Negroes is an attempt to explain the racial situation to themselves. "Who am I?" and "What am I?" and "Who are they?" and "What are they?" are urgent questions for Negroes. The demand for an answer leads not only to necessary social protest but also to the development of the creative imagination, to the search for reason and to a new concern with art and ideology. Thus, as Saunders Redding has told us, Negro literature has been a "literature of necessity," and now Negro writers in a variety of ways are brilliantly and powerfully transmitting their awareness of the racial situation into literature.

Historical and sociological research has repeatedly attempted to assess the salient characteristics of the racial situation in the United States. Usually an effort is made to understand the

so-called Negro problem within the context of America's social
development and what it means for the future of the nation.
Although a citizen of Sweden, Gunnar Myrdal typified this approach as he described the "American Dilemma" as a conflict
within the dominant white social order. But what is the Negro
version of the American society? In terms of history, what may
finally be of the greatest importance is the Negro's perception of
himself and the variety of his responses to his condition. And
this is the crucial importance and significance of the literature
of the American Negro. Here, the infinite possibilities of the
creative imagination are informed by the endless variability of
individual personality. Here, the interior meaning of race and
caste and class are apprehended and communicated.

In 1897, W. E. B. Du Bois described the feelings of a Negro
as he sees himself through the eyes of an alien world:

It is a peculiar sensation, this double-consciousness, this sense of
always looking at one's self through the eyes of others, of measuring
one's soul by the tape of a world that looks on in amused contempt
and pity. One ever feels his two-ness—an American, a Negro—two
souls, two thoughts, two unreconciled strivings; two warring ideals in
one dark body, whose dogged strength alone keeps it from being torn
asunder.*

Professor Saunders Redding, in his Introduction to a recent
edition of *The Souls of Black Folk*, tells us that the South African
Negro writer Peter Abrahams "was not alone" when he stated
upon first reading *The Souls of Black Folk* that until then he
had no words with which to voice his Negroness. It had, Abrahams wrote, "the impact of a revelation . . . a key to the understanding of my world." Mr. Redding observes that:

The Souls of Black Folk may be seen as fixing that moment in history when the American Negro began to reject the idea of the world's

* W. E. B. Du Bois, *The Souls of Black Folk*. Chicago: A. C. McClurg &
Co., 1903, p. 3. The quotation originally appeared in the *Atlantic Monthly*,
August, 1897.

belonging to white people only, and to think of himself, in concert, as a potential force in the organization of society. With its publication, Negroes of training and intelligence, who had hitherto pretended to regard the race problem as of strictly personal concern and who sought individual salvation in a creed of detachment and silence, found a bond in their common grievances and a language through which to express them.

It is within this context that we must understand the special importance of literature for the American Negro community.

Charles S. Johnson, writing in 1923, summarized the attitudes prevalent in American society and their consequences for Negro personality. The process by which these assumptions affected Negroes was described as follows:

They cannot escape being assailed on every hand from early childhood to the end of their lives with a pervading intimation of their own inferiority. From the beginning they are saturated in a tradition of their own incompetence. . . . They grow up in the system not only inferior to the other race, but to their own potential selves. They are in the midst of an advanced social system, of definite cultural influences, but denied full participation. They may never escape the insistent implications of their status and race. Attention and interest are centered on themselves. They become race conscious. Opinions and feelings on general questions must always be filtered through this narrow screen that separates them from their neighbors. Their opinions are, therefore, largely a negative product, either disparagement of difficulties or protest.*

The insights of psychoanalysis were increasingly evident in studies published during the 1930's as in Charles F. Gibson's analysis of emotional conflicts which he found to be frequently rooted in unconscious feelings that black is unclean, inferior and evil.† Studies of emotional disorders among Negroes and

* Charles S. Johnson, "Public Opinion and the Negro," *Proceedings of the National Conference of Social Work*, Washington, D.C., 1923, pp. 497-502.

† Charles F. Gibson, "Concerning Color," *The Psychoanalytic Review*, New York, 1931, Vol. XVIII, pp. 413-425.

the means by which they attempt to compensate for their alleged inferiority, with evaluations of behavioral patterns in colored communities, were conducted in several parts of the country.

Studies of Negro children by Kenneth and Mamie Clark and others* initiated a series of important research projects in the social psychology of Negroes supporting the conclusion that discrimination and segregation significantly damage Negro self-esteem. These studies of the psychological effects of racial segregation upon personality development were an important part of the social research presented to the Supreme Court in the historic school segregation cases.† Among the other social scientists who documented the extent of personality damage to American Negroes were Professors Clyde Kluckhorn, Abram Kardiner, Lionel Ovesey, and the late E. Franklin Frazier of Howard University. Although the significance and depth of the distortion and damage suffered by those born black in white America are still under intensive investigation, we must turn to the literature of American Negroes to discover the means by which survival was secured in spite of the severe psychic trauma.

What unfortunately is less understood is the Negro's perception of his own role. What of the forces summoned up to secure sanity and survival in an utterly irrational situation and the responses to that situation? Perhaps William Faulkner was right when he suggested that the most important feature of the Negro's experience in America was that "they endure." Indeed "they" do endure and, moreover, "they" have survived with great vitality.

* Kenneth B. and Mamie P. Clark, "Segregation as a Factor in the Racial Identification in Negro Preschool Children: A Preliminary Report," *Journal of Experimental Education,* Vol. VIII, No. 2 (Dec. 1939), pp. 161-63. An elaboration of this material appears as "Racial Identification and Preference in Negro Children," by the same authors, in Newcomb and Hartley's *Readings in Social Psychology,* New York, 1947, pp. 169-78. See also Joan Criswell, "A Sociometric Study of Race Cleavage in the Classroom." Archives of *Psychology,* Vol. XXXIII, No. 235 (1939).

† Brown *et al.* v. Board of Education of Topeka (Kansas); Briggs *et al.* v. Elliott (South Carolina); Davis *et al.* v. County School Board of Prince Edward County (Virginia); Gebhart *et al.* v. Belton (Delaware), Bolling *et al.* v. Sharpe (District of Columbia).

The record of that endurance and survival is to be found in the songs: the spirituals, the blues, gospel hymns and "holler-shouts"; in the music, dances, the poetry, the plays; in the stories, both in the oral tradition and in the written; in the novels, the essays, and, indeed, in all the magnificent works of the creative imagination.

For those concerned with Negro life and thought there is perhaps a special value in the study of this literature, for, as Henry James explained, the novel is "felt life," and to the Goncourt brothers the novelist was the historian of the present.

Because we live in an age of collective social depravity in the form of mass murder, genocide, atomic bombs and concentration camps, the social scientists and the psychiatrists have been examining human behavior in extreme circumstances. But for the Negro in the United States, from the very beginning, life has been lived in the extreme situation. For almost two and a half centuries before 1863 more than 90 percent of all colored people living in the United States were forced to live out their lives within a brutal and degrading system of slavery that openly declared that Negroes were not human beings but merely things, pieces of property. Tragically enough, the period after the Emancipation did not represent a fundamental discontinuity in the Negro experience. Over one hundred years ago emancipation from legal slavery was declared, but freedom was not secured for the Negro; and it is precisely this lack of freedom then and now which has consistently been the essential characteristic of Negro life in America.

But there was a great freedom in the creative imagination of Negroes, especially in the way Negroes perceived their status and tried to understand their situation. The more than two hundred slave revolts required not only courage and bravery but also imagination. In the light of what we now know through the disciplines of sociology and psychology, Negro responses to the extreme situation revealed the vigor and insistence upon survival of a people who organized slave rebellions, sabotaged the plantation economy by subtle but effective acts of passive aggression and not infrequently fled from bondage. It is also important to note that while insisting upon its survival, Negro life also created a Frederick Douglass, who would later write an enduring American literary classic, *Narrative of the Life of Frederick Douglass, an American Slave.* Thus it has always been, from Jupiter Hammon, whose poetry was published in 1760, to M. B. Tolson, Langston Hughes, Gwendolyn Brooks, LeRoi Jones and the other Negro poets of our time. Thus it has been since 1852, when William Wells Brown wrote *Clotelle,* the first novel published by an American Negro, to Richard Wright, Ralph Ellison and James Baldwin of today.

In a certain sense, for us now, Richard Wright's development as an artist will be most significant in telling us something important about freedom and the creative imagination. For here was a black writer from the backwoods of Mississippi who, in his literary achievement as well as in his life, represented a triumph of the human personality. Repeatedly in his novels Wright tells us, with an almost demonic power, how personality is corrupted by a brutal and dehumanizing society. But at the very same moment he reveals his literary talent, and in his vision as an artist he reveals that the corruption was not necessarily total, and that, indeed, Richard Wright has triumphed over it. Especially in his autobiography, *Black Boy,* Wright tells us of his struggles against the corrosive effects of the environment and of the often painful, sensitive human responses which made possible his literary creativity and his survival as a man. Thus, it must be understood that in every generation of the Negro experience in America there have been those persons who achieved freedom in their creative use of the imagination, who used the materials unique to Negro life to create a rich vernacular in speech, in music, in religious expression and in literature.

Each, of course, will choose his own individual path. For some, the creative imagination will flower in combat and struggle; for others, there will be different ways, different requirements. During the spring of 1965, a dramatic story appeared on the front page of the *New York Times* describing the arrest of hundreds of Negroes who demonstrated in the streets of Selma, Alabama, against a vicious white supremacy that still attempts to deny Negro citizens their fundamental rights. But on the next to the last page of the same issue of the *Times* was a story headlined "Asthma in Negroes Reported on Rise." The news report stated that Negroes in many cities across the country have ". . . apparently experienced a marked and mysterious increase in asthma attacks . . ." The news report quotes a well-known medical authority as saying that "Asthma attacks are known to be closely related to emotional states," and that for many years clinical psychologists have known of the relationship between emotional factors and asthma attacks.

Perhaps the stories on the front and back pages of the *New York Times* are not entirely unrelated, and perhaps they are a dramatic expression of the anxiety that accompanies self-assertion, of the deep conflict that surrounds new and uncertain self-affirmation and of the fear and guilt and the passion that co-exist with the determination to affirm the best impulses of the human personality. All of this and more is the great material of the creative imagination that now, as in the past, demands freedom and dignity. And today Negro writers are insisting upon that freedom and dignity.

Ralph Ellison tells us that:

. . . the most surreal fantasies are acted out upon the streets of Harlem. . . . Here the grandchildren of those who possess no written literature examine their lives through the eyes of Freud and Marx, Kierkegaard and Kafka, Malraux and Sartre. It explains the nature of a world so fluid and shifting that often within the mind the real and the unreal merge, and the marvelous beckons from behind the same sordid reality that denies its existence.*

Negro writers are now moving into new areas of involvement with fundamental social issues that go beyond the race question into an awareness of the tragedy, irony and absurdity of Amer-

* Ralph Ellison, *Shadow and Act*. New York: Random House, 1964, p. 246.

ican and twentieth-century life. While some are still working within the conventions of the past, other Negro writers are demonstrating the responsibility of the artist to the disciplines and traditions of art and literature. For these writers simple protest and anger are not enough and rhetoric will not be useful in masking the inadequacies of literary craftsmanship.

In confronting American society as an artist as well as a Negro, the contemporary Negro writer achieves a new strength, a new freedom for creativity. Today Negro writers have no reluctance in dealing with the absurdities and terrors of the white man's condition and at the same time they are telling the truth about Negroes, the most important truth that white America needs to know. In the future, Negro authors will not be writing as some did in the past, to please or titillate white audiences; they will not be telling of quaint and amusing colored folks or of exotic sensual Negroes who exist only in the fantasies of white people living in a society tragically obsessed by race and color. As Negro writers share all the preoccupations of contemporary literature, they will protest not only against the racial situation but against all the forces and conditions of life that artists and writers everywhere must protest against.

The unique social experience of the American Negro is the stuff of great literature. It is the material of epic poems, of heroic sagas and vast panoramic novels. It is of the substance of enduring life and creative hope that will finally triumph in a destructive world. It is a story worthy of a Balzac or a Tolstoi, of a Pushkin or a Joyce, and today there are Negro writers who are preparing to do justice to that story, which is central to an understanding of life in America.

ANGER, AND BEYOND

1.   *Saunders Redding*

The Negro Writer
and American Literature

Of the several current assumptions regarding the Negro writer in the United States, one, I think, stands out as primary. It is the assumption that there is a distinction between writings by American Negroes and writings by other Americans. It is an old assumption, and one that heretofore has been accepted blindly as a truism, and if it is now possible to call it into question, it is not before it has had a still more questionable consequence. It has led to the diversion of writing by Negroes from the main channel of American expressiveness, and to setting it off—to change the figure abruptly—as belonging, like pornography, to that class of literary works called curiosa. The critical treatment of this body of writing has also been set apart, and the standards by which so much of it—indeed, most of it—has been judged have only rarely been aesthetic and literary.

As questionable and detrusive as these consequences are, the assumption itself has validity. Of course writing by Negroes is different. The difference stems from the fact of their distinctive group experience in America. The cultural dualism of the American Negro is very real, and nearly all the Negro writers of more than local reputation have expressed it in one way or another, sometimes unconsciously—as, for instance, Phillis Wheat-

1

ley did way back in the 1770's, when, in her poetic epistle to the
Earl of Dartmouth, she wrote:

> Should you, my lord, while you peruse my song,
> Wonder from whence my love of Freedom spring,
> Whence flow these wishes for the common good,
> By feeling hearts alone best understood,
> I, young in life, by seeming cruel fate
> Was snatched from Afric's fancied happy seat:
> What pangs excruciating must molest,
> What sorrows labor in my parent's breast!
> Steeled was that soul, and by no misery moved,
> That from a father seized his babe beloved:
> Such, such my case. And can I then but pray
> Others may never feel tyrannic sway?

And just as real and as often expressed—also sometimes unconsciously—is a psychological dualism. In the autobiographical
notes that are the introduction to his first collections of essays,
Notes of a Native Son, James Baldwin is quite explicit and quite
aware of both the psychological and cultural dualism:

I know [he writes] . . . that the most crucial time in my own development came when I was forced to recognize that I was a kind
of bastard of the West; when I followed the line of my past I did not
find myself in Europe but in Africa. And this meant that in some
subtle way, in a really profound way, I brought to Shakespeare,
Bach, Rembrandt, to the stones of Paris, to the cathedral at Chartres,
and to the Empire State Building, a special attitude. These were not
really my creations, they did not contain my history, I might search
in them in vain forever for any reflection of myself. . . . At the
same time I had no other heritage which I could possibly hope to
use. . . . I would have to appropriate these white centuries, I would
have to make them mine—I would have to accept my special attitude,
my special place in this scheme—otherwise I would have no place in
any scheme. What was the most difficult was the fact that I was
forced to admit something I had always hidden from myself, which
the American Negro has had to hide from himself as the price of his

public progress; that I hated and feared white people. This did not mean that I loved black people; on the contrary, I despised them. . . .

And I take it also that this dualism is the principal thematic burden of a group of brilliant essays entitled *Shadow and Act*, by Ralph Ellison, who reminds us that when he began writing in earnest:

I was forced to relate myself consciously and imaginatively to my mixed background as American, as Negro American, and as a Negro from what in its own belated way was a pioneer background. More important, and inseparable from this particular effort, was the necessity of determining my true relationship to that body of American literature . . . through which, aided by what I could learn from the literatures of Europe, I would find my own voice, and to which I was challenged, by way of achieving myself, to make some small contribution, and to whose composite picture of reality I was obligated to offer some necessary modifications.

Measured in psychological, sociological and raw cultural terms, the distinction and the differences between writing by American Negroes and other Americans are justified. But for all that, it is only the distinction between trunk and branch. The writing of Negroes is fed by the same roots sunk in the same cultural soil as writing by white Americans. Nevertheless, both academic and popular criticism has exaggerated the distinction into a dichotomy that has been the source of grave critical injustice to Negro writing on the one hand, and that has—until recently at any rate—tended to vitiate its effectiveness as an instrument of social and cultural diagnosis and as a body of American experience through which we are enabled to understand the cultural psychology of the American world and, indeed—I think —the whole Western world. Three times within this century, writing by Negroes has been done nearly to death: once by indifference, once by opposition, and once by the enthusiasm of misguided friends.

By 1906, Charles Waddell Chesnutt, the best writer of prose

fiction the race had produced, was virtually silent; Paul Laurence Dunbar, the most popular poet, was dead. Booker T. Washington had published *Up from Slavery*, but Washington, who gave disastrous social dimensions to a literary tradition, was no writer. Though Du Bois had written *The Souls of Black Folk*, he had not yet found an audience. The polemicists and propagandists like Monroe Trotter, Kelly Miller and George Forbes were faint whispers in a lonesome wood. Indifference had stopped the ears of all but the most enlightened liberals, who, as often as not, were derided as "nigger lovers."

But this indifference had threatened even before the turn of the century. It choked off and made bitter the purest stream of Dunbar's lyricism. Yearning for the recognition of his talent as it expressed itself in traditional poetry in conventional English, he had to content himself with being represented by what he considered to be third-rate. His literary sponsor, William Dean Howells, at that time the most influential critic in America, passed over Dunbar's verse in pure English with scarcely a glance, but went on to say that:

. . . there is a precious difference of temperament between the two races which it would be a great pity ever to lose, and . . . this is best preserved and most charmingly suggested by Mr. Dunbar in those pieces of his where he studies the moods and traits of his own race. . . . We call these pieces dialect pieces . . . but they are really not dialect so much as delightful personal attempts and failures for the written and spoken language. In nothing is Mr. Dunbar's art so well shown as in these pieces, which . . . describe the range between appetite and emotion . . . which is the range of the race. He reveals in these a finely ironic perception of the Negro's limitations. I should say perhaps that it was this humorous quality which Mr. Dunbar has added to our literature, and it would be this which would most distinguish him, now and hereafter. . . .

Dunbar's non-dialect verses appeared more or less on sufferance. The very format of *Lyrics of the Hearthside*, the book in which most of his non-dialect verses appeared, suggests this. No fancy binding, no fine paper, no charming photographs such as one finds in his other books. *Lyrics of the Hearthside* was the least publicized of all his works, and four lines from his poem "The Poet" tells why.

> He sang of love when earth was young
> And Love itself was in his lays
> But ah, the world, it turned to praise
> A jingle in a broken tongue.

The indifference was due to the fact that poetry written in pure English by a Negro contradicted the Negro stereotypes, which were effective in America's thinking about the Negro. According to them, the Negro was either—and sometimes both— a buffoon, a minstrel, and a harmless child of nature or an irresponsible beast of devilish cunning, soulless and depraved. In either case, the Negro was a species of creature that was not quite man.

The influence of these concepts upon writing by American Negroes—and, of course, about American Negroes—had been and continued to be tremendous. Sterling Brown, one of the more searching scholars, had this to say as late as 1942: "The market for Negro writers, then, is definitely limited . . . and the more truthfully we write about ourselves, the more limited the market. Those novels about Negroes that sell best . . . touch very lightly upon the realities of Negro life, books that make our black ghettoes in big cities seem very happy places indeed. . . ."

Alain Locke complained that the Negro was "a stock figure perpetuated as an historical fiction partly in innocent sentimentalism, partly in deliberate reactionism. The Negro himself," Locke wrote, "has contributed his share to this through a sort of protective social mimicry . . . forced upon him through the adverse circumstances of dependence. Through having had to appeal from the unjust stereotypes of his oppressors and traducers to those of his liberators, friends and benefactors he has had to subscribe to traditional positions from which his case has been viewed. . . ."

That the stereotypes were powerful there can be no doubt, and the Negro writer reacted to them in one of two ways. Either he bowed to them, and produced work that would do them no violence and offer them no contradiction, or he went to the opposite extreme and wrote for the purpose of correcting or denying the stereotypes. Dunbar did the former. Not only his dialect poetry but his short stories depicted Negroes as folksy, not-too-bright souls, all of whose concerns are minor, and all of whose problems can be solved by the emotional and spiritual equivalents of sticks of red peppermint candy.

Charles Chesnutt's experience was both confoundingly unlike and strikingly similar to Dunbar's. When his stories began appearing in the *Atlantic Monthly* in 1887, it was not generally known that Chesnutt was a Negro. The editor of the *Atlantic*, Walter Hines Page, fearing that revealing the author's race would do harm to the reception of the author's work, kept his race a closely guarded secret for a decade. It was this same fear that led to the initial rejection of Chesnutt's first novel, *The House Behind the Cedars*, and publication in its stead of a collection of the stories that had appeared in the *Atlantic*. "At that time," Chesnutt wrote some years afterward, "a literary work by an American of acknowledged color was a doubtful experiment, both for the writer and for the publisher, entirely apart from its intrinsic merit. Indeed, my race was never mentioned by the publishers in announcing or advertising the book. . . ."

Chesnutt's later books, published after his race became known, were doomed to failure, so far as reception and sales were concerned, on another count. They were honest; they probed the problem of race; they overrode the concepts and contradicted the stereotypes that supported the folk-dialect tradition.

The indifference to the work of culture-conscious, race-conscious Negro writers seeking honest answers to real questions began to crystallize into opposition in the first decade of this century. It was opposition to the Negro's ambitions. It was opposition to the Negro writer who was honest and sincere.

But let me not too much oversimplify a complex matter. Even with the advantage of hindsight, it is hard to distinguish cause from effect. In 1902 a white minister named Thomas Dixon published a novel called *The Leopard's Spots*, the purpose of which was—as some of the advertising copy declared—"to tell the true story of the races in the South." Three years later, the same author published *The Clansman*, from which, exactly ten years later, the infamous moving picture *The Birth of a Nation* was to be made. Both Dixon's novels were vicious libels of the Negro people, and both were great commercial successes. In 1903 there was a race riot in New York. In 1904 Thomas Nelson Page published the canonical book on race relations: it was called *The Negro, The Southerner's Problem*. In 1906 there were race riots in Georgia and Texas. By 1907 practically all the Southern states had made color caste distinctions legal. In 1908 the bloodiest of riots occurred in Springfield, Illinois. And, probably the most cogent fact of all, Booker Washington had been chosen by white people as the Negro leader. He had risen to that eminence by preaching a way of life strictly in conformity to the prevailing concept, the folk-dialect tradition, which, without any important modifications whatever, embraced the stereotype of the Negro as a contented peasant, a docile menial under the stern but not unkindly eye of a white boss; a creature who had a place, knew it, and would certainly keep it unless he got "bad notions" from somewhere. The laughable and/or dangerous "coon" was also the farm hand and the city-dwelling laborer, who could be exploited for his own good and the greater glory of white men. The condition of inferior-superior race and caste could be maintained to everlasting.

What this meant to the Negro intellectual, the Negro artist and writer was that he must stick with the old forms and stereotypes and work within the old folk-dialect tradition if he wished an audience. It meant that he must do this, or that he must deny

his racial kinship altogether and leave unsounded the profound-
est depths of the peculiar experiences of his Negroness. A few
chose the first course and sedulously imitated Dunbar down
through the second decade of this century, when more skillful
white writers—Octavus Roy Cohen, Gilmore Millen, and, in a
different kind of way and with a different intent, Carl Van
Vechten and DuBose Heyward—took it up and gave it a spuri-
ous validity that has lasted almost to this time.

Other Negro writers chose the second course—apostasy. But
their motives differed from those of the first group, and their
ambitions were more steeply pitched. As Herbert Hill has said
in another context, they sought to "break through the limits of
racial parochialism into the whole range" of contemporary matters that engaged the interest of an enlightened and sophisticated
public, which public, of course, was white. I hope it is clear that
until very recently there was no Negro audience. Moreover, the
Negro writer has felt that winning a white audience was the only
adequate test of his talent and of his aesthetic standards, and that
only the judgment of a white audience had meaning. But there
is another factor here, too, and it is of equal importance: the
Negro writer has felt it to be a kind of racial duty to attract a
white audience. Until lately, when he has tried to do this in terms
of his own integrity and on the basis of the most honest exploration of the Negro experience of which he is capable, he has
failed of his objective. In the first two decades of the century,
apostasy seemed to some Negro writers the only way of escaping
complete frustration.

But if we take Alice Dunbar, the widow of Paul Laurence
Dunbar, as fairly typical of these, then there was a subtle mad-
ness in it. Born in New Orleans, married to a famous dialect poet,
later a teacher in a Negro high school, she lived all her life in a
Negro ghetto. All her ambitions and aspirations inevitably were
conditioned by the inescapable fact of her Negroness, and yet
none of this found expression in what she wrote, and all of what
she wrote ignored her racial and social heritage. That's mad.

Until our own time, when it has been followed with great popular success by such writers as Willard Motley, Frank Yerby and Will Thomas, the whole tradition had pathological overtones. And the typical issue of this tradition is naturally precious, "arty," self-conscious and, except as a symptom, empty of all meaning, of all sense—indeed, quite silly, as in a piece of William Stanley Braithwaite's called "Ironic: LL.D."

> There are no hollows any more
> Between the mountains; the prairie floor
> Is like a curtain with a drape
> Of the winds' invisible shape;
> And nowhere seen and nowhere heard
> The sea's quiet as a sleeping bird
> Now we're traveling, what holds back
> Arrival, in the very track
> Where the urge put forth; so we stay
> And move a thousand miles a day
> Time's a fancy ringing bells
> Whose meaning, charlatan history, tells.

The writers in this nonracial aesthetic tradition were all touched by absurdity. It is not strange to learn of one of them setting out to write a novel composed entirely of elliptical sentences. Though some of them developed an amazing virtuosity, they were definitely—as the saying goes—off.

Meantime, insurgency was developing in the upper ranks of Negroes. They were beginning to rebel against Booker Washington and his ideas. What had happened was that Washington, with the help of the historic situation and the old concepts, had so thoroughly seduced the minds of those white people who made up the power structure, and who professed themselves kindly disposed to Negroes, that they were his entirely. Dr. W. E. B. Du Bois tells the story in *Dusk of Dawn*. The titan of Tuskegee controlled—so far as Negroes were concerned—practically all the avenues of communication, and his control was despotic. Editors of influential journals and great publishing houses submitted manuscripts by Negroes to Washington's judgment, and rejected those that Washington told them to reject.

Led by Du Bois, the insurgents had no attention-getting voice at first. It is true that the Chicago *Defender* was founded in 1900, and Monroe Trotter's Boston *Guardian* in 1901, and they were shrill and brave organs, but neither Robert S. Abbott nor Trotter, the editors, had grown into full effectiveness. Neither, indeed, had Du Bois, but he was growing fast. In 1903 he published *The Souls of Black Folk*, which contained among other things the essay "Of Mr. Booker T. Washington and Others," a sharp criticism of the man from Tuskegee, which drew down on Du Bois' head charges of being a "perverter of our customs," an "enemy to the established order" and a "threat to the existing good relations between the races." In 1911, the first issue of *The Crisis* magazine appeared.

It was much more than the official organ of the newly formed NAACP. It was a platform for the expression of all sorts of opinions and ideas that ran counter to the old notion of Negro inferiority. Du Bois had once written, "I believe in God, who made of one blood all nations that on earth do dwell. I believe that all men, black, brown and white, are brothers, varying through time and opportunity, in form and gift and feature, but differing in no essential particular, and alike in soul and the possibility of infinite development. . . . I believe in pride of race and lineage and self. . . ."

This conviction he never lost. Month by month, in that section called "Opinion," *The Crisis* scored against reaction. Month by month it cited the significant achievements of Negroes in fields apart from those to which so many millions of people thought they belonged. Year by year it listed the outstanding Negro college graduates. It was an organ of expression for those Negroes who were tired of the tradition and apostasy, and for that handful of liberal whites who were ashamed. There were stories and poems by Fenton Johnson, articles by Benjamin Brawley, Oswald G. Villard and Kelly Miller. And there were always those incisive editorials by W. E. B. Du Bois.

Though polemic and propaganda were by far the greater part and the more important part of the magazine, there were other things in *The Crisis* as well—historical essays by Arthur Schomburg, literary pieces by Benjamin Brawley, a department of books conducted by Jessie Fauset, poems by Leslie P. Hill and Georgia Douglas Johnson. But the point about the polemic is this: excepting such liberal and non-popular journals as the *Atlantic Monthly* and *World's Work* and the two or three Negro newspapers that had not been bought or throttled by the clique at Tuskegee, *The Crisis* was the only voice the Negro had. The opposition to the message of that voice was tremendously organized around Booker Washington and his philosophy, and there is no doubt that it would have smothered that voice if it could.

It is impossible actually to measure one effect of this opposition upon writing by American Negroes. How many Negro writers of promise were discouraged and even defeated by it? There is no way to tell. But the number of Negro writers who turned to race-denial is probably even larger than that already indicated.

Nevertheless, bit by bit, protestation and revolt were becoming reagents in the social chemistry that, suddenly it seemed, produced the New Negro. Year by year more and more Negroes were transformed by it—and a lot of Negroes needed transforming. Once James Weldon Johnson himself had been content to sing:

> God of our weary years,
> God of our silent tears,
> Thou who hast brought us thus far on our way;
> Thou who hast by thy might
> Led us into the light,
> Keep us ever in the path, we pray. . . .
> Shadowed beneath Thy hand,
> May we forever stand,
> True to our God,
> True to our native land.

"Lift Ev'ry Voice and Sing" is beautiful with the soft beauty of humility and supplication. It was written in 1900, and it had the high approval of Booker T. Washington. Then followed Johnson's period of apostasy and such actually undistinguished things as "The Glory of the Day Was in Her Face," "My City," "The White Witch" and a score of similar poems. But in 1912, when he was already forty-one, he wrote the novel *The Autobiography of an Ex-Colored Man*, and by 1917 he could cry out bitterly:

> Then should we speak but servile words,
> Or shall we hang our heads in shame?
> Stand back of new-come foreign hordes,
> And fear our heritage to claim?
>
> No! stand erect and without fear,
> And for our foes let this suffice—
> We've bought a rightful kinship here,
> And we have more than paid the price.

The New Negro was only apparently phoenix-like, springing reborn from the ashes of his own degradation. Other factors than simple protest, too ponderous for elaboration here, contributed to his genesis. In the first place, as Alain Locke has said, much of the general notion—which was not so much notion as mind set—of the "Old Negro" was based on pure myth. The beginning war sloughed off some of the emotional and intellectual accretions that swathed him round, and he stood partially revealed for what he was—a fellow whose opportunities had been narrowed by historical fallacies, "a creature of moral debate," a "something to be argued about, condemned or defended, to be 'kept down,' or 'in his place' . . . a social bogey or a social burden . . ."* but, withal, a man pretty much as other men were. By 1916, the war, which made him an inter-sectional migrant, proved that he, too, sought greater freedom, more economic opportunities, the stability of education, the protection of laws even-handedly administered, the enlargement of

* Alain Locke, Introduction, *The New Negro*. New York: Albert and Charles Boni, 1925.

democracy. He, too, was a seeker after the realities in the American dream.

But when, in 1917, he was called upon to protect that dream with his blood, when he was asked to help make the world "safe for democracy," something else happened to reveal the Negro more fully. He started asking questions, and demanding answers. It was only natural. Whose democracy? he wanted to know, and why and wherefore? There followed the promises, which were certainly sincerely meant in the stress of the times. Then came the actual fighting and dying. Then peace. Then, in 1919 and after, the riots in the nation's capital, in Chicago, in Chester, Pennsylvania, in east St. Louis.

By this time the New Negro movement, with W. E. B. Du Bois, Alain Locke and James Weldon Johnson at its head, was already moving massively, and more than the students of social phenomena were aware of it. The race clashes focused the popular attention upon America's largest minority. In 1919 appeared that sonnet of Claude McKay's which is sometimes said to mark the more conscious beginning of the movement in its emotional terms.

> If we must die, let it not be like hogs
> Hunted and penned in an inglorious spot,
> While round us bark the mad and hungry dogs,
> Making their mock at our accursed lot.
> If we must die, oh, let us nobly die,
> So that our precious blood may not be shed
> In vain; then even the monsters we defy
> Shall be constrained to honor us though dead!
> Oh, Kinsmen! We must meet the common foe!
> Though far outnumbered, let us show us brave,
> And for their thousand blows deal one death-blow!
> What though before us lies the open grave?
> Like men we'll face the murderous, cowardly pack,
> Pressed to the wall, dying, but fighting back!*

* Claude McKay, *Harlem Shadows.* New York: Harcourt, Brace & Co., 1922.

In the same year, 1919, Negroes made a crack in the wall of prejudice that had confined them largely to supernumerary roles on Broadway. *Shuffle Along* was "a sparkling, all-Negro musical of unusual zest and talent." Charles Gilpin's portrayal of O'Neill's Emperor Jones was called the dramatic triumph of 1921. The Garvey movement was attracting great attention. In 1920 came Du Bois' *Darkwater*. James Weldon Johnson gave the movement fresh validity by publishing an anthology of Negro poetry, and Brawley published *A Social History of the American Negro*. Carter G. Woodson began his monumental studies of the Negro in history at about this time. *There Is Confusion*, *The Gift of Black Folk*, a remarkable first book of poetry, *Color*, by Countee Cullen, *Fire in the Flint*, Langston Hughes' *The Weary Blues*, James Weldon Johnson's *God's Trombones*, Rudolph Fisher's *Walls of Jericho*, and Claude McKay's *Home to Harlem* had all been published, read, discussed, praised and damned by 1928.

Fortunately, some of the talents that produced these works were genuine talents. All of them were interesting. Had this not been so, the New Negro movement in art and literature would surely have come to nothing. The best poetry of McKay, Johnson, Hughes, Cullen and Arna Bontemps, the early short stories of Rudolph Fisher, the best prose of Du Bois would have lived without the help of the movement, but it was the movement which brought immediate attention to many who might otherwise have attracted no attention whatsoever. It must be appreciated, too, that the interest in Negro material and Negro art expression was considerably furthered by white writers and critics. Indeed, the New Negro movement had to find scope outside the race or it would have smothered in its own cocoon. Whatever else Eugene O'Neill, Carl Van Vechten, Paul Rosenfeld, Sherwood Anderson, DuBose Heyward and Julia Peterkin did, they gave further artistic sanction to the use of Negro material for other than purposes of burlesque.

Writing by Negroes beginning with this period and continuing into the early Thirties had two distinct phases, which combined to mark the start of a psychological and artistic development that is now come to complete realization. The first of these phases was experimental, and it was a reflection of what was happening in all of American literature—of what T. S. Eliot and e. e. cummings were doing in poetry; of what Dos Passos, Anderson and Hemingway were doing in prose; of what Maxwell Anderson and Eugene O'Neill were doing in drama. That Negro writers could now afford to be touched by these influences was in itself a good sign.

But the second phase is the one that is best remembered. One searches in vain for a term to characterize it, and for the exact impulses behind it. It was chock-full of many contradictory things. It showed itself naïve and sophisticated, elemental and overwrought, hysterical and sober, frivolous and worthwhile, joyously free and yet hopelessly enslaved. It is simple enough to attribute this to the effects of the just-ended war, which were many and deep, but the atavistic release at this time of certain aberrant tendencies in writing by Negroes can nowhere be matched in contemporary literature. It seems to have been at once a period of catharsis—indeed of complete abreaction—and of ingurgitation. It produced the poignant, simple beauty of Johnson's "The Creation" and the depressing futility of Wallace Thurman's *The Blacker the Berry*. In the same period, Claude McKay could write the wholesome, picaresque *Banjo* and the utterly inexcusable filth in *Banana Bottom*. The same Hughes who wrote "I've Known Rivers" and "Mother to Son" could also find satisfaction in creating the bizarre "The Cat and the Saxophone."

In general the mind of white America fastened upon the bizarre, the exotic and the atavistic elements of this second phase and turned them into a commercialized fad. Anyone who examines, even in a cursory fashion, the social history of the Twenties is immediately struck by the influence of Harlem upon it. That this Harlem was largely synthetic did not seem to matter. The

well-advertised belief was that in Harlem gaiety was king. The
revolters from Sauk Center, from Main Street and Winesburg,
from all the villages, found carnival in Harlem. Life, the dithy-
rambics said, had surge and sweep there—freedom, an honest
savagery; and as Langston Hughes wrote in "To Midnight Nan
at Leroy's":

> Hear dat music. . . .
> Jungle night.
> Hear dat music. . . .
> And the moon was white. . . .
> Jungle lover. . . .
> Night black boy. . . .
> Two against the moon
> And the moon was joy.

The moon was also papier-mâché.

So vicious was the commercial angle that Negroes (represented as being the very gods and goddesses of unrestrained joy),
who largely had no money anyway, could not—that is, were not
permitted to—enter the best-known "Negro" night clubs in the
world.

Commercialism was the bane of the Negro renaissance of the
Twenties. Jazz music, for instance, became no longer the unin-
hibited expression of unlearned music makers, but a highly
sophisticated and stylized pattern of musical sounds. The
Charleston, the Black Bottom, the Lindy Hop went down to
Broadway and Park Avenue and were taught in Arthur Murray's
dancing school. From being an authentic form, the blues became the torch song popularized by Ruth Etting and Helen
Morgan. The stuff in which Negro writers were working passed
into the less sincere hands of white writers, and Negro writers
themselves, from a high pitch of creation, fell relatively (and
pathetically) silent.

Three times within this century writing by American Negroes
has been done nearly to death, and yet today it is in an excellent
state of health.

When Richard Wright's *Uncle Tom's Children* was published
in 1938, only the least aware did not realize that a powerful
new pen was employing itself with stern and terrible material.
Then, when *Native Son* appeared in 1940, even the least aware
realized it. If the first book, a collection of lengthy novelettes, is
a clinical study of the human mind under the stress of violence,
then *Native Son* is even more a clinical study of the social
being under the cumulative effects of organized repression. The
two books complement each other. The theme of both is *prejudice*—prejudgment, conceptual prejudgment. If one needs that
expanded a little to make it crystal-clear, the theme is the effects of prejudice upon the human personality. For what Richard Wright deals with is only incidentally, for dramatic purposes,
and because of the authenticity of empiricism, the subject of
Negro and *white*. What he deals with is prejudice. ". . . Bigger
Thomas was not black all the time," he wrote in "How Bigger
Was Born," "he was white, too, and there were literally millions
of him, *everywhere*. . . . More than anything else, as a writer,
I was fascinated by the similarity of the emotional tensions of
Bigger in America and Bigger in Nazi Germany and Bigger in
old Russia. All Bigger Thomases, white and black, felt tense,
afraid, nervous, hysterical, and restless. . . . certain modern experiences were creating types of personalities whose existence
ignored racial and national lines of demarcation . . . these personalities carried with them a more universal drama-element
than anything I'd ever encountered before; [and] these personalities were mainly consequent upon men and women living in a
world whose fundamental assumptions could no longer be taken
for granted. . . ."

Because it was not in the truest sense particular and confined;
because it was in the absolute sense universal, the stuff with
which Wright employed his pen was stern and terrible.

Some critics have said that the wide appeal of Wright's work
is due to the sensationalism in it. But it is not this. One can have
serious doubts that the girl Sue in *Bright and Morning Star* or

Bessie in *Native Son* or the opening episode in *Long Black Song* would come off very well in Chinese or in Swedish or some other tongue. What does come off well in any language is the total concept of the primary evil of prejudice. This the Chinese and the Russians and the Norwegians and the French and all other peoples would understand; and a delineation of its effects, particular though it be, interests them in the same way and for the same reason that love interests them.

Black Boy, which does not prove the point—except perhaps very obliquely—does not deny it, either. Of course, this later book is autobiographical, which excuses it from the same kind of analysis that can be brought to bear upon the works of pure creation. But even here it may be argued, and not too incongruously, that Wright depicts, delineates, and skewers home the point that "to live habitually as a superior among inferiors, be the superiority intellectual or economic, is a temptation and hubris, inevitably deteriorating. . . ." And *that*, let it be averred, has nothing to do with the extrinsic particulars of race. It has an application as universal as "power corrupteth."

So Richard Wright was a new kind of writer in the ranks of Negro writers. He had extricated himself from the dilemma, the horns of which are (1) to write exclusively for a Negro audience and thereby limit oneself to a monotypical, glorified and race-proud picture of Negro life, and (2) to write exclusively for a white audience and thereby be trapped in the old stereotypes, the fixed opinions, the stock situations that are as bulwarks against honest creation. Negro writers traditionally have been impaled upon one or the other horn of this dilemma, sometimes in spite of all their efforts to avoid it.

Langston Hughes was undoubtedly sincere when he declared of young Negro artists and writers back in the Twenties: "If the white people are pleased, we are glad. If they aren't, it doesn't matter. . . . If colored people are pleased, we are glad. If they are not, their displeasure doesn't matter either. . . ." He was sincere, but mistaken.

A writer writes for an audience. Consciously or unconsciously, he bears in mind the real or imagined peculiarities of the audience to whom he wishes to appeal. Until very recent years, Negro writers did not believe that a white audience and a colored audience were essentially alike because, in fact, they were not. They were kept apart by a wide socio-cultural gulf—by differences of concept, by deliberately cultivated fears, taboos, ignorance, and race and caste consciousness. Now that gulf is closed and the writer can write without being either false to the one audience or subservient to the other. The hope that James Weldon Johnson expressed many years ago is being fulfilled at last. "Standing on his racial foundation," the Negro author can create that which rises above race and reaches "out to the universal in truth and beauty."

Thus Margaret Walker, writing for the two audiences now becoming one, can carry away an important poetry prize. Gwendolyn Brooks, in poetry such as her *Bronzeville*, can do things with the language of imagery that appeal to all humanity. No longer fearing the ancient interdiction, Chester Himes in *If He Hollers* writes forcefully, even if somewhat irrelevantly, of the sexual attraction a white woman feels for a Negro man; and William Attaway, in *Let Me Breathe Thunder*, can concern himself almost entirely with white characters. On the purely romantic and escapist side, Frank Yerby can write *The Foxes of Harrow*, which sells well over 600,000 copies and is bought by the movies. Thus the poetry of Gwendolyn Brooks, and Robert Hayden and Moses Carl Holman. Thus *The Street* by Ann Petry, *Invisible Man* by Ralph Ellison and *A Different Drummer* by William Melvin Kelley.

Though what is happening seems very like a miracle, it has been a long, long time in preparation. Writing by American Negroes has never been in such a splendid state of health, nor with such a bright and shining future before it.

2. *Arna Bontemps*

The Negro Renaissance: Jean Toomer
and the Harlem Writers of the 1920's

That story from one of the old countries about the man with the marriageable daughter comes to mind when I think of a leading literary pundit in the second decade of this century. In a land where brides were bartered it was, of course, not uncommon for subtle salesmanship to flourish. Sometimes it could become high pressured. In this old yarn the eager parent of the bride had recited so many of his daughter's excellent qualities the prospective husband began to wonder whether she had any human faults at all. "Well, yes," the father finally acknowledged. "A tiny one. She is just a little bit pregnant."

Similarly, in the Twenties the man whose comments on writing by or about Negroes were most respected was just a little bit Negro. He was William Stanley Braithwaite, literary critic for the Boston *Transcript* and editor of an annual series, "Anthologies of Magazine Verse, 1913–1929." In "Braithwaite's Anthologies," as they were commonly known, Spoon River poems by Edgar Lee Masters, chants by Vachel Lindsay, free verse by Carl Sandburg and the early works of many other important American poets were recognized and published before the authors had received general acceptance or acclaim.

But Braithwaite did not completely disassociate himself from

Negroes, as he might have. Indeed, he was awarded the Spingarn medal in 1917 as "the Negro who, according to a committee appointed by the board [of the NAACP], has reached the highest achievement in his field of activity." His occasional observations on Negro writing in the decade preceding Harlem's golden era are therefore useful as prologue. In 1913, for example, Braithwaite took note of James Weldon Johnson's "Fiftieth Anniversary Ode" on the Emancipation and suggested that it represented a move by the Negro poet to disengage himself. A decade of near silence had followed Paul Laurence Dunbar's last lyrics, and Braithwaite's language created an image of the Negro poet in chains, seeking to free himself.

The reappearance of this Johnson poem in a collection called *Fifty Years and Other Poems*, in 1917—the same year that Braithwaite was awarded the Spingarn medal, incidentally— prompted Braithwaite to remark, in effect, that this could be the beginning of something big, like a new awakening among Negro writers, perhaps. But, actually, Johnson's most significant poetic achievement was still a decade in the future, when his collection of folk sermons in verse was to be published as *God's Trombones* in 1927. Nevertheless, Braithwaite appears to have picked the right year for the first sign of "disengagement" or "awakening" or whatever it was. The year 1917 now stands out, where Negro poetry in the United States is concerned, as the year in which Claude McKay's poem "The Harlem Dancer" appeared in *The Seven Arts* magazine under the pen name of Eli Edwards. You may know the poem. It was in sonnet form:

> Applauding youths laughed with young prostitutes
> And watched her perfect, half-clothed body sway;
> Her voice was like the sound of blended flutes
> Blown by black players upon a picnic day.
> She sang and danced on gracefully and calm,
> The light gauze hanging loose about her form;
> To me she seemed a proudly-swaying palm
> Grown lovelier for passing through a storm.

Upon her swarthy neck black shiny curls
Luxuriant fell; and tossing coins in praise,
The wine-flushed, bold-eyed boys, and even the girls,
Devoured her shape with eager, passionate gaze;
But looking at her falsely-smiling face,
I knew her self was not in that strange place.

Now this I submit was the anticipation and the theme of an early outburst of creativity later described as the Negro or Harlem Renaissance. When McKay's "The Harlem Dancer" reappeared in his collection *Harlem Shadows* in 1922, along with other poems so fragrant and fresh they almost drugged the senses, things immediately began to happen. Here was poetry written from experience, differing from poetry written from books and other cultural media in somewhat the same way that real flowers differ from artificial ones. A chorus of other new voices led by Jean Toomer, Langston Hughes and Countee Cullen promptly began to make the Twenties a decade which *Time* magazine has described as Harlem's "golden age."

Interestingly, Braithwaite recognized McKay as the first voice in this new chorus, but he spoke of him as "a genius meshed in [a] dilemma." It bothered Braithwaite that McKay seemed to "waver between the racial and the universal notes." In some of his poems, Braithwaite felt, McKay was clearly "contemplating life and nature with a wistful sympathetic passion," but in others the poet became what Braithwaite called a "strident propagandist, using his poetic gifts to clothe arrogant and defiant thoughts." Braithwaite thought this was bad. He cited McKay's "The Harlem Dancer" and his "Spring in New Hampshire" as instances of the former, his "If We Must Die" as a shameless instance of the latter. But, ironically, a generation later it was "If We Must Die," a poem that would undoubtedly stir the blood of almost any Black Muslim, that Sir Winston Churchill quoted as climax and conclusion of his oration before the joint houses of the American Congress when he was seeking to draw this nation into the common effort in World War II. McKay had written it as the Negro American's defiant answer to lynching and mob violence in the Southern states. Churchill made it the voice of the embattled Allies as he read aloud McKay's poem "If We Must Die" (see p. 13).

(see p. 13)

Obviously neither Churchill nor McKay had at that time considered the possibilities of nonviolence. The poem does show, however, how a short span of years and certain historical developments can alter the meaning of a literary work. It also demonstrates the risk of trying to separate too soon the local or special subject from the universal.

But if Braithwaite's attitude toward Claude McKay was ambivalent, it was certainly unequivocal with respect to the second, and in some ways the most inspiring, of the writers who made the Harlem Renaissance significant in the long-range development of the Negro writer in the United States.

"In Jean Toomer, the author of *Cane*," Braithwaite wrote in 1925, "we come upon the very first artist of the race, who with all an artist's passion and sympathy for life, its hurts, its sympathies, its desires, its joys, its defeats and strange yearnings, can write about the Negro without the surrender or compromise of the artist's vision. So objective is it, that we feel that it is a mere accident that birth or association has thrown him into contact with the life he has written about. He would write just as well, just as poignantly, just as transmutingly, about the peasants of Russia, or the peasants of Ireland, had experience brought him in touch with their existence. *Cane* is a book of gold and bronze, of dusk and flame, of ecstasy and pain, and Jean Toomer is a bright morning star of a new day of the race in literature."

Cane was published in 1923 after portions of it had first appeared in *Broom, The Crisis, Double Dealer, Liberator, Little Review, Modern Review, Nomad, Prairie and S 4 N*. But *Cane* and Jean Toomer, its gifted author, presented an enigma—an enigma which has, if anything, deepened in the forty-three years since its publication. Given such a problem, perhaps one may be

excused for not wishing to separate the man from his work. Indeed, so separated, Toomer's writing could scarcely be understood at all, and its significance would escape us now as it has
escaped so many others in the past.

In any case, *Who's Who in Colored America* listed Toomer
in 1927 and gave the following vita:

b. Dec. 26, 1894, Washington, D. C.; s. Nathan and Nina (Pinch-
back) Toomer; educ. Public Scho., Washington, D. C.; Dunbar,
High Scho.; Univ. of Wisconsin, 1914–15; taught schools, Sparta,
Ga., for four months, traveled, worked numerous occupations; auth.
Cane, pub. Boni and Liveright, 1923; Short Stories and Literary
Criticisms in various magazines; address, c/o Civic Club, 439 W.
23rd St., New York, N. Y.

Needless to say, no subsequent listing of Toomer is to be
found in this or any other directory of conspicuous Negro Americans. Judging by the above, however, Toomer had always been
elusive, and the interest that *Cane* awakened did nothing to
change this. Several years later Toomer faded completely into
white obscurity leaving behind a literary mystery almost as intriguing as the disappearance of Ambrose Bierce into Mexico in
1913.

Why did he do it? What did it mean?

Concerned with writing, as we are, we automatically turn to
Toomer's book for clues. This could be difficult, because copies
are scarce. *Cane*'s two printings were small, and the few people
who went quietly mad about the strange book were evidently
unable to do much toward enlarging its audience. But among
these few was practically the whole generation of young Negro
writers then just beginning to appear, and their reaction to
Toomer's *Cane* marked an awakening that soon thereafter began
to be called a Negro renaissance.

Cane's influence was not limited to the happy band that included Langston Hughes, Countee Cullen, Eric Walrond, Zora
Neale Hurston, Wallace Thurman, Rudolph Fisher and their
contemporaries of the Twenties. Subsequent writing by Negroes

in the United States as well as in the West Indies and Africa has continued to reflect its mood and often its method, and, one feels, it also has influenced the writing about Negroes by others. And certainly no earlier volume of poetry or fiction or both had come close to expressing the ethos of the Negro in the Southern setting as *Cane* did.

There are many odd and provocative things about *Cane*, and not the least is its form. Reviewers who read it in 1923 were generally stumped. Poetry and prose were whipped together in a kind of frappé. Realism was mixed with what they called mysticism, and the result seemed to many of them confusing. Still, one of them could conclude that "*Cane* is an interesting, occasionally beautiful and often queer book of exploration into old country and new ways of writing." Another noted, "Toomer has not interviewed the Negro, has not asked opinions about him, has not drawn conclusions about him from his reactions to outside stimuli, but has made the much more searching, and much more self-forgetting effort of seeing life with him, through him."

Such comment was cautious, however, compared to the trumpetings of Waldo Frank in the Foreword he contributed:

A poet has arisen among our American youth who has known how to turn the essence and materials of his Southland into the essences and materials of literature. A poet has arisen in that land who writes, not as a Southerner, not as a rebel against Southerners, not as a Negro, not as apologist or priest or critic: who writes as a *poet*. The fashioning of beauty is ever foremost in his inspiration: not forcedly but simply, and because these ultimate aspects of his world are to him more real than all its specific problems. He has made songs and lovely stories of his land. . . .

The gifted Negro has been too often thwarted from becoming a poet because his world was forever forcing him to recollect that he was a Negro. The artist must lose such lesser identities in the great well of life. . . . The whole will and mind of the creator must go below the surfaces of race. And this has been an almost impossible condition for the American Negro to achieve, forced every moment of his life into a specific and superficial plane of consciousness. . . .

It seems to me, therefore, that this is a first book in more ways

than one. It is a harbinger of the South's literary maturity: of its
emergence from the obsession put upon its minds by the unending
racial crisis. . . . It marks the dawn of direct and unafraid creation. And, as the initial work of a man of twenty-seven, it is the
harbinger of a literary force of whose incalculable future I believe
no reader of this book will doubt.

It is well to keep in mind the time of these remarks. Of the
novels by which T. S. Stribling is remembered, only *Birthright*
had been published. Julia Peterkin had not yet published a book.
DuBose Heyward's *Porgy* was still two years away. William
Faulkner's first novel was three years away. His Mississippi
novels were six or more years in the future. Robert Penn Warren, a student at Vanderbilt University, was just beginning his
association with the Fugitive poets. His first novel was still more
than a decade and a half ahead. Tennessee Williams was just
nine years old.

A chronology of Negro writers is equally revealing. James
Weldon Johnson had written lyrics for popular songs, some of
them minstrel style, and a sort of documentary novel obscurely
published under a pseudonym, but *God's Trombones* was a good
four years in the offing. Countee Cullen's *Color* was two and
Langston Hughes' *The Weary Blues* three years away, though
both of these poets had become known to readers of the Negro
magazine *Crisis* while still in their teens, and Hughes at twenty-
one, the year of *Cane*'s publication, could already be called a
favorite.

The first fiction of the Negro Renaissance required apologies.
It was not first-rate. But it was an anticipation of what was to
come later. Even so, it followed *Cane* by a year or two, and
Eric Walrond's *Tropic Death* did not come for three. Zora Neale
Hurston's first novel was published in 1931, eight years after
Cane. Richard Wright made his bow with *Uncle Tom's Children* in 1938, fifteen years later. *Invisible Man* by Ralph Ellison
followed Toomer's *Cane* by just thirty years. James Baldwin was
not born when Toomer began to publish.

Waldo Frank's use of "harbinger" as the word for *Cane* becomes both significant and ironic when we recognize the debt most of these individuals owe Toomer. Consciously or unconsciously, one after another they picked up his cue and began making the "more searching" effort to see life *with* the Negro, "through him." *Cane* heralded an awakening of artistic expression by Negroes that brought to light in less than a decade a surprising array of talents, and these in turn made way for others. An equally significant change in the writing about Negroes paralleled this awakening. Strangely, however, *Cane* was not at all the harbinger Frank seemed to imagine. Despite his promise—a promise which must impress anyone who puts this first book beside the early writings of either Faulkner or Hemingway, Toomer's contemporaries—Jean Toomer rejected his prospects and turned his back on greatness.

The book by which we remember this writer is as hard to classify as its author. At first glance it appears to consist of assorted sketches, stories and a novelette interspersed with poems. Some of the prose is poetic, and often Toomer slips from one form into the other almost imperceptibly. The novelette is constructed like a play.

His characters, always evoked with effortless strength, are as recognizable as they are unexpected in the fiction of that period. Fern is a "creamy brown" beauty so complicated men take her "but get no joy from it." Becky is a white outcast beside a Georgia road who bears two Negro children. Laymon, a preacher-teacher in the same area, "knows more than would be good for anyone other than a silent man." The name character in the novelette *Kabnis* is a languishing idealist finally redeemed from cynicism and dissipation by the discovery of underlying strength in his people.

It doesn't take long to discover that *Cane* is not without design, however. A world of black peasantry in Georgia appears in the first section. The scene changes to the Negro community of Washington, D.C., in the second. Rural Georgia comes up

again in the third. Changes in the concerns of Toomer's folk are
noted as the setting moves from the Georgia pike to the bustling
Negro section in the nation's capital. The change in the level of
awareness that the author discloses is more subtle, but it is
clearly discernible when he returns to the Georgia background.

A young poet-observer moves through the book. Drugged by
beauty "perfect as dusk when the sun goes down," lifted and
swayed by folk song, arrested by eyes that "desired nothing that
you could give," silenced by "corn leaves swaying, rusty with
talk," he recognized that "the Dixie Pike has grown from a goat
path in Africa." A native richness is here, he concluded, and the
poet embraces it with the passion of love.

This was the sensual power most critics noticed and most
readers remembered about *Cane*. It was the basis for Alfred
Kreymborg's remark in *Our Singing Strength* that "Jean Toomer
is *one* of the finest artists among the dark people, if not *the*
finest." The reviewer for the New York *Herald Tribune* had the
rich imagery of *Cane* in mind when he said, "Here are the high
brown and black and half-caste colored folk of the cane fields,
the gin hovel and the brothel realized with a sure touch of art-
istry." But there remained much in the book that he could not
understand or appreciate. Speaking of Toomer's "sometimes
rather strident reactions to the Negro," he added that "at moments his outbursts of emotion approach the inarticulately
maudlin," though he had to admit that *Cane* represented "a distinct achievement wholly unlike anything of this sort done before."

Others found "obscurity" and "mysticism" in the novelette
which comprises the last third of the book. This is not surprising, for in Toomer's expressed creed "A symbol is as useful to
the spirit as a tool is to the hand," and his fiction is full of them.
Add to puzzling symbols an itch to find "new ways of writing"
that led him to bold experimentation and one may begin to see
why Toomer baffled as he pleased readers interested in writing
by or about Negroes in the early Twenties.

Kreymborg spoke of Toomer as "a philosopher and a psychologist by temperament" and went on to say that "the Washington writer is now fascinated by the larger, rather than the parochial interest of the human race, and should some day compose a book in the grand manner."

Of course, Toomer didn't, or at least he has not published one up to now, and to this extent Kreymborg has failed as a prophet, but his reference to Toomer as philosopher and psychologist was certainly on the mark, and his rather large estimate of this writer's capacities was significant, considering its date. The "new criticism," as we have come to recognize it, had scarcely been heard from then, and apparently it has still not discovered Toomer, but the chances are it may yet find him challenging. He would have comforted them, I am almost sorry to say, incarnating, as he does, some of their favorite attitudes. But at the same time, he could have served as a healthy corrective for others. Whether or not he would prove less complex or less rewarding than Gertrude Stein or James Joyce, for example, remains to be determined.

Saunders Redding gave *Cane* a close reading fifteen years after its publication and saw it as an unfinished experiment, "the conclusion to which we are fearful of never knowing, for since 1923 Toomer has published practically nothing." He meant, one assumes, that Toomer had published little poetry or fiction, or anything else that seemed closely related to *Cane* or to *Cane*'s author. Toomer had published provocative articles here and there as well as a small book of definitions and aphorisms during that time, and since then he has allowed two of his lectures to be published semi-privately. But Redding must be included in the small group who recognized a problem in *Cane* that has yet to be explained.

To him Toomer was a young writer "fresh from the South," who found a paramount importance in establishing "racial kinship" with Negroes in order to treat them artistically. He was impressed by Toomer's "unashamed and unrestrained" love for

the race and for the soil and setting that nourished it. He saw a
relationship between the writer's "hot, colorful, primitive" moods
and the "naïve hysteria of the spirituals," which he held in contrast to "the sophistic savagery of jazz and the blues." *Cane*, he
concluded, "was a lesson in emotional release and freedom."

Chapters about Toomer were included in Paul Rosenfeld's
Men Seen in 1925 and in Gorham B. Munson's *Destinations* in
1928, and elsewhere there are indications that Toomer continued to write and to experiment for at least a decade after the
publication of *Cane*. Long stories by him appeared in the second and third volumes of the *American Caravan*. A thoughtful
essay on "Race Problems and Modern Society" became part of a
volume devoted to *Problems of Civilization* in Baker Brownell's
series on "Man and His World." Seven years later, in the *New
Caravan* of 1936, Toomer presented similar ideas in the long
poem "Blue Meridian." Meanwhile, contributing a chapter to
the book *America & Alfred Stieglitz* in 1934, Toomer was explicit about his own writing as well as several other matters.

The rumor that Toomer had crossed the color line began cir-
culating when his name stopped appearing in print. But a
reasonable effort to find out what it was Toomer was trying to
say to us subsequently makes it hard to accept "passing" as the
skeleton key to the Jean Toomer mystery. He seemed too concerned with truth to masquerade. One wants to believe that
Toomer's mind came at last to reject the myth of race as it is
fostered in our culture. A man of fair complexion, indistinguishable from the majority of white Americans, he had always had a
free choice as to where he would take his place in a color-caste
scheme. Having wandered extensively and worked at odd jobs
in a variety of cities before he began contributing to little magazines, as he has stated, he could scarcely have escaped being
taken at face value by strangers who had no way of knowing that
the youth, who looked like Hollywood's conception of an Ivy
League basketball star, but who spoke so beautifully, whose very
presence was such an influence upon them, was not only a prod-

uct of the Negro community but a grandson of the man whom the *Dictionary of American Biography* describes as "the typical Negro politician of the Reconstruction."

Men of this kind, such as Walter White of the NAACP or Adam Clayton Powell of the U.S. Congress, sometimes called voluntary Negroes when they elect to remain in the fold, so to speak, have in other circumstances been discovered in strange places in our society—in neo-fascist organizations in the United States, among big city bosses, on movie screens, in the student body at "Ole Miss"—but seldom if ever before in an organization working "for understanding between people." Yet Jean Toomer's first publication, following the rumors and the silence, was "An Interpretation of Friends Worship," published by the Committee on Religious Education of Friends General Conference, 1515 Cherry Street, Philadelphia, 1947. It was followed two years later by a pamphlet, "The Flavor of Man." The writing is eloquent with commitment. It reflects unhurried reading and contemplation, as was also true of his piece on "Race Problems and Modern Society." Toomer did not fail to remind his readers that certain racial attitudes could not be condoned. He certainly did not speak as a Negro bent on escaping secretly into white society. Jean Toomer, who, like his high-spirited grandfather, had exuberantly published his pride in his Negro heritage, appears to have reached a point in his thinking at which categories of this kind tend to clutter rather than classify. The stand he appears to have taken at first involved nothing more clandestine than the closing of a book or the changing of a subject.

Yet he is on record as having denied later that he was a Negro. That is a story in itself. Nevertheless, at that point, it seems, Jean Toomer stepped out of American letters. Despite the richness of his thought, his gift of expression, he ceased to be a writer and, as I have suggested, turned his back on greatness. His choice, whatever else may be said about it, reflects the human sacrifices in the field of the arts exacted by the racial myth on which so much writing in the United States is based. While he may have escaped its strictures and inconveniences in his personal life, he did not get away from the racial problem in any real sense. His dilemmas and frustrations as a writer are equally the dilemmas and frustrations of the Negro writers who have since emerged. The fact that most of them have not been provided with his invisible cloak makes little difference. He is their representative man. He stands as their prototype.

What, then, ordinarily happened to the Negro writer of Toomer's time in America after his first phase, after he had been published and taken his first steps? Encouraged by reviewers, assured that his talent was genuine, that he was not *just* a Negro writer but an American writer who happened to be a Negro, that his first book had broken new ground and that his next would be awaited with keen interest unrelated to any exotic qualities he may have shown but simply as arresting art, he was readily convinced. The "American writer" tag was especially appealing. It stuck in his mind, and when he got the bad news from the sales department, he coupled it with remarks he had heard from his publishers about a certain "resistance" in bookstores to books about "the problem." Obviously the solution for him, as an American writer, was not to write narrowly about Negroes but broadly about people.

So sooner or later he did it: a novel not intended to depict Negro life. The results may be examined: Paul Laurence Dunbar's *The Love of Landry*, Richard Wright's *Savage Holiday*, Chester B. Himes' *Cast the First Stone*, Ann Petry's *Country Place*, Zora Neale Hurston's *Seraph on the Suwanee*, James Baldwin's *Giovanni's Room*, along with Jean Toomer's *York Beach*. While the implication that books about whites are about people while those about Negroes are *not* should have provoked laughter, the young Negro writer was too excited to catch it. The discovery which followed was that the bookstore "resistance" was not removed by this switch. Moreover, he found to his dismay that friendly reviewers had in most instances become cool. In any case, none of these writers seemed sufficiently encouraged by the results to continue in the same direction. Whatever it was that blocked the Negro writer of fiction, that denied him the kind of acceptance accorded the Negro maker of music, for example, was clearly not just the color of his characters.

Southern white novelists from T. S. Stribling to Julia Peterkin to DuBose Heyward to William Faulkner to Robert Penn Warren had thronged their novels with Negroes of all descriptions without appearing to meet reader resistance or critical coolness. So now it could be seen that the crucial issue was not the choice of subject but the author's attitude toward it. With this knowledge the young Negro writers pondered and then made their decisions. Dunbar chose drink. Wright and Himes went to Paris to think it over, as did James Baldwin, at first. Toomer disappeared into Bucks County, Pennsylvania. Frank Yerby, on the basis of a short story in *Harper's Magazine* and a manuscript novel that went the rounds without finding a publisher, took the position that "an unpublished writer, or even one published but unread, is no writer at all." He chose "entertainment" over "literature," and worked his way out of the segregated area of letters in the costume of a riverboat gambler. His book *The Foxes of Harrow* about the Mississippi riverboat gambler became the first successful non-Negro novel by a Negro American writer.

A curious historical irony is suggested. The memoirs of George H. Devol, published in 1887 under the title *Forty Years a Gambler on the Mississippi*, relates the following about a cabin boy called Pinch:

I raised him and trained him. I took him out of a steamboat barber shop. I instructed him in the mysteries of card-playing, and he was an apt pupil. . . .

Devol recalled with much amusement a night they left New Orleans on the steamer *Doubloon*:

There was a strong team of us—Tom Brown, Holly Chappell, and the boy Pinch. We sent Pinch and staked him to open a game of

chuck-aluck with the Negro passengers on deck, while we opened
up monte in the cabin. The run of luck that evening was something
grand to behold. I do not think there was a solitary man on the boat
that did not drop around in the course of the evening and lose his
bundle. When about thirty miles from New Orleans a heavy fog
overtook us, and it was our purpose to get off and walk about six
miles to Kennersville, where we could take the cars to the city.

Pinchback got our valises together, and a start was made. A driz-
zling rain was falling, and the darkness was so great that one could
not see his hand before his face. Each of us grabbed a valise except
Pinch, who carried along the faro tools. The walking was so slippery
that we were in the mud about every ten steps, and poor Pinch he
groaned under the load that he carried. At last he broke out:

"Tell you what it is, Master Devol, I'll be dumbed if this aint
rough on Pinch. Ise going to do better than this toting along old faro
tools."

"What's that, Pinch? What you going to do?"

"Ise going to get into that good old Legislature and I'll make Rome
howl if I get there."

Of course I thought at the time that this was all bravado and brag;
but the boy was in earnest, and sure enough he got into the Legislature, became Lieutenant Governor, and by the death of the Governor
he slipped into the gubernatorial chair, and at last crawled into the
United States Senate.

Without necessarily accepting the gambler Devol as an authority on Reconstruction history we may still take his account
as substantially factual. P. B. S. Pinchback himself often referred to his career on the river. He was still a prominent public
figure when these memoirs were published. He could have denied them had he wished. That Frank Yerby, who became a
teacher in a Negro college in Louisiana after his graduation
from Fisk University, should center the story of *The Foxes of
Harrow* around a Mississippi riverboat gambler is not an odd
coincidence. But that Jean Toomer should be the grandson of
Pinchback and one of the two people to accompany his body
back to New Orleans for burial in 1921 suggests another historical irony.

The behavior pattern known sociologically as "passing for white," then, has its literary equivalent, and the question it raises is whether or not this is proper in the arts. The writer's desire to widen his audience by overcoming what has been called resistance to racial material is certainly understandable, but sooner or later the Negro novelist realizes that what he has encountered, as often critical as popular, is more subtle than that. What annoys some readers of fiction, it seems, is not so much that characters in a book are Negro or white or both as the *attitude of the writer* toward these characters. Does he accept the status quo with respect to the races? If so, any character or racial situation can be taken in stride, not excluding miscegenation. But rejection of traditional status, however reflected, tends to alienate these readers.

On the other hand, the Negro reader has little taste for any art in which the racial attitudes of the past are condoned or taken for granted. Since this is what he has come to expect in the fiction in which he sees himself, he too has developed resistance. His is a wider resistance to the whole world of the contemporary novel. To him literature means poetry, by and large. He knows Phillis Wheatley and Paul Laurence Dunbar far better than he knows any prose writers of the past. James Weldon Johnson and Countee Cullen are familiar and honored names. There is seldom a sermon in a Negro church, a commencement, a banquet, a program in which one of these or a contemporary poet like Hughes or Margaret Walker or Gwendolyn Brooks is not quoted. But the Negro novelists, aside from Richard Wright, possibly, are lumped with the whole questionable lot in the mind of this reader. When he is not offended by the image of himself that modern fiction has projected, he is at least embarrassed.

The Negro writer, like the white writer of the South, is a product of the Southern condition. Whether he wills it or not, he reflects the tensions and cross-purposes of that environment. Just as the myth of the old South weakens under close examination, the myth of literature divorced from what have been called sociological considerations dissolves in a bright light.

The fictional world on which most of us first opened our eyes, where the Negro is concerned, is epitomized by a remark made by a character in William Faulkner's *Sartoris*. "What us niggers want ter be free fer, anyhow?" asks old Uncle Simon. "Ain't we got es many white folks now es we kin suppo't?"

The elusiveness of Jean Toomer in the face of complexities like these can well stand for the elusiveness of Negro writers from Charles W. Chesnutt to Frank Yerby. What Toomer was trying to indicate to us by the course he took still intrigues, but I suspect he realizes by now that there is no further need to *signify*. The secrets are out. As the song says, "There's no hiding place down here."

3.   *Horace R. Cayton*

Ideological Forces
in the Work of Negro Writers

We are all imprisoned within our culture. It is almost impossible to break through the customary ways of perceiving the world about us in order that we may question in a fundamental sense the values held by society.

Sometimes a new critical perspective of society and its culture is stimulated by powerful ideological developments which throw new light on the everyday world of events. A new perspective can lead to insight and change. These revelations come to philosophers, scientists, political leaders and, above all, to the artist. And of all the artists, it has been the writer who, from the beginning of time, has fashioned various brave new worlds.

The creative process of the writer is difficult to describe and understand. It may be said that all men dream of freedom, but it requires the powerful revelation and perception of the artist to capture these dreams and put them into shape.

We must understand the influences of various ideological forces as they have touched the perceptions and insights of Negro writers if we are to understand the prophets and poets of the New Negro in contemporary American society.

Among the most crucial and fundamental forces affecting the Negro writer have been those of psychoanalysis and the several disciplines of the social sciences.

37

I am a sociologist by training and a writer by temperament. Many sociologists consider me one of them, and I usually tell them I am a writer. When writers think of me as a writer, I tell them I'm probably more of a sociologist. And this leads me into a fundamental concern: the question of identity.

I shall start with an autobiographical statement (perhaps because I have recently completed an autobiography) * I was born in Seattle at the turn of the century. I discovered at a very early age, perhaps three or four, that I was a Negro. And I became aware that I would always be one and that Negroes would always be underprivileged and stigmatized, a group of people set apart. I also knew that I was an American, and, in school as well as in the home, I learned that America had a dream of freedom. These two identities, both of which I had internalized, seemed to be in constant conflict. When I became aware of the conflict, I was confused.

Allen Wheelis, in his book *The Quest for Identity*,† writes:

Nowadays, the sense of self is deficient. The questions of adolescence —"Who am I?" "Where am I going?" "What is the meaning of life?" —receive no final answers. Nor can they be laid aside. The uncertainty persists. The period of being uncommitted is longer, the choices with which it terminates more tentative. Personal identity does not become fixed, does not, therefore, provide an unchanging vantage point from which to view experience. Man is still the measure of all things, but it is no longer the inner man that measures: it is the *other* man. Specifically, it is the plurality of men, the group. And what the group provides is shifting patterns, what it measures is conformity. It does not provide the hard inner core by which the value of patterns and conformity is determined. The hard inner core has in our time become diffuse, elusive, often fluid. More than ever before one is aware of the identity he appears to have, and more than ever before is dissatisfied with it. It doesn't fit, it seems alien, as though the unique course of one's life had been determined by untoward accident. Commitments of all kinds, social, vocational, mari-

---

* Horace Cayton, *Long Old Road*. New York: Trident Press, 1965.
† New York: W. W. Norton, 1958.

tal, moral, are made more tentatively. Long-term goals seem to become progressively less feasible.

Wheelis continues to observe that:

Identity is a *coherent* sense of self, it depends upon the awareness that one's endeavors and one's life make sense, that they are meaningful in the context in which life is lived. It depends also upon stable values, and upon the conviction that one's actions and values are harmoniously related. It is a sense of wholeness, of integration, of knowing what is right and what is wrong and of being able to choose.

. . . The past half century has encompassed enormous gains in understanding and in mastery; but many of the old fixed points of reference have been lost, and have not been replaced.

The insecurity I felt as a child—torn between what I had been taught and what was—has now spread to all society. While I found to an extent an identity, other Negroes and the whole of American society remain confronted by this question.

Richard Wright and Ralph Ellison were fascinated with what Herbert Hill describes as that "vast, senseless social order which destroys its victim" and which poses "the necessity to remain sane in a society where the individual personality is denied and the world appears devoid of meaning." Hill goes on to say that "Essentially the framework for *Native Son,* one of the important novels in contemporary American literature, is to be found in its implicit assumption that the social order is directly responsible for the degradation of the Negro, that American society produces conditions which distort and destroy individual human beings who are part of an oppressed group. The character in the book who functions as Wright's spokesman states that 'Taken collectively they are not simply twelve million people. In reality they constitute a separate nation, shunned and stripped and held captive within this nation, devoid of political, social, economic, and property rights.' "*

* Herbert Hill, Introduction, *Soon, One Morning—New Writing by American Negroes.* New York: Knopf, 1963.

The loss of identity ultimately leads the individual to a state of alienation both from himself and from the society at large. He is then constantly preoccupied with the seeking of "the self," and this is where his time and energy are spent. Several Negro intellectuals have protested against this. Thus Saunders Redding has written: "The obligations imposed by race upon the average educated and talented Negro . . . are vast and become at last onerous. I am tired of giving up my creative initiative to these demands."*

Before considering the psychological effects of American culture on both the blacks and the whites, I shall touch briefly upon the historical aspect of the Negro. It is unique in terms of world history. I subscribe to the school of thought that little, very little of African culture was brought to the United States and that that which the Negro did retain was isolated and died a rapid death. What I am saying is that the so-called American Negro subculture is purely a product of the Negro's experience in America; it is the American culture refracted through the prism of three hundred years of subordination.

E. Franklin Frazier, in his last book, *The Negro Church*, describes the slow growth of cohesiveness in the Negro community. The cruelty of the plantation system did not even permit the development of a stable family group. It was the Negro church that first brought some cohesion to the Negro. It was many years before Negroes as a group could even envision a free world. Certainly there were slave revolts and insurrections, but it was not until the Negro, as a group, began to have revelations (similar to the one I experienced upon learning that at Port Arthur in 1905 the Japanese, a colored race, had defeated the Russians, predominantly a Caucasian nation) that the Negro began to search for his identity, for a definition, recognition and purpose.

The only way to analyze the position of the Negro in America

* Saunders Redding, *On Being Negro in America*. Indianapolis: Bobbs-Merrill, 1951.

is to analyze the culture in its entirety. America has failed to develop a meaningful way of life that could make our country great, a way of fulfilling the vast areas of our individual personalities that are unused and truncated. This is evidenced by the indescribable loneliness that pervades our existence. We have embraced and are the victims of a configuration of shoddy values, the "get-rich-quick" compulsion, and our surrender to the bitch goddess of material success. Our emphasis is on sex for gratification rather than deep organic emotional expression, experience and communication. We are unable to formulate a meaningful religion in spite of frenetic churchgoing, and unable to rid ourselves of an archaic economic system that defies all laws of logic, humanity and downright common sense. And this in the most bountiful country in the world; a country birthed in principles both noble and bold, familiarized to us all as the American Dream.

American culture places high value on appearances, and beauty—by all means one must be beautiful—must conform to the stereotyped norms of so-called Anglo-Saxon beauty and appearance. Along with this Anglo-Saxon appearance comes the puritan ideology, engulfing one in attitudes such as "cleanliness is next to godliness." But the next step in this train of thought, as it applies to the Negro, is quite obvious. He is made to feel dirty, and consequently evil. From the point of appearance alone, the Negro is not in step with the established and accepted norms. And perhaps it is at just this point that a Negro first begins to develop his sense of shame over his very blackness. The black boy or girl learns much more early than we realize that there is something wrong with him. That he isn't just an ordinary person. That he has a stigma which he must live with for the rest of his life. This sets up great waves of shame that engulf the entire personality, the whole physical and psychological being. The reason for the all-pervasiveness of the feeling of shame is that shame has no specific focal point for cause. Shame is the result of a vague, over-all rejection. The reasons for the rejection are irrational and without structure. Shame, all too frequently, has unknown roots.

I knew that shame was something I had to fight. And for a group of people who have lived for hundreds of years as a shamed people it almost takes a conversion in the form of a religious experience to overcome that sense of shame.

Accompanying the feeling of shame is a reaction pattern, a theory which I developed in a sort of interaction between Richard Wright and myself. It is what I have called the fear-hate-fear syndrome.

Let me begin with a certain Negro girl, the only one that dared to enter an all-white school, walking the gantlet of her fellow students, who formed a double line and spat in her face as she passed. That picture was on the front page of the *New York Times* and but a few hours later was reproduced not only in *Pravda* and *Izvestia*, but in Paris, London, the Scandinavian countries, and in all of the non-white countries of the world, including those we try to buy with so-called foreign aid.

As a writer I try to imagine what went on in this cruel drama. What did the Negro girl do when she got home? What gave her such dignity and poise? And what of the little white girls who had performed this ritual of spitting? Surely we have fouled our nest, we have corrupted our children.

Do you wonder then that there are Black Muslims in the United States who have found relief from this situation by openly hating all white people? Let me confess, although I am for human dignity and would fight for whites if they were abused, humiliated and spat upon, there is a residue of hate in my heart as I think there is in most Negroes living in the United States.

To explain this I developed a theory. Several years ago I wrote a speech in which I tried to state in technical terms what I believed to be the psychology of many Negroes at that time, although it is perhaps currently changing. I quote: "I am convinced that at the core of the Negro's mentality there is a 'fear-hate-fear' complex. My assumption is that all men in West-

ern European civilization have unconscious guilt and fear of
punishment for this guilt. In the case of the dominant group this
guilt is to a large extent irrational. It can be shown to be false, a
figment of the imagination, a holdover from early childhood experiences. Guilt can more easily be resolved by psychiatric treatment or even by rational cogitation. But in the Negro the
psychological problem is ever intensified. For him, punishment
in the actual environment is ever present: violence, psychological and physical, leaps at him from every side. The personality
is brutalized by an unfriendly environment. This reinforces and
intensifies the normal insecurity he feels as a person living in our
highly complex society. Such attacks on his personality lead to
resentment and hatred of the white man. However, the certain
knowledge that he will be punished if his hate emotions are discovered only compound his fear. This is the Negro reaction to
his own brutalization, subordination and hurt. It is this vicious
cycle in which the American Negro is caught and in which his
personality is pulverized by an ever-mounting self-propelling
rocket of emotional conflict. The Negro has been hurt; he knows
it. He wants to strike back, but he must not—there is evidence
everywhere that to do so would lead to his destruction."

Each of us is well aware of the brutalities that happened only
yesterday. I shall speak autobiographically to make my point
more vivid. My father was born a slave; when I think of it now
it is unbelievable that the body of my father could have been
bought and sold like an ox or a horse. I remember hearing in my
childhood, I was ten, of a Negro who was lynched: his genitals
were cut off his living body, then he was chained to a tree and
burned alive. They tied his carcass to a car and dragged it
down the main street of the town.

Do you doubt that that left a scar on my soul? That some ves-
tige of hate and fear remains, although I have gone through
psychoanalysis and am emotionally committed to the "democratic ideal"? I learned that my problem as a person was no different from that of the Japanese or the Mexican. I learned that

it was the basic problem of adjustment to rejection and fear. Subordination, whatever the cause, produces the same result. When that subjection is based on force and violence the inevitable product in the human personality must be fear and hate.

How has the Negro dealt with his feelings of shame? There are several paths open to the Negro. Perhaps the one most in evidence today is the mass rejection of shame as the members of the mass strengthen each other by real or symbolic acts.

There is another path. It is the redefinition of the past by discovering a more glorious past as it was imagined to have been in Africa. And, of course, there have been various Negro nationalist movements from time to time. I first saw this phenomenon when Marcus Garvey came to Seattle to lead a nationalist parade. Garvey organized a million black Americans and, although his goals were foolish, the pride he stirred in black hearts was very real. I was just a young man then, for it was back in the late Twenties. There had been a parade down Second Avenue, the main street of Seattle, and thousands had followed their leader, their Messiah, who was to lead them back to Africa and to Freedom—the Honorable Marcus Aurelius Garvey, D.C.L., founder of the Black Universal Negro Improvement Association, a self-educated, eloquent and fanatically zealous Jamaican. In the parade were Negro women in the uniform of Black Cross nurses and others who wore wrapped puttees of the African Motorcycle Corps. Negro men were in the uniform of the Black Eagle Flying Corps and, in front, the Royal African Legions rode on horses.

It was ludicrous and laughable, but the black washerwomen were deadly serious, and the black men, laborers and servants, had a pride that raised the demonstration out of the absurd and struck fear or admiration in the watchers. On the dark faces, for the first time, there was pride and joy and fulfillment, reflecting limpid faith in the completeness of living which they had found. Later on, at a meeting at the Star Theatre, I heard Garvey deliver in deep resonant tones their slogan: "One God! One

Aim! One Destiny!" For the Garveyites, he was a savior, a Messiah who promised to snatch them from the edge of the abyss and turn their grief into greatness. He had put steel in the spines of Negroes who had previously been ashamed of their color. I tried to tell my parents about it later, but when I described fat black washerwomen in tight motorcycle pants they laughed. And I quickly stopped them, saying, "Don't laugh, they were proud. This is the first time I have ever seen Negroes walking down the streets of a white city with pride and dignity."

The Garvey movement was the only real mass movement among American Negroes. And it was based on glorifying things black. The Garveyites were going to have Black Cross nurses rather than White Cross or Red Cross nurses, a black house rather than a white house, a Black Star steamship line rather than a White Star line. It was ludicrous, certainly, but it fulfilled a deep hunger in the hearts of more than a million American Negroes, a valid hunger, a hunger that still exists. In the thirty or thirty-five years since Garvey, that hunger has deepened, been made more acute. If America does not allow the Negro to find pride in himself as an American, then he will inevitably seek acceptance as a black man. As for the Black Muslims, their goals are just as foolish as Garvey's. But they are appealing to the same hunger. In that sense, they are on valid ground. I will not join them, although I have been tempted. I still hope for—forgive me if I seem naïve—the fulfillment of the American Dream for all people, no matter what color. I haven't given that up yet.

James Baldwin writes to his nephew in "My Dungeon Shook":

Please try to remember that what they believe, as well as what they do and cause you to endure, does not testify to your inferiority, but their inhumanity and fear . . .

There is no reason for you to try to become like white people and there is no basis whatever for their impertinent assumption that *they* must accept *you*. The really terrible thing, old buddy, is that *you* must accept *them*, and I mean that very seriously. You must accept them and accept with love. For these innocent people have no other hope. They are in effect still trapped in a history which they do not understand; and until they understand it, they cannot be released from it.

Our failure to achieve a mature culture in which Negroes and whites alike can accomplish some aspect of personality integration has within it the seeds of political fascism. And if the emotionally truncated lives of Negroes lead many of them to give up a fruitless struggle and submit to the certainty of a harsh dictator, many whites, in their immature longing for a meaning to their lives and for a security they have not been able to find, act in a manner that would indicate they, too, are longing for the strong though cruel father who will dictate the functions of their lives.

There is another ideology that has profoundly affected the American Negro.

The Communist movement in the United States seized upon the Scottsboro case and the crisis of the Depression as a golden opportunity to seek recruits among Negroes. According to Rayford Logan, soon after World War I the Communists sought to win the support of Negro workers in the North.* However, the Communists' Sixth World Congress made a fatal mistake when, in 1928, it resolved to work toward the formation of a separate black nation within the United States. An overwhelming majority of Negroes had no more desire to settle in a separate nation than they had to go back to Africa, but the Communists, sensing the propaganda value of the Scottsboro trials, stole the Scottsboro case from the NAACP and made violent attacks on W. E. B. Du Bois, who as editor of *The Crisis* brilliantly exposed the fraudulent program of the Communist party. Since most Negroes knew of the work of men like Du Bois, and had never heard of Marx or Lenin, and also, since they were fundamentally loyal Americans despite their second-class citizenship, this Communist maneuver won little confidence among Negroes.

* See Rayford W. Logan, *The Negro in the United States.* Princeton, New Jersey: D. Van Nostrand Company, Inc., 1957.

Even in 1934, after five years of the Depression and before the New Deal had begun to reach down to Negroes, I estimate that less than 2,000 Negroes were members of the American Communist party out of a total of 24,000 party members. The frequent shifting of the Communist party position on "the Negro question" after 1934 repeated the failures of the previous years and prevented the Communists from building a permanent base within the Negro community. As Professor Wilson Record has aptly said in his authoritative study,* American Negroes refused to succumb to a siren song sung in bass.

Quite apart from the failure of the Communists to organize Negroes, they did provide a tremendous stimulant to the thinking and writing of Negroes. First, the Russian Revolution itself startled the civilized world. Then, when the Communists started working with American Negroes, they offered them the hope that if black and white would unite there would be a free world. This stimulated Negroes to a further reconsideration of the possibility of a more meaningful existence. But few Negroes were aware of the depth of their distrust toward the whites. Besides, the Communist party in America used incredibly poor tactics. The fundamental fact was that the Negroes simply did not trust the white working class and its discriminatory labor unions. And they did not trust them for good reason, for the white working class had traditionally been the Negroes' enemy and in this there has been no fundamental change.

But the issue for some was more complicated. Thus Richard Wright, for example, an Alabama boy, caught some vision of a different world as the result of the Marxist influence. He envisioned a world in which he could walk with dignity, and he was for an important period of his life seduced by the Communist vision, which, in a sense, defeated the great potential that was his, for his eventual disenchantment with the Communists caused him to devote much of his later life and energy fighting

* *Race and Radicalism: The NAACP and the Communist Party in Conflict.* Ithaca, New York: Cornell University Press, 1964.

them because they had tricked and lied to him. That same energy might have gone into brilliant literary work.

Yet, one cannot ignore the fact that the Communist party, with all its failures, still had immense influence on Wright as a writer. In his "Blueprint for Negro Writing" published in *The New Challenge*, Wright said:

. . . in the lives of Negro writers must be found those materials and experiences which will create a meaningful picture of the world today. Many young writers have grown to believe that a Marxist analysis of society presents such a picture. It creates a picture, which, when placed before the eyes of the writer, should unify his personality, organize his emotions, buttress him with a tense and obdurate will to change the world. And in turn, this changed world will dialectically change the writer. Hence, it is through a Marxist conception of reality and society that the maximum degree of freedom in thought and feeling can be gained for the Negro writer. Further, this dramatic Marxist vision, when consciously grasped, endows the writer with a sense of dignity which no other vision can give. Ultimately, it restores to the writer his lost heritage, that is, his role as a creator of the world in which he lives, and as a creator of himself.

I am inextricably concerned with the problems of the Negro and with the possibility of enriching the American culture, so I must act in some fashion, for a tremendous racial confrontation is taking place. Confrontation is an old and honorable word which has recently come into current usage. It means a direct face-to-face meeting of people or peoples with conflicting interests, ideas or values, which must be resolved. A confrontation may be resolved by a synthesis of these conflicting ideologies or beliefs or it may result in avoidance, isolation or violence. A confrontation is always a tense, meaningful and fateful phenomenon: "Me, the snares of death confronted me" is the text of Psalm 18:5.

How much time have we to convince the Americans and the world that democracy does not mean white domination? Not much. I believe that the Negro must get himself into positions of power. We need laws and the continuation of picket lines and demonstrations to awaken our people and the whole of American society.

I'd like to quote Richard Wright's introductory essay to Dr. St. Clair Drake's and my book, *Black Metropolis*: "Will the Negro, in the language of André Malraux, find a meaning in his humiliation, make his slums and his sweat-shops his modern cathedrals out of which will be born a new consciousness that can guide him toward freedom? Or will he continue as he does today, saying Job-like to the society that crushes him: Though it slays me, Yet will I trust in it."

This, for Richard Wright was a rhetorical question. Long before many he had sensed the dictates of history. If James Baldwin is the poet of the Negro revolt, Richard Wright was its prophet. In 1941, Wright wrote the text of a picture book entitled *12 Million Black Voices*,* which was both poetic and prophetic. In it he stated:

We black folk, our history and our present being, are a mirror of all the manifold experiences in America. What we want, what we represent, what we endure is what America *is*. If we black folk perish, America will perish. If America has forgotten her past, then I let her look into the mirror of our consciousness and she will see the living past living in the present, for our memories go back, through our black folk of today, through the recollections of our black parents, and through the tales of slavery told by our black grandparents, to the time when none of us, black or white, lived in this fertile land.

The differences between black folk and white folk are not blood or color, and the ties that bind us are deeper than those that separate us. The common road of hope which we all have traveled has brought us into a stronger kinship than any words, laws, or legal claims.

Look at us and know us and you will know yourselves, for *we* are *you*, looking back at you from the dark mirror of our lives!

What do we black folk want?

We want what others have, the right to share in the upward march of American life, the only life we remember or have ever known. The lords of the land say: "We will not grant this!"

* New York: Viking Press, 1941.

We answer: "We ask you to grant us nothing. We are winning our heritage, though our toll in suffering is great!" The bosses of the building say: "Your problem is beyond solution!" We answer: "Our problem is being solved. We are crossing the line you dared us to cross, though we pay in the coin of death!"

The seasons of the plantation no longer dictate the lives of many of us: hundreds of thousands of us are moving into the sphere of conscious history.

We are with the new tide. We stand at the crossroads. We watch each new procession. The hot wires carry urgent appeals. Print compels us. Voices are speaking. Men are moving! And we shall be with them. . . .

4.   *LeRoi Jones*

Philistinism and the Negro Writer

I went to a high school in New Jersey that was mainly attended by children of Italian parentage. It was about 98 percent white. At first there were only six Negroes, then twelve Negroes in the entire school. I wanted to see the other part of the world, so I went off to Howard University, a Negro school in Washington, D.C., and when I got to Howard, it shocked me into realizing the terrible sickness of my father. Later I came to understand a little more, but I hated my father in the sense of his not being a man. That is, because he was a person who did not have a college degree and who had to run an elevator, and I did not understand. Now, perhaps, I have come to understand why this occurs.

Howard University shocked me into realizing how desperately sick the Negro could be, how he could be led into self-destruction and how he would not realize that it was the society that had forced him into a great sickness. For instance, a story I told to Herbert Hill, which, I suppose, has become apocryphal, deals with life at Howard University. A student friend (he is now a lawyer in Philadelphia) and I were sitting on the campus studying one day and a watermelon truck passed, and I said, "Let's go buy a watermelon." So we bought this watermelon and went to sit on a bench in front of Douglas Hall. Tom Weaver, the boy I was with, had to go to class, and I was left there alone, sawing on the watermelon. The Dean of Men (who might still be the Dean of Men) came up to me and said, "What are you doing?" And I said, "Well, what do you mean? I'm just sitting here." And he said, "Why are you sitting there eating that water-melon?" I said, "Well, I don't know. I didn't know there was a reason for it, I'm just eating it." And he said, "Throw that away, this very instant." And I answered, "Well, sir, I can only throw half of it away, because I only own half. The other part of it is Mr. Weaver's and he's in class, so I have to wait until he comes out and gets it." The Dean, now quite agitated, replied with great emotion, "Do you realize you're sitting right in front of the highway where white people can see you? Do you realize that this school is the capstone of Negro higher education? Do you realize that you're compromising the Negro?" I was, of course, shocked. Later I had other experiences. For instance, the teacher who was in charge of the Music School there told Professor Sterling Brown, and some others who wanted to or-ganize a jazz concert at Howard, that jazz never, never would be played in the Music and Art building. When they finally did let jazz in, it was Stan Kenton. These are all examples of how American society convinces the Negro that he is inferior, and then he starts conducting his life that way. So that I find myself, now, reacting very quickly to Negroes who talk about "good hair." There are some who think that being light-skinned is somehow preferable to being dark. It's weird, especially if you are dark, to think like that—to not realize that this is another burden, something they have put on your back to carry around, so that you can't straighten up and confront them as man to man, but rather as man and something else.

When I went into the Army it shocked me into realizing the hysterical sickness of the oppressors and the suffering of my own people. When I went into the Army I saw how the oppressors suffered by virtue of their oppressions—by having to oppress, by having to make believe that the weird, hopeless fantasy that they had about the world was actually true. They actually do believe that. And this weight is something that deforms them and, finally, makes them even more hopeless than lost black men. It is because of this knowledge of the society around me that I have stated that "I write now full of trepidation, because I know the death that society intends for me. I see Jimmy Baldwin almost unable to write about himself any more. I've seen Du Bois die on another continent, Chester Himes driven away, Ellison silenced and fidgeting away in some college. I think I almost feel the same forces massing against me, almost before I've begun, but let them understand that this is a fight without quarter and I'm very fast."

The denial of reality has been institutionalized in America, and any honest man, especially an artist, suffers because of it. That is how the institution perpetuates itself, through the suffering of the honest or the naïve. For myself, I aspire to the craziness of all honest men, that is, the craziness that will make a man keep talking even after everyone else says he shouldn't. Perhaps one way Negroes could force institutionalized dishonesty to crumble, and its apologizers to break and run, would be to turn crazy, to bring out a little American Dada, Ornette Coleman style, and chase these perverts into the ocean where they belong.

The Negro writer is in a peculiar position, because if he is honest most of what he has seen and experienced in America will not flatter it. His vision and experience cannot be translated honestly into art by euphemism, and while this is true of any good writer in America, black or white, it is a little weirder for the Negro. Since if he is writing about his own life and his own experience, his writing must be separate, not only because of the intellectual gulf that causes any serious man to be estranged from the mainstream of American life but because of the social and cultural estrangement from that mainstream that has characterized Negro life in America. I have always thought of writing as a moral art; that is, basically, I think of the artist as a moralist, as demanding a moral construct of the world, as asking for a cleaner vision of society, and always asking that, no matter what your response, it be, as Ezra Pound said, "new— that you make it new, that you respond newly and personally and singularly."

I once wrote an essay called "The Myth of Negro Literature," which was published in a rather weird form in the *Saturday Review*, and the point I tried to make there was that, until quite recently, most of what could be called the Negro's formal attempt at "high art" was found in his music, and one of the reasons I gave was that it was only in music that the Negro did not have to respect the tradition outside of his own feelings—that is, he could play what he felt and not try to make it seem like something alien to his feelings, something outside of his experience. In most cases the Negro writers who usually wanted to pursue what "they" classify as "high art" were necessarily middle-class Negroes, and the art that these middle-class Negroes made tended to be an art that was, at best, an imitation of what can only be described as white middle-class literature, the popular fiction that was usually about tired white lives. The Negro writer who duplicated these tired white lives was only painting them black. Therefore he was saying essentially nothing about the Negro except that he had been desperately oppressed—so oppressed that he could not even remember his own separate experience.

Even so fine a writer as Charles W. Chesnutt, one of the earlier black writers, had to "cop out," as they say, by being a "refined Afro-American." He could not have just any sensibility. Not just any functioning intelligence that white America could recognize as being valid, as being some kind of intellectual commentary on the period or the society and the culture.

America has become a place where integration means not just dollars and cents—although that's what it is about, dollars and cents—it also means Radio City Music Hall. It means the insipidities of television, it means the impossibility of becoming a man in a place that doesn't demand manhood any more—in fact, a place where manhood has become a kind of alien grace.

So the Negro finds himself in a very weird position, that is, to be of this country but to have a culture—and it is a culture, because culture is simply the way people live, and it is reinforced by memory—to have a culture which is essentially an adjunct, separate from the mainstream of American life. The Negro either must assume culture properties that are not emotionally his own, in order to have a go at the mainstream of white America, or develop a literature (and stance) that seeks to identify and delineate the slave, the black man—the man who remains separated from the mainstream. This at least has the validity of separating oneself emotionally and, finally, intellectually from what turns out to be only mediocrity, even if it's well paid.

Disassociation from the mainstream—that is, what is said to be real by the white American image makers—is a very great virtue. The fact that Negroes moved to the city starting at the beginning of the twentieth century and became lost in the city is symbolic for the writer, who can now become more nearly anonymous—that is, he can come from anyplace and be anybody. He doesn't have to be the landed gentry. He doesn't have to be the New England aristocracy, which made most of American literature. He can be, literally, any man in the kind of anonymous circumstances that only the city provides.

The Negro writer, the Negro artist has two problems. First of all, he's got to make a break with the urge to get into the mainstream. The Negro middle class realized that in a society where black is a liability, the coolest thing is not to be that, so the first thing the Negro writer has to say is, "Well, I am a Negro," which is a great, dramatic thing. To say that is to realize that it means not only some racial delineation but a responsibility to a specific and particular culture, one that can be talked about meaningfully, simply because it is a human experience—your human experience. If I say, "I am a black man. All my writing is done by a black man," whether I label each thing I write,

"Written by a black man," it's still written by a black man, so
that if I point out a bird, a black man has pointed out that bird,
and it is the weight of that experience in me and the way I get it
from where it is to you that says whether or not I am a writer.

The Negro writer can only survive by refusing to become a
white man. If he pulls the switcheroo that the Negro middle
class wants to pull he thereby loses his memory and his writing
ability and suddenly becomes white, and then there is no trace
of him on this continent. He just never lived and never experienced a separate emotional experience. Even in the Thirties,
when Langston Hughes and what we call the Harlem School
began to refocus and describe what was really around them and
to create that place as an instrument of feeling—when they
wanted to describe literally where they were and what they felt
—they turned out a literature about poverty, a literature of violence, a literature about the seamier sides of the so-called American Dream, and the first people to jump on them were certain
middle-class Negroes who said, "Well, it's just not so. You're
talking about—you're talking about bad stuff." Which is a social concept finally. "You are talking about bad things," so that
William S. Braithwaite and George Schuyler said of such literature that "it praises degradation." Other Negroes said of the
blues, "It makes me feel like slavery." Well, the point is that the
middle class has always worked with a curious kind of fantasy.
They assume that those three hundred and some years that were
spent in this country by our fathers and our grandfathers as
slaves are to be forgotten—no one is to remember that, that it
has vanished, and we are to forget, we are to make believe that
we never did experience that and that our grandmothers were
lying.

But that's not the case. The stakeout in America that any
black man makes, if it's legitimate, will, probably, be a com-
pleter and bigger vision of what America really is than most
white men can give, because we cannot and do not forget. And
this is not necessarily racial. It's scientific, in a certain sense. If,

for instance, you live in a big house and you keep me locked in a room, and you never go in that room, you don't know anything about that room. If I come out of that room to clean many other things in the rest of the house, then I know about the whole house, and if I want to talk, I can talk about the whole house. And if you say, suddenly, that what I am talking about is degrading, is filthy, is obscene, is pornographic, then you must realize that the place that I was forced to live in is that dirty, terrible place I am now describing.

So that a man who tries to tell me that I cannot have a character in a play say "motherfucker" to describe something that my character sees is trying to deny the validity of a certain kind of experience and to deny the expression of that word as honest. He is quite clearly trying to deny a whole world of feeling because he does not know what the word means or how it is used.

But Negro literature has always been, in America, direct social response, which is, I think, the best kind of literature. We must ask the Negro writer what are his influences, and then, does he refuse to be taken in by what goes down and around as being the most admirable qualities of American culture. For example, there are certain important men who nominated Leonard Bernstein for the Pulitzer Prize in music and did not even understand that the finest composer America has produced is Duke Ellington. But they cannot even understand what Duke Ellington is, what he has been doing these many long years, and that is just sick. It's sick and it's fantastic. It's fantastic, but that is what is happening. We are labeled as not having contributed anything. And they keep on asking, "What has been the Negro's contribution to American culture?"

Well, what has it been? You think about that. What has it been? We've lived here, which is what everyone else has done, and we have memories of our particular and specific ways of living here, and that is valuable as a statement not only about this place but about the nature of the world. When I say social art, I mean not only art that is art by anyone's definition but art that will tell you how man lives, or, at least, how he wanted to live. In some black people's haste to get into straight-up America it has come to the idiocy of someone's perhaps appearing one day in *Ebony* magazine for being the first Negro to drop an atomic bomb—it goes to that kind of very dubious accomplishment, so that, as the man says, "The Negro has to be twice as good to get ahead." So are we to drop two bombs?

The Souls of Black Folk, by Du Bois, and Langston Hughes' book *Fine Clothes for the Jew* describe two different places in America—two different places in the emotional history of America. Both are equally valid, by virtue of the precision of the telling, nothing else. It is the precision of the telling that demonstrates exactly what it is you feel, by showing it rather than elaborating in some didactic but finally non-instructive way —that is, by demonstrating what art is supposed to do. So that I usually think of the Harlem writers and Jean Toomer as doing this, despite the social placement of this writing which white oriented minds might make. But Toomer not in the same way, because Jean Toomer separated himself, first as an intellectual, as a middle-class intellectual, and then as a mystic. Mysticism is, after all, the hard core of Negro culture, but mysticism of another kind. Yes, mysticism, because the spirit was always valuable—more valuable than *things* for the Negro because he never had any thing. The religious core of Negro culture still remains, is present, even in Thelonious Monk or Ornette Coleman. They are trying to get at something which is finally spiritual and has to do with the transmitting of spirit rather than "writing a biography," which might be useful for some things, like trying to get a job.

If you think of W. E. B. Du Bois, Richard Wright, Jean Toomer, Langston Hughes, Ellison, Baldwin, Chester Himes and all the others, if you think of these people you are forced to realize that they gave a top-level performance in the areas in which each functioned. The most meaningful book of social essays in the last decade is *Notes of a Native Son*, by Baldwin.

The most finely constructed archetypal, mythological novel, utilizing perhaps a Kafkaesque sense of what the world really has become, is *Invisible Man*, by Ralph Ellison. The most completely valid social novels and social criticisms of South and North, non-urban and urban Negro life, are Wright's *Black Boy* and *Native Son*.

It's all there, even to the Raymond Chandler–Dashiell Hammett genre of the detective novel, in Chester Himes' *All Shot Up* or *The Crazy Kill* or *The Real Cool Killers* which are much more interesting, not only in regard to plot but also in terms of "place," a place wherein such a plot can find a natural existence. So that the Negro writer finally doesn't have to think about his "roots" even literarily, as being subject to some kind of derogatory statement—one has only to read the literature.

It is certainly impossible to understand the Civil War or the Reconstruction period without reading Du Bois about Reconstruction. It is impossible to understand the temperament of middle-class Negro life or the America that produces it without reading E. Franklin Frazier's *Black Bourgeoisie*.

The young Negro writer has all that great material, and that of our fathers and our grandfathers, and, in addition, has the just barely plumbed innards of his own cultural history. I am writing a novel now about something my grandmother told me, and the essential reality is this: One day I ran into the house and said, "Grandmother, this boy called me a nigger." She said, "Well, you are. You are. Nobody else is." The realization of that . . . *being* that nigger, because that means you don't have the experience of being what you *think* a nigger is, is extremely significant in many ways. In jazz, people started talking about "funk," and the white man had always said: "The Negro has a characteristic smell," but then the Negro takes that and turns the term around, so that if you don't have that characteristic smell, that funk, then the music, or what you are, is not valuable. The very tools the white man gave the Negro are suddenly used against him. These very weapons he has given us.

And now we find, indeed, they are very valuable. So that even listening to the Beatles, one knows that they could not be possible without Chuck Berry or the Coasters, and it's very amusing that we can turn on television and see the Beatles but never see Chuck Berry or the Coasters. Behind American and contemporary culture, in every way that has meaning, there is the Black experience. It has become absolutely valuable for the black man to realize that he exists and that his experience is as valid as any other. My own direction is always toward spirit, which is the only thing I admit as being real. I say, "Where am I? Who am I? What's happening? Who are all these others?" And relate it to me.

So that if T. S. Eliot says something about the essential strength of language as image, I take it to mean me. If Pound says something about image as emotional and intellectual complex, I take it to mean me. If Apollinaire says something about space-time relationship or sense-drama or philosophical abstracts, that is my reality. As, for instance, the idea of Christ as an airplane pilot—I take it to mean me, something that I can use, where I am, in my ghetto or outside of that ghetto, but available as air is, or love is. It's there. You know it.

The people I know best—the young writers who are closest to me—gathered together, and when I came to New York I started a magazine called *Yugen* which published several Negro writers, many young poets like A. B. Spellman, who, I think, is among the finest of the young poets in America now. But also with these I published many others. So that I found myself publishing that writing which I thought was the most valuable. Not the writing that reflected those tired white lives again, but necessarily those people, those white and black people who were talking about a side of America that was more valuable because it hadn't been talked about. Allen Ginsberg, who gives the Jewish memory of dissent in this culture, since this culture asks and has asked all immigrants to strip themselves of the very things that would make their own culture valuable, so that the Italian who comes to America becomes an American and the Italian thing is lost. The Jew who gets into America is an American and the Jewishness is lost, and so now they want to break your back, too, Negroes, so that when you go into that place, there will be no dissent, there will be no dissent at all, so that you will be faceless, too, and your literature will reflect some kind of tired thirst for, perhaps, luxury and comfortable ignorance.

If you think about Irish literature, from Wilde on, and if you think of Wilde, Shaw, Yeats, Joyce, Synge, O'Casey, Beckett— if you think about this, those people are Irish, they are not English; and those men have been the strength of English literature for a long time.

Now that same role is being handed to the Negro, and now it has become possible for our writers to come from anyplace, young Negroes, old Negroes, as simply anonymous writers, but writing about specific experiences, which are informed by the place where they are, by what this place has made them and where they come from.

The world becomes as wide as it is because there is nothing here anyway, except what you see or want to see. And I think that consciousness can be public. It can be made public.

The writers in the ghetto will write about ghetto life and the Negroes who find themselves outside of the ghetto will go where art is and try to do it that way. Whatever the expression and the experiences available, wherever we are, our most important obligation is to tell it all exactly as it is.

5.   *Harvey Swados*

The Writer in Contemporary
American Society

Implicit in the title of my talk, "The Writer in Contemporary
American Society," is the idea that things are not as they once
were, either for the writer or for the society in which he lives. I
think this is so, and that the change is twofold. First, I believe
that the attitude of American society toward the writer is changing. Second, and partially in consequence, I believe that the attitude of the writer toward his society is in process of change.
The attitude of society seems to me primarily a sociological matter. The attitude of the writer is primarily a "literary" matter,
but here, too, I would insist that it has its social aspects.

In the nineteenth century, even during the period when the
nation's greatest writers were producing their enduring master-
pieces, this was not a hospitable place for artists of any kind.
Most of the financially successful writers were women whose
names we would not even recognize today, and most of their
readers were leisure-class women, for whom novel-reading was
a pastime to fill otherwise empty hours—a phenomenon which
has persisted down into our own time. Serious writers found
themselves regarded, when they were regarded at all, as very odd
birds indeed. Almost everyone, in short, was busy making
money; and it was not until everything came crashing down in

the 1930's and the writers had come home, broke, from self-imposed exile, that Americans and, particularly, their leaders in Washington began to consider that intellectuals and writers might have something of value to contribute to a society in a state of near-collapse.

If this seemed a temporary phenomenon during the postwar boom and the Eisenhower-McCarthy era, it is one that has reappeared in more recent years, and there are some substantial reasons for it. Education has become big business in America. The college diploma, once a prime symbol of middle- or upper-class status, has become all but a necessity for gainful employment of a worthwhile nature. This development, that began with the G. I. Bill and now, with the ghostly menace of automation and cybernation wiping out whole categories of blue-collar, white-collar, technical, engineering and even middle-management jobs, is driving people on into graduate-level studies.

It is quite possible, it is true, to get through college and obtain a degree without reading many books, and certainly without encountering any living writers. But at least there is more of a likelihood of hearing certain names uttered—and occasionally with respect—on a college campus than in a poolroom or a bar. Inevitably, the rising educational level among the American people, an irreversible phenomenon, brings in its wake a rising respect for the products of the mind.

This is one substantial reason for the increasing seriousness with which American society regards its writers. There are others, like the late Kennedy Administration's emphasis on culture, but all, including the political, are largely related to the vast increase in the number of secondary school and college students. Thanks to this rapid increase, the profitable textbook has taken American book publishing from the modest domain of family business (usually old-family business, at that) and led it by the hand to the realm of Wall Street and the big money. Affluent book publishers, bidding against each other for established writers, hunting for new writers (black as well as white, for the lesson of James Baldwin's best-sellerdom has not been lost on them)—these too have not been without effect upon the middle- and upper-class community. The young man who announces to his family that he wishes to become a writer rather than a broker, a poet rather than an engineer, a playwright rather than a salesman, is far less likely to be thrown out of the house than he would have been a generation or two ago.

He is also less likely to starve. If there is still no stable audience eager for his books at five or six dollars a copy, there are magazine editors ready to solicit him for his views on politics, movies, travel, baseball—and sometimes even to buy his fiction, for the mass circulation magazines, too, have been driven to raise their sights by an ever more sophisticated, college-educated reading public. We need only cite the *Saturday Evening Post*, the home for so long of sea stories, cowboy stories, and the homespun problems of Willie Butts and the Earthworm Tractor Corporation, which now features the work of virtually every serious writer of fiction here and abroad.

What is more, there is apt to be a refuge for the writer, while he is learning his craft, in one of those colleges and universities whose enrollment continues to skyrocket and whose English departments are now willing to give due credit for publication in periodicals less specialized than the scholarly journals. If he is established, if he is an Ellison or a Bellow, he is apt to find the colleges and the universities bidding against each other for his very presence on their campuses. And this in turn, by the simplest of circular processes, reinforces the prestige in the community at large of the writer as professor rather than as beatnik, bum, agitator or exile.

I do not wish to be mistaken as having said that paradise has arrived for the American writer, or even that his best work is having any great impact on the millions of ordinary citizens. Nothing could be further from the truth. It is still a fact that most Americans read nothing but newspapers and a magazine or two; it is still a fact that only a tiny handful of American creative artists can feed themselves and their families on the proceeds of their work; it is still a fact that no more than three or four of them can be said to have any contact with or influence on the American community at large. Nevertheless, it would be disingenuous to deny that, as I have attempted to indicate, the situation is changing.

So, too, is the attitude of the writer toward his society. It is hardly necessary to detail to you the shifts that have already taken place over the generations, and even within the life span of any one writer—to say nothing of the changes in that one writer's feelings about his country in response to the vicissitudes of his life and the alterations in the social landscape about him. But it may be helpful to make some very rough generalizations.

If America was a bad joke to those writers of the Twenties who exiled themselves or mocked at its inanities from their City Room sanctuaries in Chicago or Baltimore, it became the object of a love affair to the writers of the Thirties. Sometimes these writers were the very same people, but their attitudes were very different; they discovered that this was a beautiful land, that its traditions were those of freedom and rebelliousness, and that its people, black and white, farmer and city worker, were noble, patient, and long-suffering, and badly exploited by a tiny minority who ruled them.

The war brought a tempering of this literary patriotism rather than an intensification of it, as writers in uniform discovered that their fellow Americans were often backward, bigoted, unlettered, uninterested in the defeat of fascism, much less in making a revolution. Particularly from the new generation of novelists came book-length expressions of horror and disgust at the image of the America they encountered in the barracks.

By the 1950's the disenchantment was as complete as it had been thirty years earlier. The peculiarly miserable combination of lazy self-satisfaction and venomous chicanery which marked the Eisenhower-McCarthy era drove the American novelist into one of several positions—in some cases he utilized the gro-

tesqueries of American life in the fat and fearful Fifties as
backdrop for the picaresque adventures of his rogue-hero; in
others he turned his back on the whole ugly mess, renounced all
of its values, and quite simply cut out—either spiritually or
physically or both.

Perhaps at this point I should be specific, since I am speaking
of the immediate predecessors of the young new writers of the
Sixties. I remember writing, with considerable excitement, in a
review of Saul Bellow's *The Adventures of Augie March,* that
this was a truly ground-breaking book, that it would show the
way to a whole new generation of writers. I think that time has
proved the truth of that enthusiastic prediction, even though, to
my mind at least, none of those who have since deserted the
more formally-structured novel for the looser picaresque mode
have done so with anything like the success that Bellow achieved
in his remarkable novel.

As for those who cut out, I am thinking of course of the Beats.
It is my feeling that while the achievement of Kerouac and the
others associated with the movement has been of slight importance (in fiction if not in poetry), their *attitude* has been of considerable significance. What they did succeed in demonstrating,
in their life as much as in their work, was that it was not necessary to sign up in the Establishment, that it was not necessary
to join up in the corporation, that it was not necessary to buy all
the cant that passed for serious thinking, the slop that passed
for culture, the garbage that passed for statesmanship, and that
even in the absence of radical political currents, it was possible
to swim against the stream, to turn one's back on a swinish society—and somehow to survive.

So far in the Sixties, as I have not been the first to observe,
the leading tendency in American fiction has been one which is
loosely labeled the comic novel. As far as I am concerned it is a
misnomer, since most of the examples of the genre that I have
sampled have not been particularly comical, or even funny. I
should prefer to call it the "wild" novel, since it is usually char-

acterized by a series of disconnected incidents that could more readily be thought of as wild than as comic, and it is usually peopled by figures who are also usually wild, free-floating, and physically or spiritually grotesque.

It seems fairly clear that these novels, from *Catch-22* to whatever the latest example may be (they are now coming out in an endless stream), derive literarily from Bellow on the one hand and from the Beats on the other, and that socially they represent a kind of cultural lag, a delayed reaction to the stupidities and horrors of the Second World War, as well as to the idiocies of the postwar era. What they seem to be saying—those that have anything to say at all—is that in a ridiculous and hideous world, one in which millions of Jews were cold-bloodedly slaughtered and thousands of other human beings were blown to pieces or incinerated by hellish new bombs, the United States is as ludicrous as any spot on earth. That in the face of the stupidities, inanities, and obscenities of our countrymen, all one can do is bay at the moon.

This would be all very well if what were called for, in an era of prolonged reaction, were a fictional restatement of disaffiliation from a hopelessly rotten and moribund society. But I submit that in the 1960's, disaffiliation converted into a nihilist pose by an author's determination to gain popularity by mocking at *everything* is no longer appropriate. And that is why, despite the temporary best-seller status of some of these books, they have no more to tell us about ourselves than do, say, the French antinovels, those finicking collections of words about minute alterations in perceptions and states of being which are supposedly more scientific and hence more accurate descriptions of reality than the great fiction of the nineteenth and twentieth centuries, now presumably outdated.

For the basic truth about our time is not, it seems to me, that it is one of oppressive stagnation so hopeless that a corrosive nihilism is a civilized and reasonable reaction on the part of a sensitive man. It is rather that this is a time of explosive change without parallel in human history. What we have seen demonstrated in recent years, what we are seeing at this very moment, is that people will not submit indefinitely to oppression or to stagnation or to the threat of annihilation. There does exist in man, no matter how we tend to disbelieve it in periods of reaction, an ineradicable yearning to be free; and in this time of explosive change revolution after revolution is sweeping the world: technological revolution, social revolution, racial revolution.

It does not follow that there exists a clearly defined "task" for the writer, much less that such a task should involve the concoction of jolly uplifting fables about a brighter tomorrow. But it does follow, I do believe, that much of what is being produced nowadays by American writers who see the world as ludicrous, meaningless or absurd, and by extension as simply grotesque and comical, is in itself of no particular relevance to the rest of us who live in the world and experience it very differently.

For, need I add? the world that has produced the hydrogen bomb has also produced thousands upon thousands of active protestors and demonstrators against continued testing and against world terror. The bomb still exists, it has been used by America to destroy hundreds of thousands of human beings, it may yet be used to destroy us all; but testing has stopped, there is a détente of sorts, and we proceed, all of us (except for lunatics who must still be brought under control), on the assumption that we are not going to blow each other up. And the world that has produced Nazism, genocide, and the unspeakable holocaust visited upon European Jewry has also produced Israel, a renewed consciousness of their historical identity on the part of the Jews who were not destroyed, and a very belated but nonetheless genuine beginning of an attempt to grapple with the terrible complexities of the ethical problems raised by the holocaust— as witness the international controversy aroused by the Eichmann trial and by *The Deputy* and by their polemical aftermaths. The numbness of the Fifties has been succeeded by the questioning of the Sixties.

What is more, a continuous revolution of the oppressed and the degraded is sweeping every continent without exception. Driven from Asia, the outposts of empire still raise the flag in only a few last-ditch corners of Africa. Nor have the Russians been immune. Poznan, East Berlin, and Budapest have already warned them of what lies in store if they do not let down the barriers and allow the winds of freedom to blow. As for the Americans, we need not peer at Latin America, we need not go beyond our own borders to smell the odor of revolution in Montgomery, Greenwood, New York, and Washington, D.C.

I have no wish to be oracular or righteous. I have no wish to prescribe the tone or temper that any of my fellow writers should adopt. What I am saying is that, as a reader as well as a writer, I react with deep suspicion to writing that seems the product of a fashion, a cashing-in on what is said to be the *dernier cri*. Inevitably, it seems to me, fashions in writing must lag behind the reality that the reader himself is apprehending. Once again, however, I must pause in order to make it quite clear that I am not calling for a literature that attempts to compete with the five-star final or the eleven o'clock news. What I do seek is a literature that evidences a spirit aware of the life of our time, not just of the fashion of our time, a spirit attuned to the temper of our age, not the temper of the day before yesterday, which, in the tempo of this age, might as well be that of the pre-Civil War era.

In point of fact, the writer who is most sharply, painfully, gloriously aware of what is going on about him in the world even as he writes, all alone, may very well be concerning himself with the life of a bygone age, or with a fictional examination not of the immediate present—which is generally beyond the grasp of the imaginative writer—but of the roots of that present, of the past from which it sprang.

It should not be surprising, therefore, that some of the most interesting writers in recent years should be those who have proceeded to such an examination, unencumbered by any felt necessity to write what would be hailed as chic or modish in the reviewing media. The first novel of James Baldwin and, if I may venture the judgment, still his best fictional work to date, *Go Tell It on the Mountain*, makes meaningful for us the tortured life of a Harlem boy not simply through the vicissitudes of his own growing up but through an artist's understanding of the lives and the moving forces of those who preceded him, those who came up from the South, those who molded him and against whom he rebelled. Likewise, a younger but remarkably gifted writer, Norman Fruchter, concentrates in his most unusual first novel, *Coat upon a Stick*, not on the twelve-year-old boy whom we may reasonably identify, I should think, with the author, nor even on the boy's father, a suburban television repair man. Instead, he turns his plain and powerful prose like a searching beam upon the grandfather, an old Jew who lives alone in a decaying tenement on New York's Lower East Side. The old man is mean and crabbed, he is a cheat and a liar, he hates his own son for having wandered from the narrow path of the true faith—but he is a figure of great pathos and, at moments, even of tragic stature as he struggles to cope with the moral demands made upon him by a revolutionary figure who enters his life virtually at its close. And when we have finished this book, written by a man in his very early twenties, we sense not only the connection between the generations but the full weight of the tradition that is going to shape the life of the young boy, and many others like him, long after the story itself is concluded.

It is not by accident that I singled out a novel by a Negro and one by a Jew. A disproportionate number of the new voices now just beginning to make themselves heard in our country comes from these minorities, which is readily understandable. Their people have suffered more, they themselves have more to say, and—thanks to the factors I have already discussed—there is a growing public for their work and, in consequence, there are publishers and producers ready to back them and bring out their work. As I listen to their voices, it seems to me that they are speaking of both past and present, of a past filled with torment and glory, of a present at best troubled and at worst terrifying.

It is already apparent that we are going to witness a substantial movement of new Negroes, liberated from ignorance, self-underestimation and self-depreciation, into the fields of poetry, drama and fiction. We do not as yet have the full measure, however, of what these young intellectuals will be able to accomplish, liberated from the stultification of ghetto education and exposed to the burgeoning universities, with their writers in residence and their individual cultural boomlets. Already the eagerness with which their work is awaited is such that, speaking parenthetically, if I were a young Negro writer making my first submissions to editors and publishers, I would be wary of those who mistakenly deem it a part of the civil-rights crusade—and of good business as well—to extend the notion of preferential treatment into the literary or cultural arena. For, ultimately, the writer is a writer, no matter what else he may be, and the staying power of his work will manifest itself in its innate quality and not in such extraneous, if momentarily modish, matters as his religious ancestry or his skin tone.

I said a moment ago that the suffering of the Negro and Jewish minorities has provided the fertile soil from which talent has sprung. It ought to be noted, I think, that among the more fortunate talents of both groups, particularly among the Jewish middle-class writers, the suffering has often been vicarious, experienced, so to speak, at second hand. In such cases one of the triggering emotions may very well be guilt—and this is a phenomenon familiar to anyone who has ever been involved in a war: the civilian feels guilty that he is not in uniform, the home-front soldier feels guilty that he is not overseas, the rear-echelon soldier feels guilty that he is not in combat, the combat soldier feels guilty that he has not been hurt, the wounded soldier feels guilty that he is still alive. I need hardly labor the point, I trust, with regard to those Negroes fortunate enough to grow up out-

side the Deep South or the confines of the northern ghettoes; or
those Jews who were fortunate enough to escape the Nazi killers
or who lived, like American Jewry, beyond their grasp, and, in
some instances—irony of ironies—profited from the war in
which others gave their lives to rescue the living remnants from
the extermination camps. All I need say, I think, is that, being
human, I, too, have felt the sting of that guilt, and, what is more,
have felt it as a factor in my own writing—and I am, quite simply, sure that what is true of me must be true of others as well.

There are, of course, a multitude of factors that drive men to
write, in our society as well as in others. What I am trying to do
here is to isolate some of those that operate specifically in our
heterogeneous, explosively changing culture—as distinct from
those at work in a more stable, tradition-bound society, and as
distinct from those presumably operative universally: the desire
to gain immortality, to be popular or notorious, to be attractive
to women, to be rich, and so on. If I am at all correct in the assumption that, because of changes in our social structure, com-
manding positions on our literary front are in the process of
being taken over by writers of the new generation coming from
minority groups hitherto only marginally represented in the con-
stellation dominated by Hemingways, Faulkners, Fitzgeralds,
Frosts, Pounds, Eliots, Whartons, Jameses, Londons, Cranes,
Norrises, Dreisers, Twains, Howellses, Dickinsons, Melvilles,
Hawthornes and Thoreaus—white Anglo-Saxon Protestants one
and all—if I am at all correct in this, then it follows that American literature in the years immediately ahead will be the product
of men often driven to write by anguish at the fate of their
brothers and by guilt that in the solitude of the study they do
not always share that fate.

Great works have been created, and, therefore, once again
can and will be created, under the whip of guilt and the scourge
of anguish and despair. They have been created, too, with the
inspiration of compassion and hope. They have even been created out of hatred, but—and this I would insist upon—not very

often. For hatred—not rage, but hatred—is more sterile than nihilism and more self-destructive of the creative impulse. A literature cannot be grounded in hate. Perhaps a politics can, but not one that I would care to associate myself with. The hate politics of the recent past was fascism, and the hate politics of the present is grounded in fear—fear of the unknown, fear of the technological revolution, fear of the social revolution, fear of the racial revolution.

And besides, literature is not politics, nor can it become the willing weapon or easy tool of any politics. If we Americans learned nothing else, we should have learned that from the literary history of the 1930's.

That was the decade during which a revolution was often talked about and argued for—particularly among literary people —but never took place. This, however, is a decade during which a revolution just as much talked about *is* taking place. In consequence, the young writer of the Sixties is going to find it twice as hard as the young writer of the Thirties to determine what part of him is a writer—which means just what it always has in terms of lonely dedication and unremitting concentration on work which may seem to have no relation to life-and-death matters—and what part of him is a politician—which means, nowadays, a revolutionist. This is not a determination to be easily or glibly made, nor, if I am to judge by my own experiences (and I am not even an active participant in the Negro revolution), to be resolved even over the course of a lifetime, for some of us.

In the summer of 1961 I wrote, in the Introduction to a collection of my essays called *A Radical's America*, "In our country the Jew has moved from a marginal position to one of centrality. In the next generation it may very well be the Negro, the tenth American, who will come to be regarded by many of his fellow citizens—and by many around the world—not necessarily as Presidential timber (that old Jewish gag is already much too old, even for Irish politicians) but as the most typical American."

It is my feeling today that this typicality will come to be true not just for the Negro as American but for the Negro writer as American writer. Generation after generation of American writers has seen its obligation as one of discovering a past for its people, of inventing mythic heroes for a people who started with none, who had no history, no pantheon of gods and goddesses, no fabled kings and noblemen, nor even a common language of its own other than that of the old Empire. The Europeans, we may remember, were for a long time amused by the ridiculous presumptuousness on the part of the motley, semi-barbaric Americans in thinking that they could create a culture of their own that would go beyond hog-calling and the manufacture of cuspidors—and later of Ford cars. It was not until our own lifetime that Europe could finally bring itself to concede not only that America was capable of creating a culture in an unhistorical wilderness but that, in truth, it had already demonstrated in fiction and painting, to say nothing of music and architecture, that its vitality and originality had outstripped Europe's.

There is an interesting parallel here, it seems to me, between the case of the American artist as viewed by his European critics and that of the Negro artist as viewed by his American critics. It was granted, in fact it was insisted, patronizingly, by the white supremacists, that the Negro—all Negroes—had a sense of rhythm, "a natural sense of rhythm" I think was the way they liked to put it, and that their contribution to culture was a primitive Afro-American music known as jazz. The idea that a Negro might prefer the cello to the tenor sax, that he might as readily compose a sonata as a blues song, that he might, in fact, not be musical at all came very hard to the white who cherished his stereotypes. And, of course, we have still not arrived at the point where the Negro gains acceptance not as a Negro artist but as an artist, not as a Negro writer but as a writer.

We have not arrived there, but we are getting there. That is what is new, what is contemporary in American life: the multi-racial society, coming as a product of the racial revolution. Its consequences, not just for the Negro writer but for all American writers, are incalculable. Of one thing I think we can be sure: it will mark the end of that sense of powerlessness which has oppressed us since the Nazi death camps and the dropping of the Bomb. As I wrote last year—and I think that Mississippi in the summer of 1964 makes it a thousand times more true—young men and women are demonstrating that they can work civic wonders with their own bodies, with the power of their own minds and spirits. They are demonstrating that life is not meaningless or absurd, but wonderfully valuable. They are demonstrating, this finest and most sacrificial generation of Americans, that by believing and willing they can inspire others, and so change the world.

There is the new source of inspiration, not just for Negro writers but for all writers. And for the next generation of writers in a multi-racial society, freed from the wasteful necessity of deciding what it means to be white, to be black, to be whatever, or of struggling for things which will then be taken for granted, there will be, as a product of this racial revolution, a whole world of stories, legends and myths, replete with heroes, heroines and great deeds to equal those of any people in the dark, bloody and glorious history of mankind. From the memory of what is being struggled for now will come a new kind of literature for a newer and better kind of human being.

6.   *Nat Hentoff*

The Other Side of the Blues

I begin with an absurdity—a pronouncement from *Beyond the Melting Pot*, a 1963 book by Nathan Glazer and Daniel Patrick Moynihan. "The Negro," according to these trained observers of our society, "is only an American and nothing else. He has no values and culture to guard and protect."

That so sweepingly ignorant a conclusion can have been made in 1963 by two relatively sophisticated white social scientists is, of course, yet another index of how little is known about the American Negro experience by so many whites—both about the marrow of its past and about its widely and deeply variegated present. A corollary index is that this absurd statement was not challenged in most of the reviews of this widely praised book.

The actuality that the Negro may be "only an American" and yet also possess a distinctive, prideful culture—or subculture, if you will—not only eludes such as Glazer and Moynihan but, more damagingly, also eludes such a huge percentage of teachers from elementary school on in black, white and the so few integrated neighborhoods in this country.

It is easy enough to moralize on this point. It is also easy to become part of what Ralph Ellison has called "that feverish industry dedicated to telling Negroes who and what they are." This is an industry, he continues, "which can usually be counted upon to deprive both humanity and culture of their complexity."

76

What I am concerned with, however, is what those Negroes who *are* aware of their humanity and culture tell us and themselves about who and what they are. And how much has not yet been told?

Clearly, the Glazer-Moynihan thesis has never had any correspondence with Negro American reality—whether the reality of Leadbelly or Ornette Coleman, William Du Bois or Malcolm X, Baby Lawrence or Kenneth Clark. "In fact," as Ellison has emphasized, "all Negroes affirm certain feelings of identity, certain foods, certain types of dancing, music, religious experiences, certain tragic attitudes toward experience and toward our situation as Americans." There is also—among other distinctive elements—a Negro approach to humor, from certain kinds of blues to the infinite variations on "the dozens" to the thrusting wit of Moms Mabley and Dick Gregory.

Ellison has also pointed out the necessary qualification—"Nor should the existence of a specifically 'Negro' idiom in any way be confused with the vague, racist terms 'white culture' or 'black culture'; rather it is a matter of diversity within unity . . . due to the close links which Negro Americans have with the rest of the nation these cultural expressions are constantly influencing the larger body of American culture and are in turn influenced by them."

We are not yet sufficiently oriented, however—and I speak not only of the Glazers and Moynihans but also of those who agree with Ellison—as to the specific values in that "diversity within unity."

John Oliver Killens tells the readers of the *New York Times*: "My fight is not to be a white man in a black skin, but to inject some black blood, some black intelligence into the pallid main stream of American life, culturally, socially, psychologically, philosophically. This is the truer deeper meaning of the Negro revolt, which is not yet a revolution—to get America ready for the middle of the 20th century, which is already magnificently here."

A. B. Spellman charges that "Negroes are beating their way

into the American middle class, implementing its values while
sacrificing many of their own."

James Earl Jones, a remarkably penetrating actor, asserts:
"There's something behind the black face that has not been told
yet. I want people to look at me through my color."

Ralph Ellison adds: "We [Negroes] haven't had a chance to
discover what in our own background is really worth preserving."

Each of these statements is linked in an affirmation of the
Negro experience in America, in a conviction that there are
markedly positive—and, some would say, enviable—elements
in what Ellison has termed a Negro American style. Or rather,
styles. The diversity, subtlety and complexity of these styles still
have to be underlined. As absurd as the denial of Negro values
is the oversimplification, misunderstanding and distortion of
those values.

I mean, for example, the feverish unreality of Norman Mailer's apotheosis of the Negro hipster—as Mailer imagines him to
be. That hipster, it turns out, is only the desperate, direction-
less *golem* in Mailer's own dreams. I also mean the kind of
neon-lit, neo-Rousseauism of *One Hundred Dollar Misunderstanding* in which a black child whore is presented as the mother
wit of us all. As John Williams has speculated, "Would *One
Hundred Dollar Misunderstanding* have been quite so well received had Kitten been a social worker instead of a whore, and
the inability of man and woman, black and white, to communicate been put on an altogether different symbolic level?" Or, I
would add, if Kitten had been any kind of much more complicated *adult*?

But, removed from romanticism and removed from *voyeurs'*
exercises in wish fulfillment, what *is* the "black intelligence"
Killens cites? What *are* the diverse Negro American styles? What
are the "counter-values" to which Ellison refers as having
emerged in reaction to the persistent attempts to constrict the
Negro in America? It is evident to any white who will hear and

read that this systematic compression and oppression did create in many Negroes—who have simultaneously seen American life from below, from outside and from a narrowly intimate perspective within—a critical objectivity toward majority values. But again, what, more specifically, are the counter-values which became a corollary of that critical objectivity? What is behind the black face that hasn't been told yet?

To be sure, these questions have been answered in part. Louis Armstrong and Charlie Parker, Richard Wright and Ralph Ellison, Moms Mabley and Dick Gregory, Horace Cayton and John Lewis of SNCC, Gwendolyn Brooks and LeRoi Jones—and many more—have provided some of the answers from their own self-definitions and self-affirmations. But there is more that has not yet been fully told.

Since we are discussing the Negro writer in the United States, I shall confine my further questions to writers—to begin with, questions about the complexity of the humanity and culture of jazz. Only in recent years have we begun to learn in print something of the lives and communal values of jazz musicians—in the autobiographies of Big Bill Broonzy and Sidney Bechet; in such essays as Ralph Ellison's on Charlie Christian and Jimmy Rushing; and in the more generalized perspectives of LeRoi Jones' book *Blues People*, with its exploration of "the peculiar social, cultural, economical and emotional experience of a black man in America" as distilled in his music.

But there is so much more of jazz and the pre-jazz experience that has not yet been probed. There is no full-scale book of substance and accuracy yet on the blues as poetry, on the blues as a way of measuring resiliency and as a way of strengthening the determination not to be fragmentized by troubles, including the chronic trouble of being black.

There is not one novel so far that has been written from inside the jazz life. There is hardly any fiction and no plays yet to indicate something of the picaresque in jazz (Jelly Roll Morton, Babs Gonzales); the mockingly defiant, brilliantly resourceful and yet doomed demiurges of jazz (Lester Young, Billie Holiday); the extraordinarily diversified range of the singular survivors (Red Allen, Roy Eldridge, Duke Ellington, Dizzy Gillespie, Thelonious Monk); or the volcanic, fiercely complicated rebels (Charles Mingus, Max Roach).

Nor have enough writers yet convincingly searched before and beneath jazz into the microcosms of the folk musicians and the later gospel celebrants to extract something of the various life styles endemic to those disciplines and releases. In the context, I was told of a Sing for Freedom meeting in an Atlanta church in May of 1964. One of the performing groups was Bessie Jones and the Sea Island Singers, some of whose material and stylistic conceptions antedate the Civil War. Several of the young SNCC workers in the church were distinctly uncomfortable at having that "old-time, down-home" music superimposed onto the prerevolutionary present. Finally, one of them, a much jailed girl from Birmingham, exploded at the ignorance of the other young there. "I'm tired," she said, "of going to church and listening to teen-agers giggle and laugh when the old songs are sung. I want to know what the old songs are. I want to know that my parents were working for fifteen cents a day. I want to know what made me." It is not musicological analyses which are basically needed—though they would be welcome, too—but rather a rediscovery of the values and counter-values (to the majority hypocrisy) of those Negroes who did much more than just endure.

There are, moreover, strengths and satisfactions as well as careening challenges and brutal dead-ends in the lives and life styles of such later, urbanized communal "spokesmen" as Leroy Carr, Muddy Waters and Ray Charles. But where, with few exceptions, are their kinds of insights and self-discoveries in the work of the Negro writer in the United States?

Many more areas of the "only American" but distinctly Negro experience can, if penetrated further, detonate deeper shocks of recognition for both whites and blacks in this country. There is, for one illustration, the fascinating skein of Negro political action and reaction. Fascinating, though sometimes no less dismaying than the intersecting political folkways of the rest of America. And by politics I mean much more basic forms of relationship than what happens and does not happen at the polls. Much has been written in this vein—pre-eminently *Invisible Man*—but a great deal more of this material has hardly begun to be ordered into art, cauterizing and otherwise. I refer to the multiple forms of interaction within Negro communities and between Negroes and whites (as seen from the Negro perspective) from long before the Civil War through Reconstruction and truncated Populism to Marcus Garvey and other surges of "nationalism" to the Communist arabesques within the ghettoes in the 1930's and the present shadow play within the same ghettoes by the Trotskyites and the pro-Mao "progressives." So much more can be added to *that* chronicle of American social history.

Think, for instance, of some of today's "public figures" as potential composite subjects for literature—not biography or sociology or psychoanalytical dissection, but literature. There are the elements of farce, waste and skirmishing with tragedy—along with the mirror thereby provided of the actual moral standards of the majority—which are variously implicit in the life styles of an Adam Clayton Powell, a William Dawson, a Raymond "The Fox" Jones. And there are the abrasive triumphs, leading to acceleratingly crucial frustrations, of a W. E. B. Du Bois, or an A. Philip Randolph.

And it is particularly relevant now, as crises proliferate in what A. Philip Randolph calls "the unfinished revolution," to be more specific when one calls for the injection of "some black intelligence," some black, non-middle-class values into American life.

It can be facile to talk about not wanting to be integrated into a burning house—if one stops at that point. Those Negroes who do not intend, at this late date and after this depth of investment, to emigrate, might begin—if they have any hope left that this society can be basically changed—to expend less energy on the quick rhetoric of contempt and focus instead, as Lorraine Hansberry has urged, on rebuilding that house. The contempt is essential, both therapeutically and as a way of defining what must be discarded—but just as unalloyed emotion alone does not make a creative jazzman, so contempt alone does not make a new society.

Ralph Ellison, in the process of expressing the vital need for the persistence of a plurality of cultures in this country, has pointed out: ". . . much of Negro culture might be negative, but there is also much of great value, of richness, which, because it has been secreted by living and has made their lives more meaningful, Negroes will not willingly disregard. What is needed in our country is not an exchange of pathologies, but a change of the basis of the society. This is a job which both Negroes and whites must do together."

Or, in terms of James Baldwin's diagnostic look ahead, "There will be a Negro President of this country, but it will not be the country we are sitting in now."

But these declarations are not enough. What changes? How? Nor is it enough to claim that the way to change is the formation of a neo-Populist alliance between Negro and white civil rights actionists, between the white and black unemployed, between those few relatively awake fragments of organized labor and the more militantly Christian—in the operative sense of that word—church groups. That coalition is a resplendent vision, but it does not now exist.

With regard, therefore, to the actual present, the urgency is first how to bring that "black intelligence" into motivating and stimulating those in the ghetto to organize themselves to create as basic a series of changes in the way they now live as is possible with what potential power they now possess. As this new stage of the movement accelerates, there may then be enough dynamism to move the other putative elements of that neo-Populist alliance into the beginnings of active emulation and eventual fusion.

I am not saying that the Negro writer, in this regard, ought to abandon his primary self-expressive (and ultimately communal) concern in order to become a political block captain or strategist. But I am saying that if an artist has been self-impelled to the point at which he talks, and not only rhetorically, of changing "the basis of society," he may well owe it to himself not to stop at only the sounding of the alarm. He is not likely to be able or basically interested in drawing up overwhelming designs for political organization or for a redefinition of work in a precipitously cybernated society, but he may be able and self-driven to go beyond a by now ritualistic flaying of the "middle-class values" of the majority and become more concrete in defining and applying in such of his work as he chooses those counter-values of the black minority.

I conclude, therefore, with a question to a question. LeRoi Jones ends *Blues People* by stating:

The American Negro is being asked to defend the American system as energetically as the American white man. There is no doubt that the middle-class Negro is helping and will continue to help in that defense. But there is perhaps a question mark in the minds of the many poor blacks (which is one explanation for the attraction of such groups as the Black Muslims) and also now in the minds of many young Negro intellectuals. What is it that they are being asked to save? It is a good question, and America had better come up with an answer.

Since such otherwise disparate social critics as Paul Goodman and James Baldwin, among many others, have already made quite clear what it is that is not worth saving, the further question is what will be the function, in the future, of "black intelligence" and the "Negro American style" in buttressing those of the majority values which *are* worth preserving, and how will it substitute other values for those which ought to be discarded. In what ways, in sum, can these Negro qualities help to accelerate root changes in societal values as well as improvements in living conditions for the "under class"?

There is yet another question which requires a discussion of its own, but it has to be at least posed here. If we, indeed, begin to experience a radically integrated society, using the word radically in its denotative sense, is there any way for those Negroes who choose to remain both Negro and American to do so? Or, as has happened with minorities in America in the past—the few stubborn pockets of resistance to assimilation, such as the Hasidic Jews, excepted—will the integrated Negro lose his distinctly communal identity?

Ralph Ellison says the Negro will not. "Nor do I believe," he writes, "that as we win our struggle for full participation in American life we will abandon our group expression. Too much living and aspiration have gone into it, so that drained of its elements of defensiveness and alienation it will become even more precious to us, for we will see it ever clearer as a transcendent value." Perhaps, but that is what the Jews thought; and, nonetheless, the second and third and fourth generation Jews in this country are now mainly Jews, if they make the effort at all, in nostalgia.

"I would like to believe that Ellison is correct," a young, militant Negro at Fisk University told me, "but I do not see how we can keep our 'group expression' once we really do become a full part of the society. I would agree that, as of now, we certainly should have a major injection of 'black intelligence' and 'black counter-values' into the mainstream of American life; but how can you simultaneously inject and preserve a distinctive subculture? If one is sanguine about the future, what may happen is that our 'values' will become much more pervasive in American life as a whole; but when and if that happens, they will become less and less 'ours.' "

But, returning to the far from integrated present, what in the Negro American experience is both "really worth preserving" and will act as a spur to the redefinition of the majority American values? LeRoi Jones has said, "Just by being black in America, the Negro is a non-conformist. And the Negro uses that non-conformity as a natural fact of life." But we still need to know more about the essence of those Negro American non-conforming styles, and we need to know more about the ways in which that non-conformity can help to reshape majority American culture.

If it can. If anything can.

7.   *Robert Bone*

Ralph Ellison
and the Uses of Imagination

> *We live only in one place at one time, but far from being bound by it, only through it do we realize our freedom. We do not have to abandon our familiar and known to achieve distinction; rather in that place, if only we make ourselves sufficiently aware of it, do we join with others in other places.*
>
> WILLIAM CARLOS WILLIAMS

Some fourteen years ago an unknown writer, no longer young, published a first novel and, to no one's astonishment more than his own, won the National Fiction Award for 1952. There, suddenly, was the novel, and it spoke eloquently enough, but who was the author of *Invisible Man*? We knew only that the curve of his life was a parabola, moving from Oklahoma City to New York by way of Alabama. In the intervening years we have had some fleeting glimpses of the man and his ideas: the acceptance speech itself, an occasional interview, a fragment of his work in progress. We might have noticed his music criticism in the *Saturday Review* or the recent exchange with Irving Howe in *The New Leader*. But basically the man behind the mask remained invisible.

Now, with the publication of *Shadow and Act*,* this remark-

* New York: Random House, 1964.

86

able man emerges, at least in silhouette, to the public view. The book contains most of Ellison's essays, from the beginning of his literary career to the present. There are seven apprentice pieces, written in the Forties, which reflect the author's social and political concerns, and seven essays on jazz and the blues, which appeared principally in the late Fifties. There are three interviews of the *Paris Review* genre, and three first-rate essays on literary topics. Along the way, we learn a good deal about the author and the forces that have shaped his sense of life.

The formative years in Oklahoma City are sketched in some detail. Ellison was born in 1914, just seven years after Oklahoma was admitted to the Union. In the early days, his adopted grandfather had led a group of settlers from Tennessee to the Oklahoma Territory. Containing such elements, the Negro community of Oklahoma City developed more a Western than a Southern tone. Race relations, like all social relations, were more fluid than in established communities. Frontier attitudes persisted well into the present century, and Ellison was raised in a tradition of aggressiveness and love of freedom. He is proud of his frontier heritage, and to it may be traced his fierce individualism and his sense of possibility.

Oklahoma City was a boomtown in the postwar years—a swirling vortex of social styles and human types. There were many masks which an imaginative adolescent might try on:

Gamblers and scholars, jazz musicians and scientists, Negro cowboys and soldiers from the Spanish-American and First World Wars, movie stars and stunt men, figures from the Italian Renaissance and literature, both classical and popular, were combined with the special virtues of some local bootlegger, the eloquence of some Negro preacher, the strength and grace of some local athlete, the ruthlessness of some businessman-physician, the elegance in dress and manners of some headwaiter or hotel doorman.*

If there was no local writer for a model, there was access to a rich oral literature in the churches, schoolyards, barbershops,

* *Shadow and Act*, pp. xv-xvi.

and cotton-picking camps. And there was a curious double exposure to the exacting habits of artistic discipline. Through one
of the ironies of segregation, the Negro school system placed
particular stress on training in classical music. Ellison took up
the trumpet at the age of eight and studied four years of harmony in high school. Meanwhile he was exposed to the driving
beat of Southwestern jazz, of which Kansas City, Dallas, and
Oklahoma City were acknowledged centers. From his boyhood
onward, he was caught up in that creative tension between the
folk and classical traditions which has remained the richest resource of his art.

In 1933 Ellison enrolled at Tuskegee Institute to study composition under William Dawson, the Negro conductor and
composer. In his sophomore year, however, he came upon a
copy of *The Waste Land*, and the long transition from trumpet
to typewriter had begun. He read widely in American fiction
and, initially scorning the moderns, developed a lifelong devotion to the nineteenth-century masters. On coming to New York
in 1936 he met Richard Wright, who introduced him on the one
hand to the prefaces of Conrad and the letters of Dostoevski,
and on the other to the orbit of the Communist party. One evening he accompanied Wright to a fund-raising affair for the
Spanish Loyalists, where he met both Malraux and Leadbelly
for the first time. It was a notable occasion, symbolic of the
times and of the cross-pressures exerted from the first upon his
art.

From these cross-pressures Ellison derived his most enduring
themes. How could he interpret and extend, define and yet elaborate upon the folk culture of the American Negro and, at the
same time, assimilate the most advanced techniques of modern
literature? How could he affirm his dedication to the cause of
Negro freedom without succumbing to the stridencies of protest
fiction, without relinquishing his complex sense of life? In
Shadow and Act, Ellison returns again and again to these
tangled themes: the relationship of Negro folk culture to Amer-

ican culture as a whole, and the responsibility of the Negro artist
to his ethnic group.

As instrumentalist and composer, Ellison had faced these issues for the better part of two decades. When he began to write,
it was natural for him to draw upon his musical experience for
guidelines and perspectives. Not that his approach to writing is
merely an extension of an earlier approach to jazz and the blues;
they tend, in fact, to reinforce each other. But his experience
with jazz was formative; it left a permanent mark upon his style.
His controlling metaphors are musical, and if we are to grasp
his thought, we must trace his language to its source. There, in
the world of Louis Armstrong and Charlie Parker, Bessie Smith
and Jimmy Rushing, we may discover the foundations of Ellison's aesthetic.

MUSIC

The essence of jazz is group improvisation. Its most impressive
effects are achieved, according to Ellison, when a delicate balance is maintained between the individual performer and the
group. The form itself, consisting of a series of solo "breaks"
within a framework of standard chord progressions, encourages
this balance. "Each true jazz moment," Ellison explains, "springs
from a contest in which each artist challenges all the rest; each
solo flight, or improvisation, represents (like the successive can-
vases of a painter) a definition of his identity: as individual, as
member of the collectivity, and as a link in the chain of tradition." "True jazz," he concludes, "is an art of individual assertion within and against the group."

Here is a working model for the Negro writer. By balancing
conflicting claims upon his art, he can solve his deepest problems of divided loyalty. As an artist with a special function to
perform within the Negro group, the writer must be careful to
preserve his individuality. He must learn to operate "within and
against the group," allowing neither claim to cancel out the

other. Similarly on the cultural plane, where the Negro's group identity is at stake. Here the writer can affirm whatever is uniquely Negro in his background while insisting precisely on the American quality of his experience. "The point of our struggle," writes Ellison, "is to be both Negro and American and to bring about that condition in American society in which this would be possible."

Closely related to the question of individual and group identity is that of personal and traditional styles. Every jazz musician must strike a balance between tradition and experimentation, for "jazz finds its very life in an endless improvisation upon traditional materials." It follows that no jazzman is free to repudiate the past. The jam session, where he must display a knowledge of traditional techniques, will see to that. He must master "the intonations, the mute work, manipulation of timbre, the body of traditional styles" before he can presume to speak in his own voice. The path, in short, to self-expression lies through what is given, what has gone before.

As an American Negro writer, Ellison inherits a double obligation to the past. He must become familiar with a folk tradition which is his alone, and with a wider literary culture which he shares. Moreover, he must strive in both dimensions for a proper blend of past and present, given and improvised. In describing his response to his folk tradition, Ellison draws a parallel to the work of Picasso: "Why, he's the greatest wrestler with forms and techniques of them all. Just the same, he's never abandoned the old symbolic forms of Spanish art: the guitar, the bull, daggers, women, shawls, veils, mirrors." Similarly, Ellison appropriates folkloristic elements from Negro culture, embroiders on them, adapts them to his literary aims, and lifts them to the level of a conscious art.

In the wider context of American literature, the same principles apply. Consider Ellison's experimental idiom. Not since Jean Toomer has a Negro novelist been so inventive of new forms, new language, new technical devices. And yet none has been so deeply immersed in the American literary past. As Ellison struggles toward the realization of a personal style, he is *improvising* on the achievement of our nineteenth-century masters. It is this body of writing, he insists, "to which I was most attached and through which . . . I would find my own voice, and to which I was challenged, by way of achieving myself, to make some small contribution, and to whose composite picture of reality I was obligated to offer some necessary modifications."

Still a third balance must be struck between constraint and spontaneity, discipline and freedom. For the jazzman owes his freedom to the confident possession of technique. From his own struggles with the trumpet, Ellison learned how much the wild ecstatic moment depends on patient hours of practice and rehearsal. Freedom, he perceived, is never absolute, but rooted in its opposite. The game is not to cast off all restraint but to achieve, within the arbitrary limits of a musical tradition, a transcendent freedom. Jazz taught Ellison a respect for limits, even as it revealed the possibility of overcoming limits through technique. It was the blues, however, that taught him to discern in this paradox an emblem of the human condition.

The blues arise out of a tension between circumstance and possibility. The grim reality that gives them birth bespeaks the limits and restrictions, the barriers and thwartings, which the universe opposes to the human will. But the tough response that is the blues bespeaks a moral courage, a spiritual freedom, a sense of human possibility, which more than balances the scales. In Ellison's words, "The blues is an art of ambiguity, an assertion of the irrepressibly human over all circumstance whether created by others or by one's own human failings. They are the only consistent art in the United States which constantly reminds us of our limitations while encouraging us to see how far we can actually go."

The blues begin with personal disaster. They speak of flooded farmlands and blighted crops, of love betrayed and lovers parted, of the black man's poverty and the white man's justice. But what matters is the human response to these events. For the blues are a poetic confrontation of reality. They are a form of

spiritual discipline, a means of transcending the painful conditions with which they deal. The crucial feature of the blues response is the margin of freedom it proclaims. To call them an
art of ambiguity is to assert that no man is entirely the victim of
circumstance. Within limits, there is always choice and will.
Thinking of this inner freedom, Ellison speaks of "the secular
existentialism of the blues."

This sense of possibility lies at the center of Ellison's art. It
explains his devotion to his craft, for what is technique but another name for possibility? It explains his attitude toward protest fiction, for the propaganda novel, in portraying the Negro
primarily as victim, gives more weight to circumstance than
possibility. Ellison's is a more plastic sensibility. His heroes are
not victims but adventurers. They journey toward the possible
in all ignorance of accepted limits. In the course of their travels,
they shed their illusions and come to terms with reality. They
are, in short, picaresque heroes, full of "rash efforts, quixotic
gestures, hopeful testings of the complexity of the known and
the given."

If circumstance often enough elicits tears, possibility may release a saving laughter. This blend of emotion, mixed in some
ancient cauldron of the human spirit, is characteristic of the
blues. It is a lyricism better sampled than described. Note in Ellison's example how the painful humiliation of the bird is controlled, or absorbed, or even converted into triumph by a kind
of grudging laughter:

> Oh they picked poor robin clean
> They picked poor robin clean
> They tied poor robin to a stump
> Lord, they picked all the feathers
> Round from robin's rump
> Oh they picked poor robin clean.

The blues have nothing to do with the consolations of philosophy. They are a means of neutralizing one emotion with another,

in the same way that alkalies can neutralize an acid stomach. For the American Negro, they are a means of prophylaxis, a specific for the prevention of spiritual ulcers. It is not a question of laughing away one's troubles in any superficial sense, but of gazing steadily at pain while perceiving its comic aspect. Ellison regards this tragicomic sensibility as the most precious feature of his Negro heritage. From it stems his lyrical intensity and the complex interplay of tragic and comic elements which is the distinguishing mark of his fiction.

If the blues are primarily an expression of personal emotion, they also serve a group need. Perhaps the point can best be made through a comparison with gospel singing. When Mahalia Jackson sings in church, she performs a ritual function. Her music serves "to prepare the congregation for the minister's message, to make it receptive to the spirit and, with effects of voice and rhythm, to evoke a shared community of experience." Similarly in the secular context of the blues. When Jimmy Rushing presided over a Saturday night dance in Oklahoma City, he was acting as the leader of a public rite: "It was when Jimmy's voice began to soar with the spirit of the blues that the dancers—and the musicians—achieved that feeling of communion which was the true meaning of the public jazz dance."

We are dealing here with substitute rituals. During an epoch which has witnessed the widespread breakdown of traditional religious forms, Ellison finds in jazz and the blues, as Hemingway found in the bullfight, a code of conduct and a ceremonial framework for his art. "True novels," he insists, "arise out of an impulse to celebrate human life and therefore are ritualistic and ceremonial at their core." Ellison perceives, in short, the priestly office of the modern artist and assumes the role of celebrant in his own work. Like the blues singer, he is motivated by an impulse to restore to others a sense of the wholeness of their lives.

Finally, specific features of Ellison's literary style may be traced to his musical background. His fondness for paradox and ambiguity, for example, derives from the blues: "There is a

mystery in the whiteness of blackness, the innocence of evil and
the evil of innocence, though being initiates Negroes express
the joke of it in the blues." The changing styles of *Invisible Man*
(from naturalism to expressionism to surrealism, as Ellison describes the sequence) are based on the principle of modulation.
Chord progressions in jazz are called "changes"; they correspond
in speed and abruptness to Ellison's sense of American reality,
the swift flow of sound and sudden changes of key suggesting
the fluidity and discontinuity of American life.

LITERATURE

Let us now turn from Ellison's musical to his literary heritage.
We must begin with the picaresque novel and attempt to explain
why this form, which first appeared in Renaissance Spain, should
be revived by a contemporary Negro novelist. We must then
consider Ellison's affinity for the American transcendentalists, in
light of his commitment to the picaresque. Finally, we must examine in some detail two devices that are central to his art.

The picaresque novel emerged toward the end of the feudal
and the beginning of the bourgeois epoch. Its characteristic hero,
part rogue and part outlaw, transcended all established norms of
conduct and violated all ideas of social hierarchy. For with the
breakdown of static social relations, a testing of personal limits,
a bold confrontation with the new and untried became necessary.
Hence the picaresque journey, no longer a religious quest or
pilgrimage but a journey toward experience, adventure, personal
freedom. It was the journey of the bourgeois soul toward possibility, toward a freedom possessed by neither serf nor lord under
the old regime.

It can hardly be an accident that *Invisible Man* and *The Adventures of Augie March* should win the National Fiction Award
within two years of one another. Nor that Ellison and Bellow
should each acknowledge a major debt to Twain. For *Huckle-
berry Finn* is the last great picaresque novel to be written by a

white Anglo-Saxon American. The genre has been abandoned to the Negro and the Jew who, two generations from slavery or the *shtetl,* experiences for the first time and in full force what Ellison calls the magical fluidity of American life. A century after Hawthorne wrote *The Scarlet Letter,* our minority groups are re-enacting the central drama of that novel: the break with the institutions and authorities of the past and the emergence into an epoch of personal freedom and individual moral responsibility.

Ellison's revival of the picaresque reflects his group's belated access to the basic conditions of bourgeois existence. These consist economically of the freedom to rise and psychologically of "the right and opportunity to dilate, deepen, and enrich sensibility." The Southern Negro who is taught from childhood to "know his place" is denied these basic freedoms. He is deprived of individuality as thoroughly as any serf: "The pre-individualistic black community discourages individuality out of self-defense. . . . Within the ambit of the black family this takes the form of training the child away from curiosity and adventure, against reaching out for those activities lying beyond the borders."

The Great Migration of the Negro masses from Southern farm to Northern city was picaresque in character. In terms of Negro personality, it was like uncorking a bottle of champagne. Traditionally the journey has been made by railroad, and it is no accident that the blues are associated with freight yards, quick getaways and long journeys in "a side door Pullman car." No accident either that Ellison should emphasize his own wanderings: "To attempt to express that American experience which has carried one back and forth and up and down the land and across, and across again the great river, from freight train to Pullman car, from contact with slavery to contact with the world of advanced scholarship, art and science, is simply to burst such neatly understated forms of the novel asunder."

The bursting forth of Negro personality from the fixed boundaries of Southern life is Ellison's essential theme. And it is this, at bottom, that attracts him to the transcendentalists. For what was the central theme of Thoreau, Emerson and Whitman, if not the journeying forth of the soul? These writers were celebrating their emancipation from the Custom House, from the moral and political authority of old Europe. Their romantic individualism was a response to the new conditions created by the Revolution, conditions calling for *self*-government in both the political and moral sphere. Their passion for personal freedom, moreover, was balanced by a sense of personal responsibility for the future of democracy.

Ellison's debt to transcendentalism is manifold, but what is not acknowledged can easily be surmised. He is named, to begin with, for Ralph Waldo Emerson. In this connection he mentions two specific influences: the "Concord Hymn" and "Self-Reliance." The poem presumably inspires him with its willingness to die that one's children may be free; the essay, as we shall see, governs his attitude toward Negro culture. He admires Thoreau, plainly enough, for his stand on civil disobedience and his militant defense of John Brown. Whitman he finds congenial, for such poems as "The Open Road" and "Passage to India" are squarely in the picaresque tradition.

In broader terms, it may be said that Ellison's ontology derives from transcendentalism. One senses in his work an unseen reality behind the surfaces of things. Hence his fascination with guises and disguises, with the con man and the trickster. Hence the felt dichotomy between visible and invisible, public and private, actual and fictive modes of reality. His experience as a Negro no doubt reinforces his ironic awareness of "the joke that always lies between appearance and reality," and turns him toward an inner world that lies beyond the reach of insult or oppression. This world may be approached by means of the imagination; it is revealed during the transcendent moment in jazz or the epiphany in literature. *Transcend* is thus a crucial word in Ellison's aesthetic.

Above all, Ellison admires the transcendentalists for their active democratic faith. They were concerned not only with the slavery question but with the wider implications of cultural pluralism, with the mystery of the one and the many. To these writers, the national motto, *e pluribus unum*, was a serious philosophical concern. Emerson discerned a cosmic model for American democracy in the relationship of soul to Oversoul. Whitman, however, made the classic formulation:

> One's self I sing, a simple separate person,
> Yet utter the word Democracy, the word En-Masse.

Ellison reveals, in his choice of ancestors, the depth of his commitment to American ideals. When he describes jazz as "that embodiment of a superior democracy in which each individual cultivated his uniqueness and yet did not clash with his neighbors," he is affirming the central values of American civilization.

It remains to place Ellison in his twentieth-century tradition. What is involved is a rejection of the naturalistic novel and the philosophical assumptions on which it rests. From Ellison's allusions to certain of his contemporaries—to Stein and Hemingway, Joyce and Faulkner, Eliot and Yeats—one idea emerges with persistent force: *Man is the creator of his own reality.* If a culture shapes its artists, the converse is equally the case: "The American novel is in this sense a conquest of the frontier; as it describes our experience, it creates it." This turn toward subjectivity, this transcendence of determinism, this insistence on an existential freedom, is crucial to Ellison's conception of the artist. It finds concrete expression in his work through the devices of masking and naming.

Masking has its origin in the psychological circumstances of Southern life: "In the South the sensibilities of both blacks and whites are inhibited by the rigidly defined environment. For the Negro there is relative safety as long as the impulse toward individuality is suppressed." As soon, however, as this forbidden impulse seeks expression, an intolerable anxiety is aroused. Threatened by his own unfolding personality as much as by the whites, the Negro learns to camouflage, to dissimulate, to retreat behind a protective mask. There is magic in it: the mask is a means of warding off the vengeance of the gods.

Consider the jazz solo, one of the few means of self-expression permitted to the southern Negro. Precisely because it is a solo, and the musician must go it alone, it represents potential danger. Ellison writes of certain jazz musicians: "While playing in ensemble, they carried themselves like college professors or high church deacons; when soloing they donned the comic mask." Louis Armstrong, as Ellison reminds us, has raised masking to the level of a fine art. Musical trickster, con man with a cornet, Elizabethan clown, "he takes liberties with kings, queens, and presidents." In a later development, the bearded mask of the bopster appeared, frankly expressive of hostility, rudeness and contempt. It is a pose which still finds favor among certain Negro writers of the younger generation.

In his own prose, Ellison employs various masking devices, including understatement, irony, *double-entendre* and calculated ambiguity. There is something deliberately elusive in his style, something secret and taunting, some instinctive avoidance of explicit statement which is close in spirit to the blues. His fascination with masquerade gives us two memorable characters in *Invisible Man*: the narrator's grandfather, whose mask of meekness conceals a stubborn resistance to white supremacy, and Rinehart, whom Ellison describes as "an American virtuoso of identity who thrives on chaos and swift change." A master of disguise, Rinehart survives by manipulating the illusions of society, much in the tradition of Melville's Confidence Man, Twain's Duke and Dauphin and Mann's Felix Krull.

Masking, which begins as a defensive gesture, becomes in Ellison's hands a means of altering reality. For if reality is a process of becoming, that process can be partially controlled through manipulation of a ritual object or mask. "Masking," Ellison remarks, "is a play upon possibility," and possibility is precisely the domain of art. To clarify the matter he summons Yeats, a man not ignorant of masks: "If we cannot imagine ourselves as different from what we are and assume the second self, we cannot impose a discipline upon ourselves, though we may accept one from others. Active virtue, as distinct from the passive acceptance of a current code, is the wearing of a mask." Yeats is speaking of morality, of active virtue, but the function of the artist is implicit in his words. Before pursuing the point, however, we must come to terms with a second feature of Ellison's art.

Naming likewise has its origin in negation, in the white man's hypocritical denial of his kinship ties. For the African slaves received from their Christian masters not only European names but a massive infusion of European blood, under circumstances so brutal and degrading as to have been virtually expunged from the national consciousness. At once guilty and proud, the white man has resorted to a systematic *misnaming* in an effort to obscure his crime. Thus the use of the matronymic to conceal the slave's paternity. Thus the insulting epithets which deny not merely kinship but humanity. In some obscene rite of exorcism, the white man says "nigger" when he should say "cousin." And yet the family names persist as symbols of that hidden truth, that broken connection which will have to be restored before the nation, sick from the denial of reality, can regain its mental health.

Having been misnamed by others, the American Negro has attempted from the first to define himself. This persistent effort at self-definition is the animating principle of Negro culture. The earliest appearance of Negro folklore, for example, "announced the Negro's willingness to trust his own experience, his own sensibilities as to the definition of reality, rather than allow his masters to define these crucial matters for him." Similarly with musical expression: the jazzman who rejects classical technique is affirming his right to define himself in sound. Cultural autonomy, to Ellison, is an elementary act of self-reliance. We have listened too long, he seems to say, to the courtly Muses of white America. "Our names, being the gift of others, must be made our own."

For personal as well as historical reasons, Ellison is fascinated by the distinction between one's given and achieved identity. Named for a famous poet, it was half a lifetime before he could define, let alone accept, the burden of his given name. Acknowledging in retrospec̲t the prescience of his father, he speaks of "the suggestive power of names and the magic involved in naming." We are dealing here with the ritual use of language, with the pressure which language can exert upon reality. This is the special province of the poet, and, broadly speaking, Ellison claims it as his own. He regards the novel as an act of ritual naming; the novelist, as a "moralist-designate" who *names* the central moral issues of his time.

"The poet," writes Ralph Waldo Emerson, "is the Namer or Language-maker." As such, he is the custodian of his language and the guarantor of its integrity. In performance of this function, Ellison has discovered that the language of contemporary America is in certain ways corrupt. "With all deliberate speed," for example, does not mean what it seems to mean when uttered by the Supreme Court of the United States. He proposes a rectification of the language and, therefore, of the nation's moral vision. For accurate naming is the writer's first responsibility: "In the myth, God gave man the task of naming the objects of the world; thus one of the functions of the poet is to insist upon a correspondence between words and ever-changing reality, between ideals and actualities."

As with naming, so with the image-making function as a whole. The artist, or image-maker, is guardian of the national iconography. And since the power of images for good or evil is immense, he bears an awesome responsibility. If his images are false, if there is no bridge between portrayal and event, no correspondence between the shadow and the act, then the emotional life of the nation is to that extent distorted, and its daily conduct is rendered ineffectual or even pathological. This is the effect of the anti-Negro stereotype, whether in song or statuary, novel or advertising copy, comic strip or film. Images, being ritual objects, or masks, may be manipulated by those who have a stake in the preservation of caste lines. What is required is a rectification of the nation's icons, a squaring of the shadow and the act.

Nor can this be accomplished through the use of counter-stereotypes. Protest fiction, by portraying sociological types, holds its readers at a distance from the human person. But the problem is precisely one of identification. To identify, in the psychological sense, is to become one with. For this process to occur between white reader and Negro character, the writer must break through the outer crust of racial conflict to the inner core of common humanity. He must evoke, by his imaginative power, an act of "painful identification." To succeed requires the utmost in emotional maturity, craftsmanship and skill. For what the artist undertakes, in the last analysis, is the rectification of the human heart.

POLITICS

If Ellison had remained a jazz musician, he might have been spared a series of political attacks upon his art. No one would have complained, if he had spoken in a jazz idiom, that his riffs were lacking in protest content. No one would have accused him, as he blew up there on the bandstand, of abandoning a posture of clenched militancy. For it is not expected of a Negro jazzman that, like the first trumpet in the Dodger Fan Club, he should sit in the stands during every civil-rights contest and play at appropriate moments, "Da da da datta da: Charge!" So long as he refuses to play for segregated audiences, accepts no gigs from the State Department and does an occasional benefit for SNCC, he is allowed to go about the very difficult business of interpreting Negro experience in sound.

Not so with the Negro novelist, who works in the medium of

words. For words have a variety of uses, political exhortation being one. The ideologists, therefore, move in. The question of militancy is raised, bearing not on the novelist's conduct as a citizen or political man but precisely on his creative work, his function as an artist. To those who feel above all else the urgency of the Negro's political struggle, it is not enough that a writer demonstrate his solidarity; he must enlist his image-making powers in the service of the cause. Since no writer who understands the proper uses of imagination can acquiesce in this perversion of his talent, he must prepare to walk that lonesome valley during much of his career, and to accept a good deal of abuse from those who do not recognize the value of his art.

It was predictable enough, given the rising tempo of the civil-rights struggle, that Ellison should be under pressure from the political activists. The Freedom Movement, like all great movements of social liberation, is lacking neither in demagogues nor Philistines. But that so sophisticated a critic and humane a man as Irving Howe should join the attack is scandalous. In an article called "Black Boys and Native Sons,"* Howe takes Baldwin and Ellison to task for abandoning the "rasping outbursts," "black anger," and "clenched militancy" of Richard Wright. While he sees some signs of hope in Baldwin's recent work, he plainly regards Ellison as unregenerate. Howe's essay prompted a reply from Ellison, and the result was a sharp exchange in *The New Leader*.†

One's chief impression of this debate is that the antagonists are arguing at cross-purposes. They shout at one another, but little or no dialogue occurs. Howe's original piece is a monument to tactlessness, and Ellison is understandably provoked into a sometimes angry response. It is a bad show all around, and the issues deserve to be aired in a calmer atmosphere. It is

* *Dissent*, Autumn, 1963.
† Dec. 9, 1963, and Feb. 3, 1964. Howe's original piece has been reprinted in *A World More Attractive* (New York: Horizon Press, 1963); Ellison's rejoinder appears in *Shadow and Act* under the title "The World and the Jug."

not my intent to mediate, however, for in my opinion Howe is overwhelmingly in the wrong. Nor do I wish to repeat Ellison's arguments which—tone aside—make most of the essential points. I should like rather to explore the philosophical foundations of the controversy. If my argument seems elementary, it is best that we proceed with caution, since, plainly, each of the contestants feels threatened by the other at the center of his being.

Let me begin with a parable. Imagine a Negro writer in the late 1950's (I choose the period advisedly, for Howe describes it as a conservative decade) attempting to decide on a subject for a novel. He has before him two projects, each based on the life of a Dodger baseball hero. The one—call it the Jackie Robinson story—is alive with racial drama: the first Negro ballplayer to make the big time, the insults from the stands, the spikings by opposing players, the mixed reception from his teammates. The other—call it the Roy Campanella story—concerns an athlete who, at the height of his career, spun his car around a curve one icy morning and spent the rest of his life in a wheelchair. Within a year or two his wife divorced him, she, too, a victim of her human frailty.

Suppose, for purposes of argument, that our writer chose to tell the second story. Would that choice suggest to Howe that he was running from reality, the reality of the sharpened spikes? Or is it possible that the Campanella story also contains a reality sufficiently sharp? Nor is there a refusal to confront injustice, for the theme of the second story would have to be injustice on a cosmic scale. Perhaps Howe would attempt a political explanation of our writer's choice. He might propose that during the militant decade of the Thirties such a writer would have turned at once to Jackie Robinson, but that out of his "dependence on the postwar *Zeitgeist*" he turned instead to a subject that was safe. But perhaps these political categories are beside the point. Perhaps our writer chose as he did simply because he felt in that story a deeper sense of human life.

Not all human suffering is racial in origin, that is our initial point. Being Negro, unfortunately, does not release one from the common burdens of humanity. It is for this reason that the blues singer so often deals with other than his racial woes. And it is to this dimension of human, as opposed to racial, pain that Howe gives insufficient attention. Ultimately, Ellison and Howe are divided over the *locus* of human suffering. One stresses man's position in society; the other, his position in the universe at large.

At issue is a crucial distinction between remediable and irremediable evil. The first, roughly speaking, is the domain of politics and science; the second, of art and religion. One's sense of tragedy is linked to one's perception of irremediable evil. What we have, therefore, in the Howe-Ellison exchange, is a confrontation between Howe's political optimism and Ellison's tragic sensibility. Howe, who still believes in Progress, concentrates on the evil that can be changed to the neglect of that which must be borne.

To the white liberal, racial injustice is a remediable evil. The Negro, however, experiences it in both modes simultaneously. In historical time, things are no doubt getting better, but in one's own lifetime, white oppression is a bitter fact to which one must adjust. The Negro, as Ellison points out, must live with and suffer under the present reality even as he works to change it. Entirely apart from the Movement, he must concern himself with the strategies and techniques of personal survival. It is precisely with this necessity of Negro life that Ellison's art is engaged.

Because of Howe's bias toward remediable evil, it is difficult for him to understand redemptive suffering. Speaking of Richard Wright, he remarks, "He examines the life of the Negroes and judges it without charity or idyllic compensation—for he already knows, in his heart and his bones, that to be oppressed means to lose out on human possibilities." This half-truth, it seems to me, dehumanizes the Negro by depriving him of his human triumph over pain. For as Ellison insists, Negro life is not only a burden but a discipline. Is it idyllic to suggest that Campanella's experience as a Negro might have prepared him in some way for coping with his accident? Was it in any way relevant? Was it, in short, an emotional resource?

If one attends primarily to remediable evil, one may be tempted to make larger claims for politics than history can justify. One may end by making politics the touchstone of a man's humanity: "In response to Baldwin and Ellison, Wright would have said . . . that only through struggle could men with black skins, and for that matter, all the oppressed of the world, achieve their humanity." Perhaps the question of humanity is after all more complex. It would be impertinent to remind Howe, who is a close student of the subject, that in recent Russian history many struggled and were brutalized thereby. But the memoirs of Victor Serge suggest to me that even in the midst of revolution the artist has a special function to perform: to remind the revolution of its human ends.

It will be clear, I trust, that I am speaking out of no hostility to the Freedom Movement or to politics as such. I am arguing not for the abandonment of militancy but for the autonomy of art. There is no need for literature and politics to be at odds. It is only when the aesthete approaches politics as if it were a poem, or when the political activist approaches the poem as if it were a leaflet, that the trouble starts. Phrases like "only through struggle" urge the subordination of art to politics. We must stifle these imperialistic impulses and foster a climate of mutual respect. Emerson distinguishes between the Doer and the Sayer, and refuses to honor one at the expense of the other. "Homer's words," he observes, "are as costly to Homer as Agamemnon's victories are to Agamemnon."

And I would add that Homer's words are as valuable as Agamemnon's victories *to the Greeks*. For I am arguing throughout for the social value of art. When Howe touches on this aspect of the question, he tries invariably to pre-empt all social value for his own position. Ellison, he charges, is pursuing the essentially antisocial goal of "personal realization," while Wright is fulfilling his responsibility to the Negro community. It is a false dichotomy. The Negro writer, who is surely not free of social responsibility, must yet discharge it *in his own fashion*, which is not the way of politics but art; not the lecture platform but the novel and the poem. Without repudiating his sense of obligation to the group, Ellison has tried to express it through services which only the imagination can perform.

What is at issue is the role of the imagination in that complex process which we call civilization. The visionary power, the power of naming, the power of revealing a people to itself are not to be despised. If those who can command these powers are diverted from their proper task, who will celebrate the values of the group, who create those myths and legends, those communal rites which alone endow the life of any group with meaning? These gifts are no less precious to a people (and if you like, no more) than those of personal charisma, theoretical analysis and political organization which are the special province of the revolutionary. Let us therefore give the imaginative faculty its due, concede its social value and respect its unique contribution to the process of becoming man.

CULTURE

At least as important as Ellison's defense of the imagination is his contribution to a theory of American Negro culture. Previous work in the field, whether by Negro or white intellectuals, has stressed the autonomous character of Negro culture, viewing it as an alien or exotic tributary to the mainstream of American life. Ellison proposes a more integrated view. Negro folk culture, to his way of thinking, is an indestructible monument to the national past. Embodying as it does three centuries of American history, it is a bittersweet reminder of what we were and are as a people. Far from being isolated from the mainstream, it marks the channel where the river runs deepest to the sea.

Given the complex interplay of culture and personality, race and social class that shapes the lives of American Negroes, some degree of theoretical clarity, some modicum of sophistication in these matters is essential. Not only racial strategies but one's own sanity and peace of mind are at stake. For every American Negro responds, at some level of his being, to two apparently disjunctive cultural traditions. If this can be shown to be an arbitrary division, false to the realities of American history, not only will the personal tensions ease but the Freedom Movement will be seen in new perspective. Integration will now appear as a mutual attempt, by American whites as well as Negroes, to restore a splintered culture to a state of wholeness.

The problem of dual identity is particularly acute for members of the Negro middle class. Suspended between two cultural traditions, each with its own claims and loyalties, the educated Negro has been caught on the horns of a dilemma. To identify closely with the life-style of the white middle class has generally led to a rejection of Negro folk culture. Conversely, to identify closely with the life-style of the Negro masses has implied a disaffection with the dominant values of American civilization. This conflicting pattern of identification and rejection has produced two broad currents of thought and feeling which I have elsewhere called assimilationism and Negro nationalism. Let me describe them briefly, for purposes of contrast with Ellison's point of view.

Assimilationism is a natural response to the experience of upward mobility. As the Negro middle class becomes differentiated from the masses by virtue of income, education and social status, it looks back upon its origins with embarrassment and shame. Negro folk culture, this rising middle class would argue, is the creation of an illiterate peasantry. It is vulgar and often shocking, permeated with the smell of poverty, reminiscent of our degradation and our pain. However well it may attest to what we were, it contains nothing of enduring value for us or for our children. On the contrary, it is a major obstacle to integration. The white middle class will accept us only to the extent that we become like them. It is therefore necessary to expunge every trace of "Negroness" from our behavior.

To these arguments Ellison would counterpose the richness of his folk tradition. He insists upon the relevance of folk experience to the conditions of modern urban life and, more important still, to the condition of being man. The assimilationist demands that in the name of integration the Negro self be put to death. But Ellison regards this proposal as a projection of self-hatred. To integrate means to make whole, not to lop off or mutilate; to federate as equals, not to merge and disappear. Anything else is a denial not only of one's racial identity but of one's national identity as well. For slavery really happened on American soil, and it has made us both, Negro and white alike, what we are today.

Negro nationalism is a natural response to the experience of rejection. Rebuffed by the whites, the Negro nationalist rebuffs in turn. Rejecting the white man's civilization as thoroughly corrupt, visibly in decay and hopelessly compromised by its oppression of the blacks, he asks in anger and despair, "Why should we integrate into a burning house?" From this mood of separatism and alienation flows his attitude toward the folk culture. For here is a system of values to oppose to those of the white middle class. All that is distinctive in Negro life is thus exalted as a matter of racial pride. Traditionally, this point of view has been fortified by some sort of African mystique, the current version being the concept of *Négritude*.

Here Ellison would counter with the richness of the dominant tradition. European civilization, of which he is a part, cannot be written off so lightly. Emerson and Einstein, Mozart and Michelangelo, Jefferson and Joyce are part of his tradition, and he has paid for them in blood. He is not about to bargain them away in exchange for *Négritude*. The Negro nationalist demands that for the sake of injured pride the Western self be put to death. But if the injury is real, the remedy is disastrous. What is separatism but the sulking of a rejected child? The American Negro, after all, is no stranger to the affairs of this nation. Nor can he stand aside from its appointed destiny. For if the house burns, one thing is certain: the American Negro will not escape the conflagration.

Assimilationism and Negro nationalism both involve a maiming of the self, an unnecessary loss. Why not combine the best of both traditions? Between these opposite and symmetrical errors, Ellison steers a steady course. On the one hand, he wants in: no one, white or colored, will persuade him that he is an outsider. Talk about the mainstream! He's been swimming in it since 1619. On the other hand, he is not about to trade in his tested techniques of survival on some white man's vague promise: "Be like us and we will accept you, maybe." When he comes in, he brings his chitlins with him. If, in the process, he transforms America into a nation of chitlin eaters, so much the better for our ethnic cooking.

While assimilationism and Negro nationalism make opposite evaluations of Negro folk culture, they both regard it as in some sense un-American. To all such formulations Ellison objects that they abstract distinctive Negro qualities from the concrete circumstances of American life. The American Negro *is* different from his white countrymen, but American history and that alone has made him so. Any serious attempt to understand these differences will, therefore, lead, by a thousand devious paths, across the tracks to white America. Always there is a connection, however hidden; always a link, however brutally severed. It follows that "any viable theory of Negro American culture obligates us to fashion a more adequate theory of American culture as a whole."

To this end, Ellison offers what might be called some Notes toward a Redefinition of American Culture. There is a gross distortion, he suggests, in America's self-image. It begins with the white man's artificial attempt to isolate himself from Negro life. But Negro life is not sealed off hermetically from the historical process. On the contrary, it is the most authentic expression of that process as it has actually unfolded on the North American continent. Ellison argues, in effect, that the life-style of the Negro ghetto is *more* American than the so-called standard American culture of white suburbia because the latter, in the very impulse that gave it birth, denies a vital dimension of American experience. There is no possibility, he warns, of escaping from the past. What is required is that we bring our distorted image of ourselves into line with the historical reality.

Paradoxically, what is most distinctive in Negro life is often most American. Jazz, for example, is not simply Negro music, but the definitive rendering of American experience in sound. Similarly with folklore: "In spilling out his heart's blood in his contest with the machine, John Henry was asserting a national value as well as a Negro value." Where do we turn for the truth about American slavery: to Negro spirituals or the songs of Stephen Collins Foster? Why is the current slang of American teen-agers drawn from the speech of the Negro ghetto? Why the persistent vogue for Negro dance forms, unless we have been growing, from Charleston to Watusi, steadily less inhibited as a nation?

American culture is still in process of becoming. It is not a finished form, a house that one day will be rented out to Negroes. On the contrary, in the process of racial integration the culture will be radically transformed. This transformation will amount to a correction of perspective. By degrees, the white man's truncated version of American reality will be enlarged. The American eye will be retrained to see sights hitherto ignored or, if seen, misconstrued for venal ends. Connections formerly obscure will now be plain; the essential oneness of American civilization will emerge. Ultimately Americans will develop a new image of themselves as a nation.

"I was taken very early," Ellison remarks, "with a passion to link together all I loved within the Negro community and all those things I felt in the world which lay beyond." This passion is the driving force of his career. It can be felt in his response to jazz as well as his approach to fiction. It accounts, moreover, for his views on politics and art. For the linking together which he has in mind can barely begin in courthouse and in workshop, neighborhood and school. It must be consummated in some inner realm, where all men meet on common ground. Such are the links that Ellison would forge, the new reality he would create, the shattered psyche of the nation that he would make whole.

8.   *Albert Murray*

Something Different, Something More

Not so very long ago, as these things are reckoned in the annals of human letters, James Baldwin, then a promising young Greenwich Village intellectual from Harlem, wrote an article for *Partisan Review** about *Uncle Tom's Cabin*. It was called "Everybody's Protest Novel," and what made it especially significant was the fact that in it Baldwin, a Negro whose personal commitment to militant social and political action was unquestionable, seemed to be firmly and completely, if somewhat hastily, rejecting social protest in fiction as bad art, a mirror of confusion, dishonesty and panic, as sentimental fantasy connecting nowhere with reality.

He stated that the avowed aim of such fiction was to bring greater freedom to the oppressed. But he was unenthusiastic about this lofty purpose in itself, nor did he share the then current optimism about the effectiveness of books produced by those committed to it. In fact, he was convinced that "novels of oppression written by Negroes . . . actually reinforce . . . the principles which activate the oppression they decry."

Baldwin overstated his case, of course, but many serious students of American literature were very much impressed by what they thought all of this implied about his own ambitions as a

* June, 1949.

112

writer. They assumed that more than anything else he was stating his own personal objections to the narrowness of propaganda fiction as such. They assumed that whatever else was intended, his statements about Harriet Beecher Stowe represented his own aesthetic orientation. It is easy to see why. "She was," he wrote, "not so much a novelist as an impassioned pamphleteer; her book was not intended to do anything more than prove that slavery was wrong; was, in fact perfectly horrible. This makes material for a pamphlet but it is hardly enough for a novel. . . ."

At this time Baldwin seemed very much concerned about the fact that he was living in a mechanical and interlocking civilization which overlooked, denied and evaded man's complexity, treated him as a time-saving invention, a deplorable conundrum to be explained by science. Protest fiction, he felt, was a part of all this, a formula created "to find a lie more palatable than the truth." But as for himself, he was seeking himself and the power to free himself from himself not in mechanical formulas and in causes but within what he called a "web of ambiguity, paradox, hunger, danger, and darkness." It was the power of revelation, he declared, which was "the business of the novelist, this journey toward a more vast reality which must take precedence over all other claims."

He then went on to indict *Uncle Tom's Cabin* for its self-righteous sentimentality and its senseless and unmotivated brutality, among other things, including a theological terror of blackness and damnation. He also called it the prototype of the American protest novel, and, in the process, he described the hero of Richard Wright's *Native Son*, the most celebrated protest novel of the day, as Uncle Tom's descendant, an exactly opposite portrait, perhaps, but flesh of his flesh. But then, Richard Wright had already called the people of his previous book Uncle Tom's children. There was no argument on that score. There was, however, or so it seemed at the time, a more fundamental conflict. Richard Wright seemed to represent the very qualities in fiction which James Baldwin deplored most heatedly.

In fact, the very attempt of fiction such as Wright's to insure life was regarded by Baldwin at that time as a betrayal of life. The tragedy of the hero of *Native Son*, he wrote, was not that he was cold, hungry, black or American but that he had accepted a theology which denied him life, "that he admits the possibility of his being subhuman and feels constrained therefore to battle for his humanity." Baldwin then concluded his article as follows: "The failure of the protest novel lies in its rejection of life, the human being, the denial of his beauty, dread, power, in its insistence that it is his categorization alone which is real and which cannot be transcended."

Some two years later, Baldwin, then a very special young U.S. expatriate from Greenwich Village and the streets of Harlem living in Paris, not far from the French existentialists and among other U.S. expatriates from Greenwich Village, the Ivy League, the Big Ten and even the genteel South, and among Africans mostly from the French colonies, continued his by then much admired remarks about protest fiction. In another article, "Many Thousands Gone," also for *Partisan Review*,* he took *Native Son* to task again. A necessary dimension had been cut away, he said at one point, because the other Negroes in the story are seen only from Bigger Thomas' limited point of view, "this dimension being the relationship that Negroes bear to one another, that depth of involvement and unspoken recognition of shared experience which creates a way of life."

He also characterized the climate of *Native Son* as one of anarchy and unmotivated and unapprehended disaster, "and it is this climate common to most Negro protest novels," he went on, "which has led us all to believe that in Negro life there exists no tradition, no field of manners, no possibility of ritual intercourse, such as may, for example, sustain the Jew even after he has left his father's house." And then came the following highly suggestive statement: "But the fact is not that the Negro has no tradition, but that there has as yet arrived no sensibility sufficiently profound and tough to make this tradition articulate."

* November-December, 1951.

At the time the implications seemed unmistakable. It was assumed by almost everybody concerned about such matters that
all this was still another indication that here was a young writer-
in-progress whose single passion was to give his own fiction
greater human depth and richer historical reverberation than he
had found in any of the novels he mentioned. Overlooked in all
of the enthusiasm, however, was the astonishing fact that in addition to *Uncle Tom's Cabin* and *Native Son* Baldwin had mentioned only *Gentleman's Agreement, The Postman Always Rings
Twice, Kingsblood Royal* and *If He Hollers Let Him Go* (!) and
had alluded to *The Sound and the Fury,* one of the outstanding
achievements of modern fiction, only to protest an alleged racial
discrimination. But perhaps this was deliberately overlooked.
After all, it was the assumed promise which really mattered. The
means of fulfillment could always be evolved in the process. At
any rate, it is not erudition as such which counts in a novelist.

Or is it? At least for something? As a matter of fact, the
very same *Partisan Review* paragraph contains a significant clue
to Baldwin's subsequent difficulties and confusions as a serious
writer. "For a tradition," he continued in the very next sentence,
"expresses, after all, *nothing more* than the long and painful experience of a people; it comes out of the battle waged to maintain their integrity or, to put it more simply, out of their struggle
to survive." And then in the sentence after that he added the
following observation, which certainly implies *some* kind of erudition, perhaps Talmudic—he was, after all, writing in the *Partisan Review*: ". . . when we speak of the Jewish tradition, we
are speaking of centuries of exile and persecution, of the strength
which endured and the sensibility which discovered in it the
high possibility of the moral victory."

All of which is utterly confusing. Baldwin doesn't mention a
single Jewish novel which would justify such a statement. And
no wonder. Whatever else the great Jewish tradition in literature
represents it not only represents protest, it is *characterized* by a
great deal of protest as such. But then, perhaps Baldwin's confusion was built in at the very outset. A tradition involves *much*

more than the long and painful experiences of a people. The modern Jewish tradition, which someone has referred to as an instantly erectable wailing wall, may well represent centuries of exile and persecution, but it also represents much more—as did the ancient Greek and Roman traditions; as do the modern French and English traditions.

As for the tradition of U.S. Negroes, Baldwin may or may not realize that he is making a fundamental statement about it when he says that it is only in music that the Negro in America has been able to tell his story. Actually, this story is also told in folktales and lore, sayings, jokes and various other forms. Still there is much to be said for Baldwin's assertion. Music does contain the most comprehensive rendering of the complexities of the American Negro experience. Music, it seems, *has* been the artistic form most featured among U.S. Negroes, and there appear to be historical as well as anthropological reasons for this. At any rate there are clear historical explanations for the fact that U.S. Negro musicians have always existed in greater numbers than Negro writers. But whatever the reason, very few U.S. Negro writers or painters rank in range and achievement beside musicians like Louis Armstrong, Scott Joplin or even Charlie Parker, not to mention the great Kansas City stylists and Duke Ellington.

However, it must be noted immediately that what U.S. Negro musicians express represents far more than the fact that American black folks been 'buked and been scorned and nobody know de trouble dey seen. Distinctive as it is, U.S. Negro music like U.S. Negro life is after all or, rather, first of all, also inseparable from life in the United States at large. Thus, as an art form it is a direct product of the U.S. Negro sensibility, but it is the end-product, so to speak, of all the cultural elements which brought that sensibility into being in the first place. This goes without saying. The spirituals, for example, always expressed more than a proletarian reaction to poor pay and bad working conditions. They did reflect life on the plantation and the effects of political

bondage, but it must not be forgotten that they were also a profound and universally moving expression of Protestant Christianity—that the spirituals contained New England elements,
frontier elements and American aspirations in general, and many
other things, including an active physical existence and a rich,
robust, and highly imaginative conception of life itself.

And, of course, when one speaks of the blues, one is inescapa-
bly aware of the lamentable circumstances in which this rugged
musical tradition was formed, but the music itself represents a
sensibility which has achieved a grace, sophistication and even
elegance under pressure which seems to have eluded most psychologists but which may yet add a contemporary dimension to
the classical conception of tragic heroism.

The blues affirm not only U.S. Negro life in all of its arbitrary
complexities and not only life in contemporary America in all of
its infinite confusions, they affirm humanity in the very process
of confronting failures and existentialistic absurdities. The very
spirit of the blues moves in the opposite direction from ashes
and sackcloth, self-pity, self-hatred and suicide. As a matter of
fact, the dirtiest, meanest and most low-down blues are not only
not depressing, they function like an instantaneous aphrodisiac!

There are, incidentally, also significant implications of affirmation inherent in the basic fact that U.S. Negro music has always been a part of a great tradition of dance and physical labor.
Perhaps even more significant is the fact that U.S. Negro life itself, for all of its assimilated complexities and for all its involvement in the processes of mechanization, has always remained
basically oriented to the use of dance rhythms for practical as
well as aesthetic purposes.

All of which would seem to be of the most immediate and
fundamental interest to any serious student of American culture,
to say nothing of a serious writer of American fiction. And yet
James Baldwin, for all his understandable dissatisfaction with the
thinness of Richard Wright's characters and situations, and for
all his fine, youthful arrogance about a "sensibility sufficiently

profound and tough" to make the Negro tradition articulate, has never written in terms of any of the sustaining actualities of that tradition in any of his own stories.

Instead, he has relied more and more on the abstract categories of academic research and less and less on the poetic insights of the creative artist. So much so that the very characteristics of protest fiction which he once deplored in the work of Harriet Beecher Stowe and Richard Wright now seem to be his stock in trade; they are, in any case, the things he is now world-famous for. His best-selling novel, *Another Country*, for instance, reflects very little of the rich, complex and ambivalent sensibility of the novelist, very little, indeed—no more than does the polemical essay *The Fire Next Time*. What Baldwin's writing actually reflects, in this connection, is the author's involvement with oversimplified library and laboratory theories and conjectures about the negative effects of racial oppression.

And like *Native Son* it does so for a very good reason. It was designed to serve a very worthy cause—the cause of greater political, social and economic freedom and opportunity for Negroes in the United States. And the current civil-rights movement has profited from his books and from his position as a public figure in many very tangible ways. In fact he has become one of the best known heroes of the Negro Revolution—a citizen spokesman, as eloquent in his own way as was citizen polemicist Tom Paine in the revolution of '76—a major achievement in itself.

Polemics, however, are not likely to be epics. They are likely to be pamphlets, even when they are disguised as stories and plays. Thus, ironically enough, Baldwin's historical role in the civil-rights struggle has also been all but indistinguishable from the one played by Harriet Beecher Stowe in the Civil War. And with some of the same exasperating confusion. For, in spite of what he once declared about raging near-paranoiac novels of oppression actually reinforcing the principles which activate the conditions they decry, he himself has found it expedient to degrade U.S. Negro life to the level of the subhuman in the very process of pleading his humanity—something he once said one had only to accept!

Baldwin writes about Harlem, for example, with an evangelical sense of moral outrage, and his declarations on this subject are said to have stirred the conscience of the nation. But he never really accounts for the tradition which supports Harlem's hardheaded faith in democracy, its muscular Christianity, its cultural flexibility, nor does he account for its universally celebrated commitment to elegance in motion, to colorful speech idioms, to high style, not only in personal deportment but even in the handling of mechanical devices. Intentionally or not, much of what he says implicitly denies the very existence of Harlem's fantastically knowing satire, its profound awareness and rejection of so much that is essentially ridiculous in downtown doings. Sometimes he writes as if he had never heard the comedians at the Apollo Theatre.

Life in Harlem is the very stuff of romance and fiction, even as was life in Chaucer's England, Cervantes' Spain, Rabelais' France. But what Baldwin writes about is not really life in Harlem. He writes about the economic and social conditions in Harlem, the material *plight* of Harlem. And far from writing in terms of a U.S. Negro tradition he confuses everything with the Jewish tradition and writes about life in a black *ghetto*! In point of fact, James Baldwin, like most native-born U.S. Negroes, is probably a part white Anglo-Saxon Protestant of Southern derivation, and sometimes he likes to say that he comes from a long line of field hands and maybe a Texas sheriff or so, too; but he often writes as if he were really a black, brown or beige New York Jewish intellectual of immigrant parents. During these times there is very little to indicate that the spellbinding power of much of his polemical eloquence really comes out of his background as a boy-preacher in a Harlem store-front church.

A serious novelist, like all other good citizens, should, needless to say, support worthy political causes; but that he should distort his work to do so is another matter altogether. Baldwin once strongly implied that protest and distortion were inseparable, that protest fiction insists on false categories, rejects life, decries the beauty and power of human beings. This is not necessarily so. One has only to think of the basic and very clear-cut element of protest in all of the fiction of James Joyce. And, among other outstanding novels of the twentieth century, what of *The Sun Also Rises, Light in August, The Magic Mountain, The Castle, The Great Gatsby*? Actually, much goes to show that the element of social protest as such underlies as much of the action in the upper middle-class world of *The Great Gatsby* as it does in the revolutionary proletarian milieu of André Malraux's *Man's Fate*.

Nor is the element of propaganda in itself necessarily detrimental. The advertisement of alleged values is a fundamental aspect of all literature, as is the damnation of all that would jeopardize or destroy what is held to be of value. In this very elementary sense, Henry James, of all people, produced some of the best propaganda ever written. There is no doubt in anybody's mind that the author of *The Ambassadors* and *The Turn of the Screw* was for goodness and against evil—and he made a convincing case for his position—but he did not oversimplify the virtues of his heroes, the vice of his villains, the complexity of their situation or the ambiguity of their motives.

But perhaps Baldwin had in mind political propaganda as such, which of its very nature almost always tends to gear itself to expedient means and immediate action. Perhaps this does create very special problems for the artist. Perhaps it leads him, in spite of himself, to oversimplify all situations in terms of the remedial program to which he is committed, and, of course, this could easily involve him in the kind of writing which produces election campaign slogans and advertising copy for cure-all medicines. But even in this, political propaganda contains no truly unique dangers. Propaganda which oversimplifies life in terms of faith, hope, charity or romantic love produces a distortion of reality which is every bit as misleading.

Nevertheless, there are many reasons why it is all but impossible for a serious writer of fiction to engage his craft in a political cause, no matter how worthy, without violating his very special integrity as an artist in some serious way. All of these reasons are complicated and some may seem downright questionable, but perhaps none is more important than the fact that, as well meaning as he may be, the truly serious novelist has what almost amounts to an ambivalence toward the human predicament. Alarming as this may seem, however, it is really very fundamental to his open-minded search for the essential truth of human experience.

There is, first of all, his complex awareness of the burdensome but sobering fact that there is some goodness in bad people, however bad they are, and some badness or at least some flaw or weakness in good people, however dear. In fact, sometimes the artist comes pretty close to being politically suspect; because, on the one hand, he is always proclaiming his love for mankind and, on the other, he is forever giving the devil his due!

And then there is a crucial ambivalence in his eternal and even infernal involvement with the ironic actualities of *antagonistic cooperation*! He is all for achieving the good society, the salubrious situation, the excellent environment. But at the same time he insists that the beautiful community does not automatically produce beautiful people who stay good or sweetness and light that lasts for ever afterward. Not only this, but he actually seems to be more excited about the fact that sorry situations, ugly communities, trying circumstances and impossible environments, along with whatever else they do, also, *of their very nature*, produce not only good people but incomparable *heroes* who come from the awful darkness but bring sweetness and light!

II

For several years before Baldwin's articles, Richard Wright had been a famous U.S. Negro expatriate living in Paris among the most famous French existentialists, who, incidentally, were hav-

ing a field day protesting against U.S. canned goods, refrigera-
tors, automobiles and, most of all, U.S. dollars in the hands of
U.S. citizens. Wright, who seemed to regard himself as U.S.
Negro-in-residence, so to speak, gave them other U.S. absurdities
and atrocities to protest about. He also liked to function as American political pundit for the African colonials along the boule-
vards and around the old Latin Quarter.

But, meanwhile, he was by way of becoming something of an
existentialist himself, although he was still given to ripping red-
hot pages of accusations from his outraged and smoldering typewriter and angrily flinging them all the way back across the
Atlantic and into the guilt-ridden lap of America. During this
time he also flung one at the guilt-ridden face of pagan Spain
and two or three at the guilt-ridden face of white folks everywhere.

It was bad enough that the fiction Wright began to turn out
during this time was even worse than that of Jean-Paul Sartre
(which was really going some, by the way); much more important is the fact that, for all the down-home signifying and uptown
sassiness he put Sartre and Simone de Beauvoir hip to—or maybe
precisely because of it—he was unable to keep the ever square
but news-prone Mister Sartre, the world's fastest academic hip-
shooter, from being sucked in on the politically benevolent, racist
notions of *Négritude*, an all but hopelessly confused theory or
doctrine of international Negroism, or is it Black Nationalist in-
ternationalism?

At any rate *Négritude*, notion or doctrine, not only tends to
confuse tradition (or cultural inheritance) with racial inheritance
(or racial mysticism), it also encourages the kind of aesthetic
nonsense which has involved an alarming and increasing number of young and not so young U.S. Negroes in programs, movements and organizations which can only make it even more
difficult for them to realize the infinite potential of the *American* Negro elements in the *American* tradition.

Most of the devices for the promotion of what is now called

Black Arts are more political than anything else, and naïvely political at that. Many so-called Black Artists identify themselves not with the United States but with Africa, which is political naïveté coupled with an incredible disregard for the dynamics of socio-cultural evolution. Politically naïve also is their amusing disregard for the national boundaries on the continent of Africa. Americans that they are, they seem to be forever confusing the *countries* of Africa with the *states* of the United States. And if this is pan-Africanism, then how naïve can you get?

Some of the Black Arts affiliates are anti-American, anti-American white folks, that is. At least they pretend to be, some belligerently so. But so far, what they intend to accomplish either in government or the arts is not very clear. So far, it has only added up to a whole lot of black anarchy, which, of course, is considered to be a legitimate enough objective by some ideologies, and not for such pseudo-sanguinary–pseudo-nasty aesthetic reasons as may be bragged about during some obscene intellectual séance in some Greenwich Village night club, where the speakers say another four-letter word when they really mean spit and confuse blood with stage make-up.

Whatever their objectives and however political, even, every last one of these so-called Black Arts movements seems to be commercially oriented toward white American audiences above all others, and, curiously enough, not one is seriously considered to be subversive—far from it. As a matter of fact, most of the promotion, encouragement and financial underwriting which is not smuggled in from abroad comes from devoted white patrons. But that is a very special story in itself, as is the fact that for his own perverse reasons, both personal and political, the U.S. white involved seems to regard the whole thing as some new fashionable, outrageous, but very safe game in which he is not so much rejected as envied and not so much ignored as wooed! Roughly, perhaps, but he seems to like it like that.

In some ways it all seems like one of those boring acts from

one of those third-rate but ever-clever clown shows by Jean
Genet, the grand old off-Broadway darling of the beatniks and
Susan Sontag's campfire girls, the French scatologist whom J. P.
Sartre calls a modern saint! Indeed, for all its homemade overtones of Uncle Tom's chillun scandalizing Miss Ann and Mister
Charley in front of company, most of the pretentiously aggres-
sive racism in the Black Arts movement in New York seems to
come from the Genet play, which has been translated as *The
Blacks*. Incidentally, the French title of this play is not *Les Noirs*
but rather *Les Nègres*, which to U.S. Negroes *usually* means
something else altogether!

In other ways, however, one is also reminded of some of the
less political but by no means less naïve capers which characterized so much of the so-called Negro Renaissance back in the
Twenties. This New Negro movement, as it was sometimes
called, was also a black arts movement encouraged and supported by white people. It grew directly out of the effete tradition of aesthetic decadence, which in race-oriented America
confused black U.S. peasants with African natives and financed
more "primitive abandon" between the Hudson and Harlem
rivers than ever existed anywhere in the Congo. After all, actual
primitive life is nothing if not formal. Primitive behavior is the
very opposite of wild abandon. It conforms to taboos. Abandon,
like bad manners and crime, is not inherent in the restrictions of
primitive discipline by any means. It is rather one of those natural products of the freedom and individuality which comes with
what is called civilization. It is the super-civilized avant-garde
bohemian, not the superstition-ridden savage, who is forever
and ever in wild-eyed, hot-collar, soap-box street-marching or
window-breaking rebellion against all sorts of restrictions—some
of them purely imaginary.

The current Black Arts movement, like the one before it, is
nothing if not avant-garde, ersatz tiger noises underneath the
bamboo tree boom-boom and all. But the avant-garde sort of
thing is not exclusive to the cognoscenti these days. It also makes

sensational news copy for the New York dailies, *Time, Life, Look, Newsweek,* NBC-TV, CBS and ABC. Some of it gets staged through the angelic efforts of New York theatrical patrons, some of them female. Some of it gets printed by the big, fat publishing firms, and some of it comes out on Columbia and RCA-Victor records.

Meanwhile, one can only hope that, in spite of the current popularity of *Négritude* in some circles, there are also U.S. Negro writers whose literary insights will enable them to do much more than turn out shrill, defensive and predictable counter-propaganda against the doctrine of white supremacy, as important as this propaganda is. *Such insights should also enable these writers to realize that they have as much responsibility for representing the mainstream of U.S. life as anybody else. It is always open season on the truth, and there never was a time when one had to be white to take a shot at it.*

Indeed, if there is one thing that all U.S. Negroes think they know about American literature it is that white writers seldom deal with the realities of American experience. Negroes think they know far too much about the everyday doings of the white people around them to be taken in by the phony bedtime stories in most of the books and magazines, in spite of the fact that most white people seem to allow themselves to be taken in by them. Negroes think they know quite a bit about the lives of white people, and much more. One can only hope they learn how to get some of what they really know and how they truly feel into fiction, rather than what a book like *An American Dilemma* tells them they are supposed to know and how somebody tells them they're supposed to feel.

Most white writers go on year after year turning out book after solipsistic book in which they pretend that the world is white. In this they go hand-in-hand with most U.S. journalists, photographers and motion-picture producers. But any U.S. Negro share cropper surrounded by a field of snow-white cotton knows better than that. And he knows that the world is not

black, either. He knows that the only color the world really has
is the color of infinity, whatever that is. This particular U.S.
Negro knows very well that the white man, for all his relative political and economic power, is not free. He has not read *The
Waste Land* but he has heard the blues, and some of them really
are about Miss Ann and Mr. Charley. But he is not cheered by
the fix they're in; he is sobered by it—as his great-great-grand-
father was sobered by the spirituals which sometimes whispered,
*Nobody knows the trouble I seen when I seen what was really
happening in the BIG HOUSE.* No wonder great-great-grandpa
took religious salvation so seriously.

And yet your *Négritude* promoter, for all his bamboo boom-
boom, often gives the impression that he is out to paint the world
black only because *he* believes it's white, and that white is really
all right, but he's going to change it out of spite! But who knows?
Perhaps this is only a part of the political fakery involved in this
kind of confidence game. How *could* one know? Your *Négritude*
promoter also identifies himself with the most militant integra-
tionist!

Thus does the American species of *Négritude* bring itself, by
a commodious vicus of recirculation, back to protest fiction and
Marxist environs. Whereupon enter the old effeterati, now become the politerati, doing an ofay version of the one-butt shuffle
to the fading but still audible strains of the old 1930's dialectical
boogie-woogie.

These white friends of the Negro, that is to say, friends and
friends-in-print of Negro Causes, or is it the Negro Cause?, are
very sincere in many ways, and they have done much good in
some ways but they have also done and continue to do untold
harm in a number of perhaps unrecognized but very fundamental ways. They encourage inferior standards and values by
accepting or pretending to accept shoddy and immature work-
manship. They sanction inadequate education by going along
with what they know is intellectual rubbish and aesthetic nonsense, if they know anything. And, furthermore, only the most

snobbish and most self-indulgent condescension would permit
them to tolerate so much arrogant stupidity and subversive ir-
responsibility.

It is about time U.S. Negro writers realized that whether or
not these particular white friends themselves have any literary
taste and maturity (and one wonders), they do not assume that
Negro writers have any. Nor do they assume that Negro writers
have any major literary ambitions. They seem to assume that
for the Negro literature is simply incidental to protest. And it is
about time Negro writers began to wonder why. It is about time
they started asking themselves why these people are happiest
when Negroes are moaning and groaning about black troubles
and miseries. It is undeniable that these friends also tolerate and
seem to enjoy being insulted, accused or "baldwinized" from
time to time. But that is another one of those stories about
choosing one's own punishment.

And it should also be remembered that these people never
show any real enthusiasm for the affirmative elements in U.S.
Negro life (and there are affirmative elements in all human life,
even in hillbilly life). Quite the contrary. These are the selfsame
people who insist on explaining away qualities such as tough-
minded forbearance and faith, compassion, musical expressiveness, and even physical coordination, as being marks of
oppression or even pathological evidence of racial inferiority.

U.S. Negro writers, and would-be writers who have any valid
literary ambitions whatsoever, obviously cannot afford to allow
themselves to be overimpressed by the alleged superiority of the
academic or professional background of their white-friends-in-
print. Only people who have learned nothing from literary biography and have no fundamental understanding of the ironies
involved in the creative process would hold, as these so often do,
that Negroes will be able to write first-rate novels *only after* all
oppression is removed, *only after* such time as Negroes no longer
feel alienated from the mainstream of U.S. life.

What could be more misleading? Writers have always thrived

on oppression, poverty, alienation and the like. Fëodor Dostoevski, for example, was very poor, much oppressed and, in addition to all sorts of other personal problems, he was epileptic.
He was certainly alienated. He was imprisoned, and one time he
came within minutes of being officially lynched. But he wrote
good books. Because he liked good books. Because his mind
and imagination functioned in terms of good books. Even in jail.
A writer who is oriented toward good books will at least try to
write good books. But the sad fact is that there is very little to
show that very many U.S. Negro writers have ever actually
tried to write major novels.

There is certainly justification for some doubts and even sus-
picions about the *literary* value of the white-friends-of-the-Negro-
Cause. One can only doubt that they know how art comes into
being or suspect that they know only too well. But be that as it
may. They *could* provide a literary atmosphere in which Negroes
would become oriented toward major works of art. But they do
not. They do something else altogether. They actually discourage
interest in art by overemphasizing and oversubsidizing the social
sciences and by insinuating that Negroes who are interested in
great art are not really interested in the everyday problems and
realities of life by accusing them of trying to escape the rigors of
oppression by fleeing to the Ivory Tower!

None of this is intended as any excuse for U.S. Negroes
themselves. Many things may be segregated, but great books
and great ideas are not. Not really. Not even the Ku Klux Klan
has shown any great concern because a Negro was sitting somewhere in a quiet corner reading Goethe or Thomas Mann. (They
are much too busy seeing to it that the white pupils get to the
trade schools first!) No—this is only to indicate the literary
quality of the Negro's white well-wishers. But, to make a long
story short, all you have to do is compare the kind of encouragement given by the typical white literary patron with the aspirations of the managers and promoters of Negro prize fighters.
Financial double-dealing aside, the backers of Negro boxers are
out to produce champions of the world.

It is about time all U.S. Negroes took a closer look at all their friends-of-the Cause. To be conned by such self-styled good will as is usual with so many of these cheap-note aristocrats is not only to invite contempt, and not only to encourage it, but also to deserve it.

III

Ralph Ellison wrote an article about Richard Wright which was published in the *Antioch Review* in the summer of 1945. This was four years before James Baldwin came to write "Everybody's Protest Novel" and some six before he was to do "Many Thousands Gone." Baldwin, as has been seen, was sharply critical of Wright, who, incidentally, was an old personal friend and one-time benefactor. Ellison, also an old personal friend, was generous almost to a fault. So much so that when Wright encountered him shortly afterward all Wright could do was shake his head in pleased bewilderment—somewhat, one imagines, as the original tunesmith of "Body and Soul" must have done upon meeting Coleman Hawkins—and all he could say was almost exactly what one imagines the tunesmith must have said: "Man, you went much further than the book. Much further." (Wright was never to go as far again.)

All Ellison, a former trumpet player and student of music composition, could do was shake his head in turn and smile reassuringly and reply, "Well, what you wrote made it possible for me to say what I said about it. All I was trying to do was use what you put there. All I was trying to do was play a few riffs on your tune. It was your tune, I just hope I didn't embarrass you. I just hope I did it justice." He did it more than justice.

Ellison's article was a commentary on *Black Boy*. This autobiographical record of Wright's childhood and youth employed all the techniques of fiction and was obviously intended to be a literary work of art as well as a personal document. Ellison called it "Richard Wright's Blues," and his remarks did go far beyond the book itself. They included what was stated and, like all really perceptive literary criticism, he suggested what was represented, symbolized, ritualized.

Richard Wright, in spite of the shifts in his formal political affiliations, was always essentially a Marxist thinker. It is true that he maintained and no doubt believed that Marxism was only a starting point for Negro writers, and he himself was certainly the kind of intellectual who realized that Negro folklore had important literary significance. He also had a very extensive knowledge of world history and cultures, of ideas as such and of contemporary world literature. But although his wide intellectual interests, so much broader than those of most other U.S. Negro writers, were a very active part of his everyday writing equipment, he remained primarily a Marxist. He read Eliot, Stein, Joyce, Proust, Hemingway, Gorki, Nexö and most of the others, and he used much of what he learned, but he was almost always restricted by the provincial limitations of dialectical materialism. He used Freud, for example, primarily to score Marxian points, and even his later involvement with existentialism seemed to have political revolution as its basic motive.

Ellison was very much aware of the comprehensive range of Wright's intellectual and literary background, and, in passing, he suggested parallels between *Black Boy* and Nehru's *Toward Freedom*, Joyce's *Portrait of the Artist as a Young Man*, Dostoevski's *House of the Dead*, Rousseau's *Confessions* and Yeats' *Autobiographies*. But what impressed him most was that, knowingly or not, Wright had written a book which was in essence a literary equivalent to the blues. "The blues," Ellison wrote,

is an impulse to keep the painful details and episodes of a brutal experience alive in one's aching consciousness, to finger its jagged grain, and to transcend it, not by the consolation of philosophy but by squeezing from it a near-tragic, near-comic lyricism. As a form, the blues is an autobiographical chronicle of personal catastrophe expressed lyrically. And certainly Wright's early childhood was crammed with catastrophic incidents. In a few short years his father deserted his mother; he knew intense hunger; he became a drunkard begging drinks from black stevedores in Memphis saloons; he had to flee Arkansas, where an uncle was lynched; he was forced to live with a fanatically religious grandmother in an atmosphere of constant bickering; he was lodged in an orphan asylum; he observed the suffering of his mother, who became a permanent invalid, while fighting off the blows of the poverty-stricken relatives with whom he had to live; he was cheated, beaten and kicked off jobs by white employees who disliked his eagerness to learn a trade; and to these objective circumstances must be added the subjective fact that Wright, with his sensitivity, extreme shyness and intelligence, was a problem child who rejected his family and was by them rejected.

Thus, along with the themes, equivalent descriptions of milieu and the perspectives to be found in Joyce, Nehru, Dostoievsky, George Moore and Rousseau, *Black Boy* is filled with blues-tempered echoes of railroad trains, the names of Southern towns and cities, estrangements, fights and flights, deaths and disappointments, charged with physical and spiritual hungers and pain. And like a blues sung by such an artist as Bessie Smith, its lyrical prose evokes the paradoxical, almost surreal image of a black boy singing lustily as he probes his own grievous wound.

"Their attraction," he added, referring to the blues again near the end of the article, "lies in this, that they at once express both the agony of life and the possibility of conquering it through sheer toughness of spirit. They fall short of tragedy only in that they provide no solution, offer no scapegoat but the self."

Baldwin, who made no mention of *Black Boy* or of Ellison's commentary when he wrote about the Negro tradition and the Negro sensibility in "Many Thousands Gone," stated in an address at a Negro writers conference at The New School in New York during the spring of 1965 that as a writer he had modeled himself on none of the white American writers, not even Hemingway or Faulkner, but on black musicians, black dancers and so on, even on black whores (or did one hear right?), but most assuredly on the blues singers. He then spoke lovingly about Billie Holiday and lamented the current personal and legal difficulties of Ray Charles.

But his recent Broadway play, *Blues for Mister Charlie*, has very little if anything to do with the blues. It fills the stage with a highly stylized group of energetic and militant self-righteous Negroes hollering and screaming and cussing and accusing and talking out of school and under other folks' clothes, and threatening to raise hell and all that, but generally feeling as sorry for themselves as if they had all just come from reading *An American Dilemma, The Mark of Oppression* and most of the "liberal" magazines. There is an up-tempo beat, which could go with a classic Kansas City shout, but what comes out sounds more like the reds than the blues. (Incidentally, when down-home people used to speak of having the reds, the mean old reds, they meant they were in a fighting mood, that they could see red. But being down-home blues people, and Joe Louis people to boot, they did what they were going to do and talked about it later, if at all.)

Baldwin's criticism of *Native Son* was essentially valid. The people, the situations and the motivation in that quasi-realistic novel were more than oversimplified. They were exaggerated by an overemphasis on protest as such and by a very specific kind of political protest at that. Oversimplification in these terms does lead almost inevitably to false positions based on false assumptions about human nature itself. Every story, whatever its immediate purpose, is a story about being man on earth. This is the basis of its universality, the fundamental interest and sense of identification it generates in other people.

If you ignore this and reduce man's whole story to a series of sensational but superficial news items and editorial complaints and accusations, blaming all the bad things that happen to your characters on racial bigotry, you imply that people are primarily concerned only with certain political and social absolutes. You imply that these absolutes are the *sine qua non* of all human fulfillment. And you also imply that there are people who possess these political and social absolutes, and that these people are on better terms with the world as such and are consequently better people. In other words, no matter how noble your mission, when you oversimplify the reasons why a poor or an oppressed man lies, cheats, steals, betrays, hates, murders or becomes an alcoholic or addict you imply that well-to-do, rich and powerful people don't do these things. *But they do.*

Baldwin once seemed sensitive to this sort of embarrassment. He had accused Wright of trying "to redeem a symbolical monster in social terms," and he had already spoken of the truth as implying "a devotion to the human being, his freedom and fulfillment; freedom which cannot be legislated, fulfillment which cannot be charted." He had also seemed firmly convinced that categories were not real and that man "was not, after all, merely a member of a society or a group [but] something *resolutely indefinable, unpredictable.*"

These seem like the assumptions of a writer who is interested in literature. Assumptions like these underlie all of the world's great stories. The unpredictable is the very stuff of storytelling. It is the very stuff of dramatic power, suspense, thrills, escapades, resolutions; the very stuff of fears, hopes, quests, achievements. It is the very stuff of the human condition.

That a sophisticated intellectual like Richard Wright knew all of this goes without question. But he chose to operate within the framework of his basic political commitment. This was an unfortunate choice. But in spite of his arbitrarily circumscribed point of view he wrote a number of things which were politically useful, and there were also times, especially in certain parts of *Uncle Tom's Children* and *Black Boy*, when the universal literary values automatically went beyond the material objectives of political ideology.

Baldwin began by rejecting Wright's achievements as being inadequate and also dangerous. And at the time, as has been shown, the grounds for his rejection seemed solid enough. And, besides, he, himself, seemed to promise not only something different but something more.

So far he has not fulfilled that promise. The only thing really different to date has been his special interest in themes related to the so-called sexual revolution. And this is only different from Wright; it is not at all different from a lot of other writers these days, all of them white. Otherwise, Richard Wright is the author that James Baldwin, the novelist, playwright and spokesman, resembles more than any other, including Harriet Beecher Stowe.

Baldwin once complained about the climate of anarchy and unmotivated and unappreciated disaster in *Native Son*. But in his own recent novel, *Another Country*, he seems to think this sort of climate has some profoundly absurd existentialistic significance. It does not. Wright's existentialism, such as it was, had led to the same mistake in *The Outsider* that Baldwin had already spotted in *Native Son*.

Both Baldwin and Wright seem to have overlooked the rich possibilities available to them in the blues tradition. Both profess great pride in Negroes, but in practice seem to rate the theories and abstract formulations of French existentialism over the infinitely richer wisdom of the blues. Both, like most other intellectuals, and even anthropologists, seem to have missed what should be one of the most obvious implications of the blues tradition. *It is the product of the most complicated culture, and, therefore, the most complicated sensibility in the modern world.* The United States has all of the complexities of all the other nations in the world, has many of its own which most other nations are either not yet advanced enough or powerful enough to have.

But perhaps many people underrate the philosophical relevance of the blues tradition for modern life because it was not created by certified intellectuals. If so, they should examine the dynamics of cultural interaction and artistic feedback more carefully. Negro experience includes all areas of life in the United States. Negroes are always there in one capacity or another, and they are always reacting to what is happening, and their reactions become elements in the blues tradition. Racial snobbishness and U.S. provincialism and deference to things European keep many Americans from realizing it, but the most old-fashioned elements in the blues tradition are often avant-garde by the artistic standards of most other countries in the world. Europeans seem to appreciate this better than most Americans.

Somehow or other, James Baldwin and Richard Wright seem to have missed the literary possibilities suggested by this. Ralph Ellison has not. He went beyond Richard Wright in the very process of commenting on *Black Boy*, and he went beyond every other American writer of his generation when he wrote his first novel. The possibilities he had talked about in "Richard Wright's Blues" were demonstrated most convincingly when he published *Invisible Man*, probably the most mature first novel, American or whatever, since *Buddenbrooks*. It was certainly more mature both in craftsmanship and in vision than *This Side of Paradise*. And, of course, Hemingway's first was not *The Sun Also Rises* but *Torrents of Spring* and Faulkner's was *Soldier's Pay*!

Ellison had referred to the *Portrait of the Artist as a Young Man* in placing *Black Boy* in the genre of literary autobiographical writing. He did not imply that Wright's artistic achievement was comparable. *Invisible Man* in some ways recalls *Ulysses*. James Joyce's great contemporary masterpiece was an Irish *Odyssey*. *Invisible Man* is an American one. This certainly is not intended as a suggestion that Ellison is yet the great writer that Joyce became. But anyone who is shocked at the juxtaposition should remember, all pieties aside, that Ellison actually already excels Joyce in sustaining dramatic intensity and in outrageous narrative inventiveness, and that his rhetorical resonance is at least as close to much of Joyce as is that of any other contemporary American novelist, with the possible exception of Faulkner, who, by the way, also excels Joyce in dramatic impact and sheer narrative intrigue.

Invisible Man was *par excellence* the literary extension of the blues. It was as if Ellison had taken an everyday twelve-bar blues tune (by a man from down South sitting in a manhole up North in New York singing and signifying about how he got there) and scored it for full orchestra. This was indeed something different and something more than run-of-the-mill U.S. fiction. It had new dimensions of rhetorical resonance (based on lying and signifying). It employed a startlingly effective fusion of narrating realism and surrealism, and it achieved a unique but compelling combination of the naturalistic, the ridiculous, and the downright hallucinatory.

It was a first-rate novel, a blues odyssey, a tall tale about the fantastic misadventures of one American Negro which was at the same time a prototypical story about being not only a twentieth-century American but also a twentieth-century man, the Negro's *obvious* predicament symbolizing everybody's *essential* predicament. And like the blues, and echoing the irrepressibility of America itself, it ended on a note of promise, ironic and ambiguous, perhaps, but a note of promise still. The blues, with no aid from existentialism, have always known that there were no clear-cut solutions for the human situation.

Invisible Man was mainstream American writing in the same sense that U.S. Negro music is mainstream. This music, far from being simply Afro-American (whatever that is, the continent of Africa being as vast and varied as it is), is, like the U.S. Negro himself, All-American. This is why so many other American musicians, like Paul Whiteman, George Gershwin, Benny Goodman, Woody Herman, Gerry Mulligan and all the rest, identify with it so eagerly. The white American musician (excluding hillbillies, of course) sounds most American when he sounds most like an American Negro. Otherwise he sounds like a European.

White Americans may strike Negroes as being almost embarrassingly awkward on the dance floor, but all Americans, even those committed to segregation, are, culturally speaking, closer to the blues than any song-and-dance group or tribe anywhere in Africa. The blues tradition is not indigenous to Africa. It is a U.S. Negro tradition, and it is indigenous to the United States. The authentic and mature Negro jazz musician is probably fully aware of this, if only as a result of his practical involvement in show business. And perhaps this awareness is another factor which has made him a mainstream American artist in the richest sense of the word. And there is much that all U.S. writers can learn from him about working with American experience in aesthetic forms that are vernacular and sophisticated at the same time, particularly and peculiarly American and universally contemporary at the same time.

In spite of his status as an entertainer, or sometimes, perhaps, as a very direct result of it, the Negro jazz musician, representing the very spirit of American life, has, it seems, always been oriented to something different and something more.

Duke Ellington, for instance, is an object lesson in cultural assimilation for creative purposes, and his music, at its best, is All-American *because it sounds as if it knows the truth about all the other music in the world and is looking for something better.* Perhaps someday one will be able to say the same thing about American fiction. Negro writers can do much to bring about that day, and there is every reason why they should.

9.   *M. Carl Holman*

The Afternoon of a Young Poet

In the late winter of my senior year in high school I entered a
poem in an annual literary competition sponsored by the Arts
Club of St. Louis. Because I was almost pathologically shy, and
because I was not sure I actually intended to go through with it
until I was picking my way back up the icy street from the corner
mailbox, I told no one what I had done. Until that night I had
submitted poems to Negro newspapers and magazines and had
won one or two small prizes, but I had never before ventured to
enter a "white" contest.

I had found the announcement of the Arts Club competition
in the section of one of the white dailies where I read avidly
about plays, concerts and ballets which might just as well have
been taking place on the moon. During that period of my life I
was strongly influenced by three or four university-trained teachers on our high school faculty who were still caught up in the
afterglow of the Negro Renaissance. Mr. Watts, Miss Armstrong, Mr. Blanton and Miss Lewis taught us from the "lily-
white" textbooks prescribed by the St. Louis school system,
but they also mounted on their bulletin boards the works and
pictures of Langston Hughes, James Weldon Johnson, Claude
McKay, Sterling Brown, Countee Cullen and Jean Toomer.

Entering the contest, however secretly, represented unusual

daring for me, though it would have been as easy as breathing for Miss Armstrong, a vibrantly energetic mahogany-skinned woman whose voice flayed our budding manhood with contempt when she read McKay's poem "If We Must Die." (Her voice accused and disturbed me, conjuring up two confusing memories from my childhood downtown on Carroll Street—the first, that day in the depths of the Depression when half the fathers on the block straggled back from their protest march on City Hall, their heads broken and bleeding. Some of them weeping, but only one of them laughing. The potbellied little man next door who came stumbling up the alley apart from the others, tittering like a drunken woman, one eye puffed shut, his bloody rag of a shirt dragging in the dust. Giggling and whispering, *"Don't hit me no mo, Cap'n. You the boss. You sho God is the boss. . . ."* And less than five years later, Big Crew, standing in the middle of the yard, his lips drawn back from his blue gums in a wolfish grin, smashing his black fist like a hammer into the rent man's face, picking the man up like a sack of flour and knocking him down again. All the time talking to him as quietly as one friend to another: *"Git up and fight, you peckerwood sonuvabitch. Git up and fight for your country."*)

I yearned during those high school years to write something as defiantly bitter as McKay's "If We Must Die" or Sterling Brown's "Strong Men." My temper was capable of flaring up and consuming me so utterly that during a period of a few months I found myself in wildly hopeless fights with the older boys. Deep in hostile north St. Louis I had placed my life and those of two boys with me in jeopardy when, without thinking, I spat in the face of a young white boy seated on the stoop surrounded by at least seven members of his beefy family, because he called me a "skinny black nigger" as my friends and I were passing. My mother's long campaign to curb my temper had only taught me at last to swallow my feelings, hiding them so deep that I could not have dredged up my rages and despairs and found words for them even if I had wanted to. The long poem I finally mailed to the Arts Club was called "Nocturne on a Hill." Though it was probably honest enough in its way, it echoed more of the white writers I had been reading and told more about my reactions to the shapes and sounds of the city than it did about the people I loved and hated, or the things which delighted, hurt or confused me most.

We had moved from Carroll Street downtown three years earlier and we were living that year on Driscoll Avenue in midtown, halfway between the river on the east and that section of West End the whites had ceded to the Negro doctors, schoolteachers and postal workers. For a long time after the move to Driscoll Avenue I had continued to go back to the old neighborhood. In part this was because the customers to whom I sold Negro weekly newspapers lived there (ranging from an ancient self-ordained bishop, whose wife was never permitted to expose anything more than a slender wax-yellow hand and a black-clad sleeve as I handed the paper through the double-chained door, to the heavily powdered ladies in the big house on Seymour Street who had bought a dozen papers from me every Friday for a month before I learned how they made their living). But even on days when I had no papers to sell, Carroll Street for a long time continued to have the same love-fear magnetism for me it had exercised when I lived there; racked by sweaty nightmares on nights when the patrol wagons and ambulances pounded past our house, listening by the hour to the Italians singing from the backyards where they had strung light bulbs for the parties that left the alley littered with snail shells and the discarded bottles the winos fought over the next morning. On Carroll Street we had lived closely, though not intimately, with whites: the Italians on Bouie Avenue to the rear, the Jewish storekeepers, the Germans who worked in the bakery and the bank, the Irish truck drivers and policemen (and one saloon keeper who reconverted his storefront when Prohibition ended, returning to its old place in the window the faded, flyspecked sign whose legend we chanted up and down the street: "Coolidge Blew the Whistle,

Mellon Rang the Bell, Hoover Pulled the Throttle and the Country Went to Hell").

Driscoll Avenue was a less impoverished and more self-contained world than Carroll Street. Except for the merchants and bill collectors, it was possible to walk through midtown for blocks without seeing a white face. We lived on the first floor of a three-story brick house set on a concrete terrace from which three stone steps led down to the street. My chores during that long winter included keeping the steps salted down and making sure the heavy hall door was kept tightly shut.

My mother was ill for a long time that winter, and the grown-ups came to visit her, stamped into the house wrapped like mummies with only their eyes showing, bringing pots of stew, pickled preserves and the latest tale of some drunk who had been found frozen stiff in an alley or a neighbor who had been taken to "Old Number Two" with double pneumonia. Number Two was the nearest city hospital, and the neighborhood saying was that they did more killing there than Mr. Swift did over at his packing house. Old people in the neighborhood sometimes clung stubbornly to their beds at home, hiding the seriousness of their ailments, for fear they would be sent to Number Two to die. My mother was not old, but I lay awake many nights that winter, listening to her rasping breathing and praying that she would not have to be taken to Number Two. Sometimes, after her breathing had smoothed out and she had fallen asleep, I would get out of bed and go over to the window, raising the shade enough to let in the white winter moonlight. Fumbling for a pencil and piece of paper, I would write lines and fragments which I could not see, then fold the paper and stuff it into my hiding place back of the piano which nobody in the house played.

My mother's conviction that both her children were going to finish high school and college and "amount to something" had persisted in the face of the bleakest realities her native Mississippi and a half-flat near the tracks in south St. Louis could

marshal against her. Even in her illness, hollow-eyed and feverish, she wanted to know what we had done in school daily, what
the teachers had said, whether our homework was done. A gifted
seamstress and a careful manager of small change for most of
her life, she never doubted she would one day find the proper
use for the patterns, scraps of cloth, Eagle stamps, buttons and
pins she scrupulously put aside, each in its proper place. She
cooked huge pots of soup, with opulent aromas suggesting mag-
nitudes of power and promise out of all proportion to the amount
of meat in the pot. She felt she had ample reason to sing "He
Leadeth Me," and when we had amazed ourselves and our
teachers by prodigies of nerve-straining effort she only said
mildly, "Didn't He promise He would make a way out of no
way for those who believed in Him?"

Lacking her faith, I was so beset with premonitions and terrors during those months of her illness that I lost all recollection
of the poem I had mailed to the Arts Club. The cousin I loved
most had died in childbirth just two years before, at the age of
nineteen, and I had been tormented ever since by the fragility
of the web separating life and death. Though she met the slight-
est ache or pain visited on her children as if it were an out-
rider of the Devil's legions fully armed, my mother regarded
her own illnesses as nuisances to be gotten through with as little
fuss as possible. By the time the snow had melted in the gutters
she was on her feet again, halfway through her spring cleaning
and fretting to have the last frost gone so that she could start
planting the narrow rectangle of earth out front she called her
garden.

I came home from school one afternoon in early May to find
a letter from the Arts Club in our mailbox. I was afraid to open
it until I had first made sure it was not bulky enough to contain
the rejected poem. There was only a single sheet inside, a note
typed on the most elegant stationery I had ever seen, congratu-
lating me on the selection of my poem as one of the five best
works submitted in that year's contest and inviting me to meet
the other winners at the club two weeks later.

The first surge of surprise and pleasure was followed almost at once by a seizure of blind panic. How could I go out there to Westmoreland Place, a street I had never seen, to meet a group of strangers, most if not all of them white—when I stammered or fell silent whenever I had to talk to one of my teachers without the supporting presence of the rest of the class? Reading the note again I saw that the meeting had been scheduled for mid-afternoon of a school day. For most of that next week I debated whether I should accept the club's invitation or prepare to be sick on that day. Finally, just forty-eight hours before the date set in the letter, I went down to the principal and secured permission to be excused from my afternoon classes to attend the Arts Club meeting.

That same afternoon I showed my mother the letter. She knew me well enough to play down the pride she felt, complaining instead about people who would miss Heaven one day because they always waited until the last minute. She consulted with a friend who worked in the section where the club was located and wrote down the directions for me, dryly reminding me to have the conductor give me a transfer when I boarded the trolley outside the school. I had once had to walk home a distance of some six miles away because I forgot to ask for a transfer. Actually, I was less concerned about the transfer than about the possibility that on the way out to the club I might develop motion sickness. This often happened when I rode the trolleys. Usually I got off the car as soon as the first queasy stirrings began in the pit of my stomach, and walked the rest of the way. But this time I would be in a part of town that I did not know at all. I resolved to ride standing up all the way, trusting that my mother's God would not let me be sick.

I left school on a hazily bright afternoon alive with the tarry tang of smoke and the green smell of growing things which I associate still with spring in St. Louis. It was good to be a privileged truant with the whole block in front of the school to myself, the typewriters clicking behind me in the principal's office and the unheeded voices of the teachers floating out of the

classroom windows overhead. The first trolley was a long time
coming. When I got on I remembered to ask for the transfer,
and though over half the seats were empty on both trolleys, I
stood up all the way. But when I got off the second car I found
that I had managed to lose the directions my mother had given
me. I could not remember whether I was to go north or south
from the trolley stop. My palms promptly began sweating and I
took out the letter from the Arts Club, reading the address again
as if that would give me a clue. In my neighborhood most of the
houses were row houses, or were separated from each other by
nothing more than a narrow passageway. Even houses like the
one we lived in, though not flush with the pavement, were close
enough so that the addresses could be easily read from the side-
walk. But out here the houses were set back from wide lawns
under shade trees and there was no way of making out the addresses without going up a long walk to the front door. No
small children were playing outside, there were no stores into
which a stranger might go and ask directions, and the whole
neighborhood was wrapped in a fragrant but forbidding stillness.
Remembering that my mother had said the club was only two
blocks away from the trolley stop, I started walking south, deciding that if it turned out I was going the wrong way I could
always come back and go two blocks in the other direction. I
walked three blocks for good measure without finding Westmoreland Place, then turned and started back.

A red-faced old man with bushy military whiskers that reminded me of pictures I had seen of the Kaiser came down one
of the walks with a bulldog on a leash. I braced myself to ask
him where Westmoreland Place was, but before I could speak,
his china blue eyes suddenly glared at me with such venomous
hatred that I had the feeling he was about to set the dog on me.
I averted my eyes and walked on, trembling suddenly with an
answering hatred as senseless as his. Not noticing where I was
going, I was about to cross into the next block when I looked
up at the street sign and found that I was on Westmoreland

Place. It was a street of thick hedges and houses which, if anything, were more inaccessible than those I had already passed. I
walked up the street in one direction, then crossed and reversed
my course. By now the letter was wilting in my hand. The
trolley ride had taken longer than I had estimated and I was
sure I was already late. One of the last things my mother had
said to me that morning was, "Now try to be sure not to get out
there on Colored People's Time." My mind groped for a plausi-
ble lie that would let me give up the whole business and go
home. I thought of saying that the meeting had been called off,
that the place was closed when I got there, that I had caught the
wrong car and gone too far out of the way to get back in time.
At one point, I almost convinced myself that I should go back
to the trolley stop and catch a car that would take me downtown to my old refuge, the main public library. I could stay
there reading for an hour or two, then claim I had actually attended the tea. But my spirit quailed at the prospect of inventing answers to all the questions that would follow. And what if
in the meantime someone from the club had already called my
home or the school? I hated myself for entering the competition
and felt sick with envy when I thought of my schoolmates who
by now were idling down the halls on free period or dreaming
their way through the last classes before the liberating bell.

I was plodding down the same block for the second time
when around the corner of a big stone house across the street
came an unmistakably colored man in work clothes, uncoiling
a garden hose. We might have been the only two living souls on
a desert island. Almost faint with relief I angled across the street
toward him. But the handyman, his high shiny forehead fur-
rowed in elaborate concentration, adjusted the nozzle and began
playing rainbow jets of spray across the grass. I halted at the
edge of the lawn and waited for him to take note of my presence.
In due time he worked himself close enough so that I was able
to ask him if he knew where the Arts Club was. I held out the
letter as I asked him, but he merely turned his rusty deepset eyes

on me with a look that plainly said, *I hope to God you ain't come out here to make trouble for the rest of us.* In later years I have seen that look in the eyes of Negro businessmen, schoolteachers, college presidents, reverend ministers—and a trio of cooks and dishwashers peering through the swinging doors of a restaurant kitchen at the dark-skinned students sitting at counters where no one of their color ever presumed to sit before.

But I was of another generation, another temperament and state of mind from those students. So when the handyman flicked one hand in the direction from which I had just come and said, "There 'tis, over there," I thanked him—rather thanked his back, which was already turned to me.

I would never have taken the two-story brick building at the end of the flagstone walk to be anything other than the residence of a comfortably well-off family. Just before I pushed the button beside the broad door it occurred to me that the handyman might be playing his notion of a joke on me. Then I looked down at the thick mat on which I was standing and saw the letters "A-C." I pressed the button, waited and was about to press it again when the door swung open. The rake-thin white maid standing there had composed for her plain freckled face a smile of deferential welcome. The smile faded and her body stiffened in the neat gray uniform. For an instant I thought she would close the door in my face, but she braked it so that it was barely ajar and said, "Yes?" I mumbled something and held out the letter. She squinted at the envelope and said, "You wait here." The door closed and I stood there with my face burning, wanting to turn and go away but unwilling to confront the expression of sour satisfaction I expected to see on the face of the handyman across the street. After what seemed fifteen full minutes a gray-haired woman in a blue uniform with starched cuffs came to the door. "All right, what is it now?" she said, sounding like a very busy woman. I held out the letter and she took it, measured me up and down with her shrewd eyes and said to the younger woman hovering behind her, "I'll be right back." The freckle-faced thin one looked miles above my head toward the street but we shared the unspoken understanding that I was not to move from where I stood and that she was to watch me.

I stood rooted there, calling myself every kind of black fool for coming in the first place, my undershirt cleaving to my damp skin. It had become clear to me that I had received the invitation by mistake. And now that I had surrendered the letter, the only proof that I had been invited, my sole excuse for being there at all was gone. I pictured them huddled inside, talking in whispers, waiting for me to have the good sense to leave. Then I heard voices coming toward the door. My keeper faded back into the gloom of the hallway and an attractive woman in her forties held the door open and smiled at me. Everything about her, her fine-textured skin, the soft-colored dress and the necklace she was wearing, her candid gaze, defined an order of relationships which did away with any need for me to deal further with the other two women. "Hello," she said. "So you're the boy who came over to tell us Mr. Holman couldn't come?"

I stared dumbly at her, wondering how I could have been fooled into thinking she was one of those white women my mother would have described approvingly as "a real lady, as nice as they come."

"Please tell him we hope he'll be feeling better soon," the woman said. "We had so hoped to meet him."

"I'm—I got the letter saying to come out here," I blurted. We stood there for a minute staring at one another and then her pink skin flushed red. "Oh, you mean you—oh, I *am* so sorry," she said. "Please do come in. I didn't know." She glanced back at the maids. "I mean, we thought—"

It was finally clear to all of us what she had thought. That the white boy who wrote the poem had been unable to come so his family had thoughtfully sent their colored boy to tender his regrets.

"You come right on in," the woman said. "I'm your hostess. All the others are already here and we've been waiting for you."

She drew me inside the cool, dim hallway and guided me up the stairs like an invalid. I could not remember ever walking on such thick carpets. I had a hazy impression of cut flowers in vases, and paintings hanging along the walls like those I had seen in the Art Museum in the park. As she went up she kept on talking, but I made very little of what she was saying because now I could hear the murmur of other voices and laughter coming from the floor above us. I had the feeling that an intimate and very pleasant family party was in progress which we were about to ruin and I wanted to ask my hostess if I might not be excused after all. Instead I let myself be piloted into a sunny high-ceilinged room which at one and the same time seemed as spacious as a playing field and so intimate that no one could move without touching the person beside him. A blur of white faces turned toward us, some of them young, some middle-aged, some older, but all of them clearly belonging to a different world from that of the uniformed women downstairs. A different world from mine. For a flickering moment there was a drop in energy like that sudden dimming of lights during a summer storm and then I was being introduced in a flurry of smiles, bobbing heads and a refrain seeming to consist of variations on "Delightful . . . delighted . . . so good you could come . . . a pleasure."

Whenever I have tried to recollect that afternoon since, the faces in that upstairs room elude me like objects seen through sunlit water. I remember that one of the girls was blonde and turned eagerly from one speaker to another as if anxious not to miss one word, that there was a boy there from a school out in the country who talked and moved with the casual, almost insulting assurance which for a long time afterward I automatically associated with private schools. All of the other students there who had won prizes or honorable mentions in the area-wide competition were either from private schools or from white high schools whose very names were new to me. One of the girls was from a Catholic school and one of the sisters from the faculty had come along with her. I discovered that other winners were accompanied by their teacher and I mentally kicked myself for not realizing that I might have been buttressed by the presence of Miss Armstrong or Mr. Blanton. Certainly they would have been much more at home in this company than I was. Gradually, as cookies, tea and punch were passed and the talk again swirled back and forth, I began to relax somewhat, content to be on the periphery of that closed circle. I kept stealing glances around the room, taking in the wide fireplace and the portrait above the mantel of some famous man whose identity kept eluding me, the rows of books in the recessed shelves along the wall, and the magazines scattered tantalizingly just out of reach on the long oaken table in the center of the room.

In school, except to recite, I had rarely ever talked even to my English teachers about poems, books and writers. But this group, comfortably seated or standing about the pleasant room with the haze of spring sunlight sifting through the windows, shared a community of language and interests which enabled them largely to ignore differences of age and individual preference and to move from one idea or work to another as effortlessly as fish in a pond. They talked of Shakespeare and Keats, Milton and Shelley, but there were other writers whose lines I had spoken aloud, sometimes in puzzlement, when I was alone. Now they were being argued over, attacked, defended, ridiculed: Eliot, Frost, Sandburg, Millay, Vachel Lindsay, Amy Lowell, Yeats. There were moments when someone touched on something I had read and I was tempted to speak out in agreement or disagreement. At other times I was overcome by the gloomy conviction that I could never in the years that were left to me read all the works some of them seemed to know by heart. I felt particularly lost as the talk shifted to novels only recently written, to concerts they had attended and plays seen at the American Theatre downtown or "on our last trip to New York." (I had been drunk for days on the free concert given for Negro high school students by the St. Louis Symphony the year before, shutting myself off in my room with an umbrella spoke for a baton, trying to be all the voices of the orchestra and graceful Mr. Golschmann conducting the *New World Symphony*. Later I was to go to the American as often as I could to see the road companies in performance and, during intermissions, to devour the posters advertising the plays I would not be able to see. Often my companion and I were among less than a dozen Negroes present. (Years afterward, on a trip back to St. Louis I was triumphantly informed that Negroes were no longer segregated in the second-balcony seats at the American. Second-balcony seats being all we could afford, my friend and I had never asked for anything else, a neat dovetailing of covert discrimination and economic necessity.)

Toward the end of the long afternoon, it was proposed that the young writers read their poems. Once again I was plunged into sweaty-palmed agony. My torment only increased as the first two readers read their poems like seasoned professionals, or so it seemed to me. When my turn came I tried to beg off, but the additional attention this focused upon me only increased my discomfort and I plunged in, at first reading too fast and almost inaudibly but finally recollecting some of the admonitions my teachers had dinned into my head in preparation for "recitations" before Negro school and church audiences as far back as the second grade. I had not realized how long a poem it was when I was writing it and I was squirmingly conscious of certain flaws and failures which had never before loomed so large. The applause and praise that followed when I finished, if anything, exceeded that given the others; a situation which, even then, aroused the fleeting suspicion that the dancing bear was being given higher marks than a man might get for the same performance. One of the older women murmured something about Paul Laurence Dunbar. Someone else asked me if I liked Pushkin. I could only look blank, since at that time I knew almost nothing about the great Russian's poetry and even less about his Negro lineage. Inevitably, there was a flattering and irrelevant comparison to Langston Hughes. A wavy-haired gentleman took his pipe out of his mouth to ask if I didn't think "The Negro Speaks of Rivers" was a marvelous poem. I said I certainly did. (But stopped short of trying to explain why the Mississippi always made me think not of Lincoln at New Orleans but of the playmate on Carroll Street drowned during an Easter baptism, the cold, feral grin of the garfish skeleton which two of us stumbled on as we moped along the riverfront toward the pickle factory and the high platform beyond where the city garbage trucks dumped their loads into the frothing stream, and the dimly remembered "high waters" sucking at the edge of the roadbed as the train brought my father and me back to St. Louis from our grandfather's funeral.)

Gradually, as the light faded outside the window, people began looking at their watches and saying good-by. One of the club members thanked all of us for coming and said she could not remember when the Arts Club had had such a fine and talented group. The blonde girl clapped her hands for attention, her eyes shining with the enthusiasm of the born organizer. Why, she wanted to know, did this year's group really have to scatter? It seemed to her that we should not let our companionship, our new friendships die. Some of us were going away for the summer, but there were still several weeks left yet before school would be out. Some might be going off to college in the fall, but others would not, and probably some of those who would be entering college would be going no farther away than the University of Missouri at Columbia, or St. Louis, Washington, or one of the other schools in the St. Louis area. I was silent as the others chimed in, suggesting that we meet at the various high schools or rotate meetings from one home to another before and after summer vacations. Such a point was made of including me in and I felt already so much the witch at the wedding party that I was not inclined to remind them that I would have a much harder time getting into a meeting at the schools they attended or the colleges in the area than I had had getting into the Arts Club that afternoon. To say nothing of what their parents and friends and mine would make of those meetings in the homes. I tried to picture those well-dressed and half-assured young white poets strolling past the cleaning and pressing shop to a meeting at my house. Nevertheless, my Driscoll Avenue cynicism began crumbling under the effervescent pressures of their youth and mine. We made our way down the thick-carpeted stairs, true poets and comrades, a verbal skyscraper of plans and projects rising as we descended. We would exchange our favorite original poems by phone and by mail. We would do a volume of poems together and a famous novelist who was a good friend of our hostess would get the book published for us. The Arts Club would serve as secretariat and haven, keeping track of addresses and phone numbers and providing a place where we could meet, read and write.

Good will, mutual admiration, flowering ambition united us as we parted in the gathering spring dusk. The air was scented with the watermelony smell of freshly cut grass. The lights were on in the stone house across the street, but the handyman was gone.

I did not hear from the young men and women I met that afternoon at the Arts Club the next week, the next month, or ever. But I had a great many more serious disappointments than that, along with a decent amount of good fortune, in the two remaining years I spent in my home town. Like many other young men similarly situated I was involved during those pre-war years in a quiet but no less desperate scramble simply to hold on to life and not go under. By the end of that period of twenty-odd months I had run an elevator, worked as a machine operator, delivered parcels, patrolled a lake stocked with fish nobody ever tried to steal, and stood in half a hundred job lines with white and black men who showed up every morning less out of hope than the need to put off as long as possible that time of day when they must once again face their families. For me and a good many others my age it was not a question really of having something to eat and a place to sleep. The battle was, rather, to find ways of withstanding the daily erosion, through tedium, through humiliation, through various short-term pleasures, of the sense of your own possibilities. Necessary, too, was some sensitivity to possibilities outside yourself. Here I do not exclude chance, the lucky break. For me it came with the opportunity to become a part-time student at a college I might have attended full time two years earlier.

On the night before I left for college my mother gave a party for me, inviting a dozen of my friends. Some of them brought gifts. As I was walking past the Catholic church on Garth Avenue, shortly after midnight, going home to the flat I shared with my father, a squad car pulled up and two officers jumped out. Night sticks at the ready, they flashed a light in my face and wanted to know where I was coming from and where I had picked up all that stuff. They pawed through the presents I was carrying until they came across an anthology of poetry autographed for me that night by my friends. The first officer grunted and snapped off his light. The second seemed tempted to take a swipe at me anyhow for wasting their time. They got back in the car and drove off, leaving me to walk the two blocks remaining between the church and home.

The next morning, on a cold, sooty, old-style St. Louis day, I left home. I got on a bus and headed for Jefferson City, Missouri. That trip away from home has been a much longer journey than I had anticipated and a very much different one. On certain occasions, as when my poetry was published or while lecturing at Atlanta University, I have remembered that afternoon. And I have thought that perhaps when I next visited St. Louis, I would try once again to find my way to the Arts Club. I never have and it is probably just as well. It may be that I got as much as could reasonably be expected on that first visit.

10.   *Ossie Davis*

The Wonderful World
of Law and Order

As an entertainer I'm an author. If you say that I am a writer, I will reply, "I am an actor." And if you accuse me of being an actor I will say, "No. I am a writer." If you say that I am a Negro I will escape by saying, "Of course not. I am an American." But if you accuse me of being an American, I will then dodge behind the fact that I am a Negro. Now, this kind of duplicity, this kind of double-sidedness to my character and personality is not unusual. We all know about it. We are faced with it and live with it. It is part of the Negro characteristic, and it's a major part of the basic problem that other Americans are confronted with: that is, the question of identity. Who am I? Who am I not? What do I do? What don't I do? All of these things confront us as individuals, groups and classes.

Those persons seriously involved in literature, which may be in itself a search for identity, especially in our times, will realize that though I begin in perhaps a facetious tone, I am really quite serious in my jokes. I am greatly concerned with literature, and I am deeply involved with social action, and I am fortunate enough (or, perhaps, unfortunate enough) to see no fundamental difference between the one and the other. I can appreciate and enjoy fully the literary traditions out of which contemporary

154

Negroes and other writers have developed, and I respect and admire and enjoy their works. I have my opinions and have formed judgments as an individual and as an artist about what I consider to be their respective merits. However, though I consider myself primarily a literary man, I am also an entertainer, so, once again, if you say that I am a literary figure, I will say, "I am an entertainer." If you say that I am an entertainer, I will say, "No. I am a clown." My reason for telling you this is that these dualities are the basis of my approach toward certain important matters. One of the functions of the study of literature is to enlighten those whose interest is with the writer himself. Now, I have chosen, in my writing, to address myself primarily to those people who are living in the ghettoes of our country, who are still left on the streets, who are still down in the cotton patch, and whose literary experiences are nil because of the circumstances of their entire lives.

But does this mean that the riches of literature are to be denied this important class of Americans, white and black? I think not. I believe that the joys and the wealth of our culture belong to all. But I would like to go a step further and deliberately aim my message at the involvement of that lowest stratum in our culture and our economy, the Negro people. I would like, if possible, to carry my revolutionary message to them in a language which I think they can immediately perceive, without, at the same time, being patronizing or choosing to speak down to them from the heights of literary eminence.

By that I mean I attempt to use all of the elements of popular folk culture and try to weld them into an instrument of communication, because in addition to being the expression of what a person is, of what his personality is and what his point of view is, literature is also fundamentally communication.

More fully, it is not enough, in my point of view, merely to expose myself and all of the truth and the wonder and the awe I feel at being a person upon the face of the earth. I have, in addition, to communicate that feeling and insight to others.

But even to communicate is not the final result, as far as I am concerned. I deliberately set out to communicate in order to elevate. I must clearly assume an exaggerated point of view, an exaggerated measure of my own importance to think that I have something which, when communicated to a larger mass of people, can elevate them, but without that egotism, without that assumed divine right to inform and direct and educate, I think no artist ever gets off the ground. The Negro in this country has to write protest, because he is a protestant. He can't help but be. He cannot accept the situation in which he finds himself, so, therefore, he is driven to scream out against the oppression that surrounds him, that suffocates him. So that what he writes will be in the nature of protest. The protest has been, and still is and must continue to be, loud, bitter and haranguing. It must irritate. It must shake. It must disturb. It must move the very bowels of compassion. It must be angry. It must be aimed at corrective action and now.

But those are not the limits of protest, and I have chosen to approach the whole problem from another direction. I say that we can protest about an unjust situation on an intellectual level by saying that in addition to being unjust the situation is also ridiculous, and that we can show that it is ridiculous, and perhaps even laughable, and, therefore, not worthy of the behavior of educated, culturally advanced human beings, such as must be the kind of people, both white and black, who inhabit America at this late date.

I have chosen to make my protest in the form of revealing the ridiculous institutions that have brought us, in our national life, to a very critical point in our cultural, economic, political and social history. And I think that such a protest is valid. The theatre, as you know, has long been given to pointing the finger of ridicule at that which it found to be ridiculous. I can imagine no other institution on the face of the earth more ridiculous than the institution of segregation, and, though it is cruel, though it is capable of committing murder and destroying me and oppressing me physically and brutally, emasculating me, still, there is a possibility that I can maintain enough of my own balance and point of view to say that in addition to being oppressive and in addition to killing me it is also absolutely ridiculous. Because, sometimes, those who will not respond to the validity of your argument as an experience in logic or rationality will respond if your argument is presented in another form, in another light altogether. And I happen to believe that one of the traditions by which my people have been able to survive in the oppressive atmosphere of American culture has been the tradition of corrective and educational humor.

We told jokes, one to another, but we weren't telling jokes for the sake of getting off fast quips and gags. That stream of humor had to carry our sense of self, our sense of history, our hope of the future, our religious concern about man's relationship to man. It had to point us to the future and tell us to "Wait, bide your time. The day is coming when you can stand up and be a man." Humor, the folk humor of the Negro people, is, of course, not the only way in which the Negro chose to stand up and assert his manhood. Those of us who were gifted enough to play trumpets and beat drums in New Orleans and other places of oppression could stand up and, with our horns, declare our manhood. We couldn't say it in the English language. We couldn't say, "I, too, am a man," because that could get you killed. But there was a chance that when you had a horn at your lips you could communicate fully the fact of your manhood, as long as you didn't do it in intelligible English. This is the nature of jazz, so far as I felt it and understand it. But I am discussing humor and I am dealing in terms that I hope are socially responsible. I would like to give back to the Negro people the humor they themselves created, give it back in the form in which they created it and let it begin, once again, to serve the function for which it was originally created.

There was a man, who has become synonymous with some of the aspects of our trouble, named Stepin Fetchit. Now, we know that Stepin Fetchit was earning a living; he almost made himself a rich man by caricaturing a certain attitude about Negro people which we know not to be true but which certain people wanted to believe, and this idea was that all Negroes were lazy and stupid and they drawled and said, "Yowsah."

This man was, perhaps, not very bright, and he became a good stereotypical justification of what was wrong with Negroes and why they lived in ghettoes and why they'd never make it. Because they just didn't have it. They were all shiftless. They were all lazy. And they never thought for themselves and always waited for somebody to do something for them. On this basis, we rightly protested the use of Mr. Stepin Fetchit and his character and his talent to demean the whole Negro race, because we realized that the community about us was drawing conclusions from his behavior which we knew to be incorrect and using his behavior to justify the continued oppression in which we found ourselves.

But let's look a little deeper into what originally was behind the meaning of Stepin Fetchit's lazy character. As you will remember, those of you who have a long memory, we were slaves in this country, and we were required to work from sunup to sundown and there was no time off, no coffee breaks, no Social Security, none of the few benefits that we have only lately acquired. Slavery was straight labor, even above and beyond the devotion required of a mule. And we were required, for the benefit of our masters, to work ourselves, literally, to death. If you could—if you were an honest man, an honest Negro, and if you had no way to escape—you would literally work yourself to death, because it was cheaper for a master to work a slave to death and get all the work out of him and later buy a replacement. Now, a slave like Stepin Fetchit, who really was a smart man, who understood the ways of the white folks, would suddenly discover that he was regarded as a very unintelligent creature, so when the master would send him to get a rope he would come back with maybe a plow, until finally the slaveowner would get the idea that this man was so dumb and so inefficient and so shiftless that nothing could be done but to let him sit under a tree.

You might ask why. Why didn't the man take Stepin Fetchit and sell him or get rid of him? Because unconsciously this behavior identified, confirmed and reinforced the slaveowner's prejudices against the possibility of Negroes being responsible, thoughtful and efficient people. So that the Negro achieved two purposes. He saved himself by being too dumb to do the work that the mules and the other slaves were doing, and therefore he survived. And he also gave the overlord the satisfaction of believing that all Negroes were dumb and lazy.

However, I must now protest against the wrong, the invalid use of a stereotype, by whites or by others, after it has been disembodied and the protest content has been removed. Most of the stereotypes we know about Negroes were invented by Negroes for the purposes of survival and social correction. We do this all the time. It is a way in which a society tries to control its members. It will criticize its leaders. It will state its aims, through stereotypes, through jokes and humor. But our humor has been taken away, emptied of its bitter protest content, and has been used against us. And this has led us, sometimes, to rebel against our own humor. In my play *Purlie Victorious* I have tried to restore the protest content of the Negro's humor. I attempted to comment upon the world of law and order, especially in a particular scene.

It is the second scene of the play, and it takes place in the commissary. The commissary is a place on the cotton patch where the man who owns the cotton patch sells food and seed and goods to the people who work the cotton patch for him. He sells these things at such an exorbitant price that no matter how hard you work on the farm you will never be able to pay the bill, and until you can pay the bill you can't leave. Therefore, this is an arrangement which ensures him a permanent supply of cheap labor, and his instrument of control is the company store, the commissary. Now, our hero is Old Captain Cotchipee, who represents the old, unreconstructed South. He has a benevolent attitude toward "his" Negro people, as you will understand, but he has a son, young Charlie Cotchipee, who is our hope in the white liberal community in the South and in the North, and I think you will recognize some of his possibilities and his great limitations in the character as we see him.

Charlie Cotchipee has been brought up, subversively, by the Negro woman who runs the house. She has taught Charlie Cotchipee to revere Abraham Lincoln. This immediately throws him into a tremendous disturbance, because he has been taught the value of freedom and dignity and he has to live in the South where these values are denied. So right away our young liberal is in hot water. Now, into the scene comes the greatest stereotype of them all, "Uncle Tom." I called him Gitlow, because the question arises, "How low can you git?" The answer: "Git low!" We at first recognize Gitlow as a man who is a masterful Uncle Tom, but as the scene goes along, I think we will understand a little bit more of what Gitlow really is all about. I offer this brief scene which is not entitled in the play "The World of Law and Order," but which is basically concerned with the world of law and order. It was taken from *Purlie Victorious* or *A Non-Confederate Romp Through the Cotton Patch.*

We are now in the little business office of the commissary, where all the inhabitants of Cotchipee Valley buy food, clothing and supplies. At the rise of the curtain, a young white man, twenty-five or thirty, but still gawky and adolescent in outlook and behavior, is sitting on a high stool, downstage right center.

His face is held in the hand of IDELLA, *a Negro cook and woman of all work, who has been in the family since time immemorial. She is the only mother* CHARLIE, *who is very much oversized, even for his age, has ever known.*

IDELLA *is as little as she is old and as tough as she is tiny, and she is busily applying medication to Charlie's black eye.*

The scene begins as follows:

CHARLIE: Ow, Idella. Ow.

IDELLA: Hold still, boy.

CHARLIE: But it hurts, Idella.

IDELLA: I know it hurts. Whoever done this to you must have meant to knock your natural brains out.

CHARLIE: I already told you who done it to me. Ow!

IDELLA: Charlie Cotchipee. If you don't hold still and let me put this hot poultice on your eye, you better. First the milking. Then the breakfast. Then the dishes. Then the washing. Then the scrubbing. Then the lunchtime. Next the dishes. Then the ironing. And now, just where the plucking and picking for supper ought to be, you!

CHARLIE: You didn't tell Paw?

IDELLA: Of course I didn't. But the Sheriff did.

CHARLIE: *(Leaping straight up.)* The Sheriff!

IDELLA: Him and the Deputy come to the house less than an hour ago.

[I'd like to observe that the Sheriff and the Deputy are representatives of law and order.]

CHARLIE: Are they coming over here?

IDELLA: Of course they're coming over here. Sooner or later.

CHARLIE: What should I do, Idella? What will I say?

IDELLA: "He that keepeth his mouth, keepeth his life."

CHARLIE: Did they ask for me?

IDELLA: Of course they asked for you.

CHARLIE: What did they say?

IDELLA: Well, I couldn't hear too well. Your father took them into the study and locked the door behind them.

CHARLIE: Well, maybe it was about something else.

IDELLA: It was about you. That much I could hear. Charlie, do you want to get us both killed?

CHARLIE: I'm sorry, Idella. But—

IDELLA: "He that openeth wide his lips shall have destruction."

[Now, here is a situation where the Negro is telling the white liberal, "You talk too much. You're going to get me in trouble." You know? "You're opening wide your mouth. Cool. Easy. We've got to work this thing out together."]

CHARLIE: But it was you who said it was the law of the land.

IDELLA: I know I did.

CHARLIE: It was you who said it's got to be obeyed.

IDELLA: I know it was me.

CHARLIE: It was you who said everybody has to stand up and take a stand.

IDELLA: I know it was me, but dammit, I didn't say stand up and take a stand in no barroom.

CHARLIE: Ben started it. Not me. And you always said never to take low from the likes of him.

IDELLA: Not so loud. They may be out there in the commissary. (*She goes and takes a look to see if the* SHERIFF *and the father are out in the commissary. She comes back and says, lovingly:*) Look boy. Now, everybody down here don't feel as friendly toward the Supreme Court as you and me do. Now, you big enough to know that. And don't you ever go out of here and pull a fool trick like you done last night and not let me know about it in advance. You hear me?

CHARLIE: I'm sorry.

IDELLA: When you didn't come down to breakfast this morning and I went upstairs and looked for you and you just settin' there looking at me with your big eyes, and I seen how they done hurt you, my, my my. Whatever happens to you happens to me. You big enough to know that.

CHARLIE: I didn't mean to make trouble, Idella.

IDELLA: I know that, son. I know it. (*She puts poultice on his eye.*) Now, no matter what happens when they come, I'll be right behind you. Keep your nerves calm and your mouth shut. You understand?

CHARLIE: Yes.

IDELLA: And as soon as you get a free minute, come over to the house and let me put another hot poultice on that eye.

CHARLIE: Thank you. I'm very much obliged to you, Idella. . . . Idella?

IDELLA: What is it, son?

CHARLIE: Sometime I think I ought to run away from home.

IDELLA: I know, honey, but you already tried that.

CHARLIE: Well, sometimes I think I ought to run away from home again.

(*At this moment, his father* OLD CAPTAIN COTCHIPEE, *comes in from the commissary.*)

OLD CAPTAIN: Why don't you, boy? Why don't you?

(*He is aged and withered a bit, but by no means infirm. He is dressed in the traditional Southern linen, the white hat, shoestring tie, long coat, twirling mustache of the Old Southern Colonel. In his left hand, he carries a cane. In his right hand, a coiled bull whip. His last line of defense. He stops long enough to establish the fact that he means business, threatens them both with a mean, cantankerous eye, then hangs his whip—the definitive answer to all who might foolishly question his Confederate power and glory—upon a peg.*)

(CHARLIE *freezes at the sound of his voice.* IDELLA *tenses, but she keeps on working on Charlie's eye.*)

OLD CAPTAIN: (*Crosses down and rudely pushes* IDELLA'S *hand aside and lifts* CHARLIE'S *chin up so he may examine the damage done to his eye. He shakes his head in disgust*): You don't know boy, what a strong stomach it takes to stomach you. Just look at you settin' there, all flopped over like something the horses dropped, steaming, stinking—

IDELLA: Don't you dare talk like that to this child.

OLD CAPTAIN: When I think of his grandpaw, God rest his Confederate soul, hero of the battle of Chickamauga—get out of my sight. (CHARLIE *tries to get up and leave.*) Not you. You! (*Meaning for* IDELLA *to go.*) Wait a minute, Idella. Now, you've been closer to this boy than I have, even before his Maw died. Now, any thought ever entered his head you didn't know about it first? Have you got anything to do with what my boy's been thinking lately?

IDELLA: (*Pauses a moment.*) Well, I didn't know he had been thinking lately.

OLD CAPTAIN: Don't play with me, Idella. You know what I mean. Now, who's been putting these integrationary ideas into my boy's head? Was it you? I'm asking you a question, dammit! Was it you?

IDELLA: Well, why don't you ask him, Captain? Ask him. Ask him.

OLD CAPTAIN: He ain't going to say a word unless you tell him to, and you know it. I'm asking you again, Idella. Have you been talking integration to my boy?

IDELLA: I can't rightly answer you any more on that than he did.

OLD CAPTAIN: By God, you will answer me. I'll make you stand right there. Right there, all day and all night long, till you do answer.

IDELLA: Well, that's just fine.

OLD CAPTAIN: What's that? What's that you say?

IDELLA: Well, I mean, I ain't got nothing else to do. Supper's on the stove. Rice is ready. Okra's fried. Turnips simmered. Biscuits baked. Stew is stewed. In fact, them lemon pies you wanted special for supper are in the oven right now. Just getting ready to burn.

OLD CAPTAIN: Get out of here! Get out of here!

IDELLA: Oh, no hurry, oh Captain.

OLD CAPTAIN: Get the hell outta here! . . . Now, I'm warning you, both of you. That little lick over the eye is a small skimption to what I'm going to do. Now I won't stop until I get to the bottom of this. (IDELLA *still ignores him.*) Get out of here, Idella. Before I take my cane. (IDELLA *looks at him and gives a chuckle. And walks out of the door.*) OLD CAPTAIN: (*Sticks his head out of the door.*) And save me some buttermilk to go with them lemon pies. Do you hear me? (*Captain turns to his son, the last of a long line of Cotchipees, who was supposed to carry on the tradition of the old South, and is not doing very well at it. Looks at his son.*) The Sheriff was here this morning.

CHARLIE: Yes, sir.

OLD CAPTAIN: Is that all you got to say to me? Yes, sir?

CHARLIE: Yes, sir.

OLD CAPTAIN: You are a disgrace to the Southland.

CHARLIE: Yes, sir.

OLD CAPTAIN: Shut up. Shut up! I could kill you, boy. I could kill you with my own two hands.

CHARLIE: Yes, sir.

OLD CAPTAIN: Shut up! I could beat you to death with that bull whip! Put my pistol to your good-for-nothing head, my own flesh and blood, and blow your blasted brains all over the valley. If you wasn't the last living drop of Cotchipee blood in Cotchipee County, I— I—

CHARLIE: Yes.

OLD CAPTAIN: (*Grabs the boy by his collar and stands him up.*) Are you trying to get non-violent with me?

CHARLIE: (*Dangles until calm is restored.*) Paw, I'm ready with the books. That is, when you're ready.

OLD CAPTAIN: (*Flings him into the chair.*) Thank you. Thank you. What with all your Yankee propaganda, your barroom brawls, and your other non-Confederate activities, I didn't think you had the time.

CHARLIE: (*Takes up the account book and begins to read.*) Cotton report. Fifteen bales picked yesterday and sent to the cotton gin, bringing our total to three hundred and fifty-seven bales to date.

OLD CAPTAIN: (*Is impressed.*) Three hundred and fifty-seven! Boy! That's some picking. Who's ahead?

CHARLIE: Gitlow Johnson. With seventeen bales up to now.

OLD CAPTAIN: (*Happily.*) Gitlow Johnson. Well, I'll be

damned! Did you ever see a cotton-pickiner darkey in your whole life?

CHARLIE: (*Disturbed.*) Commissary report.

OLD CAPTAIN: (*Still lost in his dreams of law and order.*) Did you ever look down into the valley and watch ole Gitlow pickin' his way through that cotton patch? Holy St. Mother's Day. I'll bet you—

CHARLIE: Commissary report.

OLD CAPTAIN: (*Wakes up from his dream.*) All right. Commissary report.

CHARLIE: Yes, sir. Well, first, sir, there's been some complaints that the flour is spoiled. The beans are rotten. And the meat is tainted.

OLD CAPTAIN: Cut the price on it.

CHARLIE: But it's also a little wormy.

OLD CAPTAIN: Well, then, sell it to the Nigras.

CHARLIE: (*Can't swallow that.*) Well—

OLD CAPTAIN: Is something wrong?

CHARLIE: No, n-n-no, sir. I mean, I mean, sir, that we can't go on doing that, sir.

OLD CAPTAIN: (*Innocently.*) Why not? It's traditional.

CHARLIE: Yes, sir. But, but—times are changing. All this debt—according to this book, every family in this valley owes us money they'll never be able to pay back.

OLD CAPTAIN: Of course. It's the only way to keep them working. Didn't they teach you nothin' in school?

CHARLIE: We're cheating them. And they know we're cheating them. How long do you expect them to stand for it?

OLD CAPTAIN: As long as they're Nigras.

CHARLIE: But how long before they start a-raring up on their hind legs and saying, "Enough, white folks. Now that's enough! Now, either you start treating me like I'm somebody in this world or I'll blow your brains out."

OLD CAPTAIN: Stop it. Stop it! Stop it! Stop it! Boy, you're tampering with the economic foundation of the Southland. Are you trying to ruin me? One word more like that and I'll kill—I'll shoot—I'll— One more word like that and I'll fling myself on your Maw's grave and I'll die of apoplexy. I'll— Shut up, you! Do you hear me! Shut up! Shut up!! Shut up!!!

(*At the height of his passion, into the store comes good old* GITLOW. GITLOW *has a patch on his head, because Missy tried to put a progressive thought into it and had to rely on a baseball bat to accomplish that particular feat.*)

OLD CAPTAIN: (*looks at Gitlow.*) What the hell do you want?

GITLOW: Nothin', sir. Nothin'—that is, well, Missy, my old woman, well, sir, to get to the truth of the matter, I got a little business.

OLD CAPTAIN: Nigras ain't got no business. If you don't get the hell back to that cotton patch, you'd better. Git, I said!

(GITLOW *starts to beat a hasty retreat.*)

OLD CAPTAIN: No. Don't—don't go, Uncle Gitlow. Good old faithful Gitlow. Don't go. Don't go.

GITLOW: Well, you're the boss, boss.

OLD CAPTAIN: Now, just the other day, the other day I was talking to the Senator about you. What's that great big knot on your head?

GITLOW: Missy—I mean, a mosquito.

OLD CAPTAIN: (*Examines the bump.*) Mmm. Must have been wearing brass knucks. And he was telling me, the Senator was, how hard it was, impossible, he said, to find the old-fashioned, solid, hard-earned, Uncle-Tom-type Negro nowadays. I laughed in his face.

GITLOW: Yes, sir. By the grace of God, there's still a few of us left.

OLD CAPTAIN: I told him how you and me growed up together. Had the same mammy. My mammy was your mother.

GITLOW: Yes, sir. Bosom buddies.

OLD CAPTAIN: And how you used to sing that favorite spirit-

ual of mine. "I'm a comin'. I'm a comin'. For my head is bend-
ing low." (GITLOW *joins in on the harmony.*) "I hear the gentle
voices calling Old Black Joe."

(*Now, this proves too much for* CHARLIE *who, remember, is
our liberal friend and can't stand Gitlow's behavior. He starts to
sneak off. His father catches him.*)

OLD CAPTAIN: Where you goin'?

CHARLIE: Well, maybe they need me out in the front.

OLD CAPTAIN: Come back here. Turn around. Show Gitlow
that eye.

(CHARLIE *shows* GITLOW *the eye, which is black.*)

GITLOW: Great God Almighty! Somebody done cold cut this
child! Who hit Mr. Charlie? Tell Uncle Gitlow who hit you?

(CHARLIE *doesn't answer.*)

OLD CAPTAIN: Now, would you believe it, all of a sudden,
he can't say a word. And just last night the boys wuz telling me
this son of mine made himself a full-fledged speech.

GITLOW: You don't say?

OLD CAPTAIN: Um mm. All about Nigras. Negroes, he calls
them. Four years of college and he still can't say the word right.
Seems he's quite a specialist on the subject.

GITLOW: Well, shut my hard-luck mouth.

OLD CAPTAIN: Yes sirree. He told the boys over at Ben's Bar
in town that he was all for mixing the races together.

GITLOW: You git on away from here.

OLD CAPTAIN: He says white children and darkey children
ought to go to the same schoolhouse together.

GITLOW: Well, tell me the truth!

OLD CAPTAIN: He got hisself so worked up, somebody had
to cool him down with a Coca-Cola bottle.

GITLOW: Tell me the truth again.

CHARLIE: Now, that wasn't what I said.

OLD CAPTAIN: You callin' me a liar, boy?

CHARLIE: No, sir, but I just said that since it was the law of
the land—

OLD CAPTAIN: It is not the law of the land. No such a thing.

CHARLIE: I didn't think it would do any harm if they went to school together. That's all.

OLD CAPTAIN: I know. That's enough.

CHARLIE: Well, they do it up North.

OLD CAPTAIN: Why, this is down South. And down here they'll go to school together over me and Gitlow's dead body. Right, Git?

GITLOW: You the boss, boss.

CHARLIE: (*Still pressing the liberal point of view.*) But this is the law of the land.

OLD CAPTAIN: Never mind the law, boy. Look here. You like old Gitlow? Hm? You trust him? You always did, didn't you?

CHARLIE: Yes, sir.

OLD CAPTAIN: And Gitlow here—why, he would cut off his right arm for you if you was to ask him. Wouldn't you, Git?

GITLOW: You the boss, boss.

OLD CAPTAIN: Now, Gitlow—Gitlow ain't nothing if he ain't a Negro. Ain't you, Git?

GITLOW: Oh, two—three hundred percent I calculate.

OLD CAPTAIN: Now, if you really want to know what the Nigra thinks about this here integration and all the like of that, don't ask the Supreme Court. Ask Gitlow. Go ahead. Ask him.

CHARLIE: (*Knowing where this is going to lead.*) I don't need to ask him.

OLD CAPTAIN: Then I'll ask him. Raise your right hand, Git. (GITLOW *raises his right hand.*) Do you solemnly swear to tell the truth, the whole truth, nothing but the truth, so help you God?

GITLOW: I do.

OLD CAPTAIN: Gitlow, as God is your judge and maker, do you believe in your heart that God intended white folks and Nigra children to go to school together?

GITLOW: No, sir. I do not.

OLD CAPTAIN: Do you, so help you, God, think that white folks and black should mix and associate in street cars, buses and railway stations, in any way, shape, form or fashion?

GITLOW: Absolutely not.

OLD CAPTAIN: And is it not your considered opinion—God strike you dead if you lie—that all my Negroes are happy with things in the Southland just the way they are?

GITLOW: Indeed, I do.

OLD CAPTAIN: Do you think ary a single darkey on my place would ever think of changing a single thing about the South? And to hell with the Supreme Court, as God is your judge and maker?

GITLOW: As God is my judge and maker and you are my boss, I do not.

OLD CAPTAIN: (*Turns to* CHARLIE.) The voice of the Negro himself. What more proof do you want, boy?

CHARLIE: I don't care whose voice it is. It's still the law of the land and I intend to obey it.

OLD CAPTAIN: (*This is more than he can take.*) Get out of my place, boy. Get out of my place before I kill you out. I'll kill you. I'll kill you. (*He is so carried away that he has an apoplectic fit.*)

GITLOW: (*Seeing his source of economic security about to vanish.*) Easy. Easy, Captain. Easy. Easy. (OLD CAPTAIN *groans.* GITLOW *sets him in the rocking chair and goes to the shelf and picks up a few little bottles.*) Some aspirin, sir?

OLD CAPTAIN: Gitlow?

GITLOW: Yassir, Captain? Gitlow is here. Right here.

OLD CAPTAIN: Quick. Quick, old friend. My heart. It's my heart. Quick. A few passels, if you please. Of that old spiritual.

(GITLOW *begins to sing,* "Gone are the days when my heart was young and gay." OLD CAPTAIN *begins to sing with him. And it begins to ease him.*)

OLD CAPTAIN: I can't tell you, Gitlow, how much it eases the pain. (*Then he remembers the source of his troubles.*) Why can't he see what they doing to the Southland, Gitlow? Why can't he see it like you and me? If there is one responsibility you've got, boy, above all others, I said to him, it is these Nigras. Your Nigras, boy. Good, honest, hard-working cotton choppers, if you keep after them.

GITLOW: Yes, Lord.

OLD CAPTAIN: Something between you and them, boy, no Supreme Court in the world can understand. If it wasn't for me, they'd starve to death. What's gonna become of them, boy? After I'm gone.

GITLOW: (*Looks to heaven.*) That's a good question, Lawd. You answer.

OLD CAPTAIN: They belong to you, boy. To you. Every one of them. My old Confederate father told me on his deathbed, "Feed the Nigras first, after the horses and cattle." And I've done it every time.

(GITLOW *continues to sing.*)

OLD CAPTAIN: (*Being soothed back into the state of spiritual grace.*) Ah, Gitlow. Old friend. There is something absolutely sacred about that spiritual. I live for the day you will sing that thing over my grave.

GITLOW: Me, too, old Captain. Me, too.

I have tried in that scene to sketch broadly what I knew to be the psychological and personal truths of the lives of many people and what I knew were the economic and social foundations against which those lives had, necessarily, to be lived.

Each actor, each human being, you will notice, is caught up in a role, in a stereotype, and he behaves in accord with that stereotype. Now, I have tried to put in the stereotype what I know to be the truth of the situation out of which the stereotype grew in the first place, and I am happy to say that I think I have succeeded.

But these were not stereotypes that I created. They were created a long time ago on the plantations and then were taken by white-faced minstrels and emptied of their ammunition and protest and bite and made into something altogether different. I merely tried to bring them back where they belong.

But what is my larger intent? Is it merely to show you that we can laugh? That we look at the situations of life with more than angry eyes?

No. I have a specific reason for writing a play like *Purlie Victorious* in the manner in which it was written. To me, my intent was to have a handbook of consolation, information and struggle, which my people and their friends could use to understand, explain the situation in which they found themselves and point the way toward a possible solution.

This particular play was situated in the South, where the Negro is in economic servitude on a plantation. Now, another kind of play needs to be written about the Negro in Harlem, who is in a different kind of servitude, but nonetheless real and nonetheless disturbing and about which something must be done. That play could be done with humor, and it could point the same kind of moral and teach the same kind of lesson in the same kind of way. For it is equally ridiculous that people live in slums in this day and age of automation, when we have in our power all that it takes to create better housing and decent communities. It's ridiculous, in addition to everything else it is, that people are required to live in rat-infested decaying slum houses.

But to turn again to *Purlie Victorious*. One of the things that always intrigued me was the relationship between the iambic pentameter verse form, that came down to us through the King James version of the Bible and from Shakespeare, and the use of it, consciously and unconsciously, by the Negro ministers who wouldn't know an iambic pentameter from a hole in the ground. And yet they have adapted this particular structure to their use, and it seems to me that part of my literary job is to make conscious use of this technique.

Now, Purlie Victorious is a minister who has ordained himself. He is a stereotype of that Negro minister. If you ask him what time it is, he has to intone the answer. He can't give you a straight answer without intoning it. And Lulubelle Gussie Mae Jenkins is the updated version of Topsy, a little Negro girl who has never learned to value herself as a person and, therefore, wanders around, willy-nilly, wanting to be loved but not knowing exactly how to demand it, because she doesn't think that she's worthy of anybody's love, especially the white folks'.

But Purlie sees her and he sees something altogether different.

Listen to this, in which Purlie Victorious, our young minister, talks about Lulubelle Gussie Mae Jenkins. He is speaking to his sister, Missy.

PURLIE:
How wondrous are the daughters of my people,
Yet knoweth not the glories of themselves!
Where do you suppose I found her, Missy—
This Ibo prize—this Zulu Pearl—
This long lost lily of the black Mandingo—
Kikuyu maid, beneath whose brown embrace
Hot suns of Africa are burning still: where—where?
A drudge; a serving wench; a feudal fetch-pot:
A common scullion in the white man's kitchen.
Drowned is her youth in thankless southern dishpans;
Her beauty spilt for Dixiecratic pigs!
This brown-skinned grape! this wine of Negro vintage—
MISSY: (*Who has no tolerance for the iambic pentameter.*) I know all that, Purlie. But what's her name?

LULUBELLE: (*Looking at Missy.*) I don't think he likes my name so much. It's Lulubelle, Ma'am. Lulubelle Gussie Mae Jenkins.

MISSY: (*Gushing with motherly assurance.*) Lulubelle Gussie Mae Jenkins. My, that's nice.

PURLIE: Nice! It's an insult to the Negro people.

MISSY: Purlie. Behave yourself.

PURLIE: A previous condition of servitude, a badge of inferiority, and I refuse to have it in my organization. Change it.

MISSY: You want me to bosh your mouth for you?

PURLIE: Lulubelle. Gussie Mae. Jenkins. What does it mean in Swahili? Cheap labor.

MISSY: Swahili?

PURLIE: One of the thirteen silver tongues of Africa—Swahili, Washingo. . . . (*He names the thirteen tongues.*) A language of moons, of velvet drums, hot days, of rivers, red splashed and bird song bright. Black fingers in rice white at sunset red. Ten thousand Queens of Sheba.

MISSY: Just where did Purlie find you, honey?

LULUBELLE: It was in Dawson, Alabama, last Sunday, Aunt Missy. Right in the Junior Choir.

MISSY: The Junior Choir? My. My. My.

PURLIE: (*Carried away.*) Behold, I said, this dark and holy vessel, in whom should burn that golden nut brown joy which Negro womanhood was made to be.

Ten thousand queens. Ten thousand Queens of Sheba, Ethiopia, herself, in all her beauteous wonder. Come to restore the ancient thrones of Kush.

Parenthetically, this is iambic pentameter, if nothing else. I can attest to that. But what—what am I trying to do?

I am trying to correct a distorted image of Negro womanhood that has persisted in our culture down to this very day. I could, of course, do this clinically, by describing in ones and twos and yeses and nos, what I think happened, but I chose to do it in a poetic form, because it's more concise and it allows me to express what I actually feel and know by my senses and by my emotions to be true.

Because that is beautiful which has somewhere excited love, and this is the definition of beauty, and if a woman is loved, she is beautiful, and I must tell my women that they are beautiful, first, because I find them to be so, and, second, because they need it as an extension of my manhood and my confidence in myself.

I can say to them, "You are beautiful; you are not scrubbing the floors. That is not you. You are a queen. Ten thousand Queens of Sheba. Scrubbing floors on your knees. Get up. Walk. Talk. Be what you are. My queen. My woman, whom I will defend and fight for to the death." And this is what I tried to say in a comedy. In a farce, mind you, to Negro womanhood.

Now, you begin to get the reason for my choice of an outlandish form—because, unfortunately, I cannot express those same sentiments in realistic prose.

This is not to suggest that I have anything against realistic prose; it is merely that what I have to say creates for me a need of expression in another form, and I think that the reconstruction of the beauty of Negro womanhood will be the beginning of the emancipation of Negro manhood. This is the way I approach that particular problem.

Toward the end of the play, Purlie at last confronts his archenemy Old Captain Cotchipee, and he goes up the hill and gets the old man whipped and gets money from the old man—not by a direct confrontation—but when he comes down the hill his desire to impress his beloved gets the better of him, so he preaches a tremendous sermon of hell-fire and damnation in which he puts Old Captain on trial and consigns him to whip lashes. But this is all a sermon. It's all an extension of his need as a man to express himself, even violently. But it's done in a sermon.

Old Captain, of course, comes in during this sermonizing and there is Purlie talking to the man he has just gotten through burying as a result of his tremendous power.

After Old Captain comes in, his son, Charlie, is dragged in by the Deputy. Old Captain thinks Purlie has done some stealing, but the guilty culprit is really his own son. The Sheriff says:

SHERIFF: Southern justice strikes again.

OLD CAPTAIN: Oh, Charlie, Oh, no.

IDELLA: Charlie. My baby.

OLD CAPTAIN: Release him, you idiots. Release him at once. What have they done to you, my boy?

IDELLA: What have they done to you?

CHARLIE: (*After he is freed from his gag.*) Hello, Paw. Idella. Purlie.

OLD CAPTAIN: (*Talking to the servitors of law and order.*) I'll have your thick, stupid necks for this.

SHERIFF: It was you who gave the orders, sir.

OLD CAPTAIN: Not my son, you idiot.

DEPUTY: It was him broke into the commissary.

OLD CAPTAIN: What?

SHERIFF: It was him stole the five hundred dollars. He confessed.

OLD CAPTAIN: Steal? A Cotchipee? Sir, that is biologically impossible. Son, Charlie my boy. Tell them the truth. Tell them who stole the money. It was Purlie, wasn't it, boy?

[Old Captain makes the assumption which is automatic in his circumstances. Purlie had to steal because Purlie was a Negro.]

CHARLIE: Well, as a matter of fact, Pa, it was mostly me that broke in and took the money. I'd say—in fact, it was me.

OLD CAPTAIN: No.

CHARLIE: It was the only thing I could do to save your life, Pa.

OLD CAPTAIN: Save my life? Idell, he is delirious.

CHARLIE: When Purlie come up that hill after you last night, I seen him, and lucky for you I did. The look he had on his face against you was not a Christian thing to behold. It was terrible. I had to get him into that commissary right then and there and open that safe and pay him his inheritance. Even then I had to beg Purlie to spare your life.

OLD CAPTAIN: (*Turns to Purlie.*): You spare my life? Boy, how dare you? Charlie, my son, I know you never recovered from the shock of losing your mother almost before you were born, but don't you worry. It was Purlie who stole that money and I'm going to prove it. Gitlow, my old friend, arrest this boy. Gitlow, as Deputy for the colored, I order you to arrest this boy for stealing. (OLD CAPTAIN *takes out his pistol and puts* PURLIE *under arrest.*) (GITLOW, *in the meantime, has changed his mind. Instead of helping* OLD CAPTAIN, GITLOW *snatches the pistol out of his hand and casually points it in his direction and sings once again his old song, "Gone Are the Days," which by now has a brand-new meaning.*

OLD CAPTAIN (*amazed*): Er, er, stealing.

PURLIE: Well, I'm going to really give you something to arrest me for. (*He snatches the whip from* OLD CAPTAIN'*s hand and is getting ready to wreak justice with a bull whip for all the years of suffering.*)

OLD CAPTAIN: Have a care, boy. I'm still a white man.

PURLIE: Congratulations. Twenty years ago, Old Captain, I told you this bull whip was going to change hands one of these days.

MISSY: Purlie, wait.

PURLIE: Stay out of my struggle for power.

MISSY: You can't do wrong just because it's right.

[She picked that up from Martin Luther King.]

GITLOW: Never kick a man when he's down, except in self-defense.

LULUBELLE: No matter what—you always are and always will be the hero of Cotchipee Hill.

PURLIE: Am I?

LULUBELLE: Ten thousand Queens of Sheba.

PURLIE: I bow to the will of the Negro people. (*He decides not to beat* OLD CAPTAIN *because, really, not that he is angry at* OLD CAPTAIN, *but another change has taken place.*) But one thing, Old Captain. I am released of you. The entire Negro people is released of you. No more shouting Hallelujah every time you sneeze. Nor jumping jackass every time you whistle Dixie. Now we're going to love you, if you'll let us, and laugh as we leave, if you don't. We want our cut of the Constitution and we want it now. And not with no teaspoon, white folks. Throw it at us with a shovel.

I've tried to sketch for you, briefly, what the content of *Purlie Victorious* is, and why I chose to express my sentiments in the style and manner that I did. Satire, farce, slapstick, but, underneath it all, a true appreciation of some important aspects of life.

In the book of the play is my apologia—the reason I wrote the book in the first place—and it reads as follows:

"Our churches will say that segregation is immoral because it makes perfectly wonderful people, white and black, do immoral things. Our courts will say segregation is illegal because it makes perfectly wonderful people, white and black, do illegal things. And, finally, our theatre will say segregation is ridiculous because it makes perfectly wonderful people, white and black, do ridiculous things. That was the point I had in writing the play and that was the point I hope I have gotten across."

But we were talking about the wonderful world of law and order. If you'll recall, in the scene between Old Captain and Gitlow and Charlie, Old Captain was defending what was, to him, ordained by God. He believed that anyone who attempted to change the world of law and order, this peaceful ordained relationship between the two groups, was threatening the very foundations of civilization. Because Old Captain believed, as quite a few of us believe, white liberals and black liberals, that law and order is the essence of civilization. But this is not necessarily true. Justice is the essence of civilization, and when law and order is imposed upon a basically unjust situation there is bound to be a clash, sooner or later, between law and order—no matter how respectably law and order is presented and preserved—and those forces whose cry and need for justice makes them unable to maintain a real respect for law and order.

I do not say that I have been liberated from all respect for law and order. On the contrary, I realize what chaotic conditions could come about if the skeins of law and order were to vanish, if violence and brute force were the only resort to settling our disputes.

I know what would happen. I really want law and order, but I realize that law and order presuppose justice. When we speak of young people in the streets of Harlem as having no respect for policemen we must remember that the policemen had no respect for those young people in the first place. And when we describe young people as "punks" or "hoodlums"—words I hate to use; I don't use those kinds of words because it gives permission for a policeman to shoot a human being and forget that he is a human being—who loot, break stores open and rob jewelry and socks and underwear and garments—and we deplore these things —let us not forget the other looting that goes on silently and quietly, even on the level of the policeman, who, at a certain time every week, goes to a certain store or apartment and picks up a brown paper bag filled with money.

Who is the more successful of the looters, those unfortunate young people who were out on the streets of dismal cities on hot August nights or the policeman who has, for years, made it in a middle-class society by looting every day in the black community, by turning his back on dope, by turning his back on gambling and prostitution, by not insisting upon the preservation of even the most basic rights for the members of that community? I think one should know where the looting began in the first place.

If there is to be respect for law and order it must be based upon mutual understanding and a respect for those who are under the law, and order must be maintained for the benefit of all of those who are under the law.

We face a great crisis in our country today. We have been called upon by some of our leaders to refrain from demonstrations and protest because they might be construed as an attack upon law and order. We are told that attacks on law and order might give ammunition to the white backlash, and there are those who think that this is the greatest harm that could come to the cause of the Negro people.

Now this is a debatable point. I am forced to ask, if there is a white backlash, what is it lashing back from? Where was it all the time? Am I sure that those who are lashing back were not waiting for someone to come along and give them an excuse to lash back?

I am not so certain. I fear greatly that the Negro people, after mounting a magnificent struggle for their freedom, as they have done so often in the past, will be asked, once again, in the name of some vague larger freedom, in the name of the larger community, in the name of law and order, to halt their struggle and, once again, we'll come out of that struggle, as I personally came out of World War II, to find that we have lost the war that we thought we had won. And I would hope that those who ask for patience, those who ask us to wait will meet us with a real concrete program of action, with real remedies, so we will have something to be patient about, something to wait for, something that we can understand and appreciate and explain to ourselves and our children.

We wait now, at the darkest hour of the night, in order to make it peaceable and to prepare ourselves better for the action which is certain to come at dawn.

11. *Melvin B. Tolson:* An Interview

A Poet's Odyssey

TOLSON: This is M. B. Tolson speaking "From My Books." I relive again the last two lines of Keats's famous sonnet, "On Looking into Chapman's Homer," when I recall the exciting Christmas Eve of 1943. It brought me the good news that my first volume of poetry was to be published. I was forty-three years old. I had lived on hope, and, as Robert Lowell says, "Hope lives in doubt." I had kept the faith; but, sometimes, as Lowell says again, "Faith is trying to do without faith."

INTERVIEWER:* Since every man is a philosopher, what was your philosophy during those years?

TOLSON: I think my philosophy, at that time on the darkling plain, was summed up in a poem that appeared in my first book, *Rendezvous with America.* The poem was quoted in the *Saturday Review of Literature* when Stephen Vincent Benét reviewed the book. The lyric was called "The Poet." It brings back to me those salad days, like Cleopatra's memories of Caesar after she had fallen in love with Mark Antony.

INTERVIEWER: Do you mind reading the poem?

* The interviewer was M. W. King, professor of English, Lincoln University, Jefferson City, Mo.; the interview took place at Langston University, Langston, Oklahoma, March 10, 1965.

181

The Poet

The poet cheats us with humility.
Ignored by *Who's Who* among his peers
And *Job's News* also, yet this lapidary
Endures the wormwood of anonymous years:
He shapes and polishes chaos without a fee,
The bones of silence fat no pedigree.

His ego is not vain,
Stuffs not on caviar of smile and phrase.
He comes of nobler strain,
Is marrowed with racier ways:
The beggar Vanity feeds on the crumbs of praise.

He stands before the bar of pride,
Gives not a tinker's dam
For those who flatter or deride
His epic or epigram:
The potboy, not the connoisseur, toadies for a dram.

Peep through his judas-hole
And see the dogma of self at work,
The nerve and verve of soul
That in the sky-born lurk:
The eagle's heart abides not in the mole,
The poppy thrives not at the arctic pole.

A freebooter of lands and seas,
He plunders the dialects of the marketplace,
Thieves lexicons of Crown jewel discoveries,
Pillages the symbols and meccas of the race:
Of thefts the poet's magic leaves no trace.

An Ishmaelite,
He breaks the icons of the Old and New,
Devours your privacy like a parasite,
Parades the skeletons closeted with God and You:
The poet's lien exempts the Many nor the Few.

An anchoret,
He feeds on the raven's bread,

Candles worlds whose suns have set,
Leads Nature to the nuptial bed,
Bathes in pools that never mortals wet:
The poet unlocks the wilderness with an epithet.

A Champion of the People versus Kings—
His only martyrdom is poetry:
A hater of the hierarchy of things—
Freedom's need is his necessity.
The poet flings upon the winds blueprints of Springs:
A bright new world where he alone
    will know work's menacings!

INTERVIEWER: That was over twenty years ago. Would you make any changes now, either in content or in form?

TOLSON: "The only thing that does *not* change is the law that everything changes." The poet-protagonist in the lyric just quoted, Heraclitus, says the poet, any poet in the Greek sense, "shapes and polishes chaos without a fee." He is *poiētēs*—the maker. The word *art* comes from *ars* (to put together)—that is, human contrivance acquired through experience, study, observation, and knack. You know what Ezra Pound did to the original manuscript of T. S. Eliot's *The Waste Land*, bringing order out of chaos. The premise becomes more obvious when we examine the deletions and alterations in Poe's "To Helen" and the first four lines of Yeats's "Leda and the Swan."

INTERVIEWER: One cannot re-do a work of art.

TOLSON: Remember that Cocteau, who said that, *did* re-do his syntax and orthography. Of course, he believed in *Ex*piration instead of *In*spiration—a breathing out of the inner thing. I have tried both of those and also another, in the last fifty years —*Per*spiration. The work sheets of a poet may be very shocking to his starry-eyed admirers. Eliot has expressed for time and eternity the wrestling of Jacob the Poet with his Angel of Words —words that "slip, slide, perish, decay with imprecision, will not stay in place, will not stay still."

INTERVIEWER: Let us come back to this poem, "The Poet," written some twenty years ago. I am not the first to observe in it the striking metaphors that appear in your subsequent books, namely, *The Libretto for the Republic of Liberia* and *Harlem Gallery*. It seems to me that, like the Metaphysical Poets and the French Symbolists, you take an extraordinary delight in figures of speech—especially the metaphor.

TOLSON: I would add another group to the Metaphysicals and the Symbolists: the Negro people. Remember Karl Shapiro's words, in his Introduction to *Harlem Gallery*: "Tolson writes in Negro." I am no soothsayer talking to Virgil's dark Aeneas, before his descent into the lower world of the black ghetto; however, I hazard that Shapiro has pillaged my three books and discovered that I, as a black poet, have absorbed the Great Ideas of the Great White World, and interpreted them in the melting-pot idiom of my people. My roots are in Africa, Europe, and America.

INTERVIEWER: I understand that you have lived a varied and, in many instances, a hazardous life?

TOLSON: Tennyson's protagonist says in *Ulysses*, "Much have I seen and known . . ." And, again, "I am a part of all that I have met . . ."—as shoeshine boy, stevedore, soldier, janitor, packinghouse worker, cook on a railroad, waiter in beach-front hotels, boxer, actor, football coach, director of drama, lecturer for the NAACP, organizer of sharecroppers' unions, teacher, father of Ph.D.'s, poet laureate of a foreign country, painter, newspaper columnist, four-time mayor of a town, facer of mobs. I have made my way in the world since I was twelve years old.

INTERVIEWER: Am I to understand that your ideas and images, the blood and bone and sinews of your idiom, have come out of the lives you have led?

TOLSON: Yes. I like to go about places, hobnob with people, gather rich epithets and proverbs in churches and taverns, in cotton fields and dance halls, in streets and toilets. The rhythms and imagery exorcise white magic. The man in the ears is my jack-in-the-box. My catholicity of taste and interest takes in the Charleston and the ballet, Mr. Jelly Roll and Stravinsky, the Congolese sculptor and Phidias, the scop and the Classicist.

INTERVIEWER: I remember the *Partisan Review* observation that, although critics had identified your technique of juxtaposition with Eliot's *Waste Land* and Pound's *Cantos*, its kinship to the associative organization of the blues is obvious.

TOLSON: That acute observation surprised me, for, in the *Libretto*, to which it referred, there was no surface sign of the blues; however, I do write jazz ballads, but the *Libretto* is very literary, to say the least. I thought the Establishment, the Academy, would like it.

INTERVIEWER: Allen Tate said: "For the first time, it seems to me, a Negro poet has assimilated completely the full poetic language of his time and, by implication, the language of the Anglo-American poetic tradition." You "out-pounded Pound," according to Karl Shapiro.

TOLSON: Well, I did go to the Africans instead of the Chinese. Let me read some of those metaphysical African proverbs, in the Fifth Section of the *Libretto*. Gertrude Stein's judgment that the Negro suffers from Nothingness revealed her profound ignorance of African cultures.

> "*Seule de tous les continents*," the parrots
> chatter, "*l'Afrique n'a pas d'histoire!*"
> *Mon petit doigt me l'a dit:*
>
> "Africa is a rubber ball;
> the harder you dash it to the ground,
> the higher it will rise.
>
> "A lie betrays its mother tongue.
> The Eye said, 'Ear, the Belly is
> the foremost of the gods.'
>
> "Fear makes a gnarl a cobra's head.
> One finger cannot kill a louse.
> The seed waits for the lily.
>
> "No fence's legs are long enough.
> The lackey licks the guinea's boot
> till holes wear in the tongue.

"A camel on its knees solicits
the ass's load. Potbellies cook
no meals for empty maws.

"When skins are dry the flies go home.
Repentance is a peacock's tail.
The cock is yolk and feed.

"Three steps put man one step ahead.
The rich man's weights are not the poor
man's scales. To each his coole.

"A stinkbug should not peddle perfume.
The tide that ebbs will flow again.
The louse that bites is in

"the inner shirt. An open door
sees both inside and out. The saw
that severs the topmost limb

"comes from the ground. God saves the black
man's soul but not his buttocks from
the white man's lash. The mouse

"as artist paints a mouse that chases
a cat. The diplomat's lie is fat
at home and lean abroad.

"It is the grass that suffers when
two elephants fight. The white man solves
between white sheets his black

"problem. Where would the rich cream be
without skim milk? The eye can cross
the river in a flood.

"Law is a rotten tree; black man, rest
thy weight elsewhere, or like the goat
outrun the white man's stink!"

INTERVIEWER: I can see the reason for the remark by Melville Herskovits [then director of the Program of African Studies
at Northwestern University]: "More and more, African modes

of creative expression are receiving attention as we seek to understand the thinking of Africans."

TOLSON: Saul Bellow, who was a student under Herskovits, sent his hero, Henderson the Rain King, to Africa to find a cure for the sickness of his soul. "What's past is prologue." Last year Jacob Drachler, teacher and artist, published a book called *African Heritage*. As you probably know, Mr. Drachler was kind enough to use three sections of my *Libretto* as Prologue, Interlude and Epilogue of this odyssey in African culture.

INTERVIEWER: The Negro has been the victim of ethnic stereotypes. Since you are a realist, may we assume that you take your characters from life?

TOLSON: If the house in which I was born had been located on the other side of town, I would not write about the characters I write about. Selah! In the *Harlem Gallery* I have a few characters from my life, who are designated by name: Louis Armstrong, for example, about whom Hideho Heights, a fictitious character, has composed a poem; however, I cannot vouch for the truth of Hideho's interpretation of Satchmo. The analysis of a real person's tridimensionality is never complete—his biology, his sociology, his psychology. A person may be, from day to day, from mood to mood, from situation to situation, a different jack-in-the-box. So one never knows what figure will be revealed when the lid is removed. This apocalypse of a personality on its Isle of Patmos often shakes the beholder with disbelief. In consternation one may say, sometimes even in terror, "After all these years, I thought I knew him!" To change the metaphor, a person in his lifetime may wear not one mask, but many, which are revelations of his complex nature and nurture. There is no such thing as a flat character in life—stereotypes notwithstanding. The candid camera of intimacy always reveals a personality in the round. People are the fruits—bitter or sweet—of the Heraclitean law of change. A work of art is an illusion of life—a world of make-believe. Its person, place or thing never existed except in the alchemy of the imagination. Yet, I dare say, we understand the people of that other world better than we understand the people of this world. My knowledge of Aeneas, Bloom, Prufrock, Captain Ahab, Othello, and Herzog is more comprehensive than my knowledge of my immediate friends and enemies. Each of these real persons is a multiple jack-in-the-box. Clyde Griffiths in *An American Tragedy* has a clearer identity than Lee Oswald, in spite of the voluminous *Report* of the Warren Commission. In fact, I think Robert Penn Warren could have done a better job in motivation than did Justice Earl Warren. The only Julius Caesar I know is the one Shakespeare created, although I read Julius Caesar's *Commentaries on the Gallic Wars* in the original Latin when I was a fledgling student.

INTERVIEWER: Do you mean that the only persons we can know totally are the characters in fiction—never people in everyday life?

TOLSON: Yes. The abysses of the unconscious are beyond the soundings of even a Freud. Yet, delineations of characters in the poem, the novel, the drama can give us a better understanding of people in a society. In order to get a comprehension of persons and classes, my old professor of sociology used to make his students read and analyze contemporary novels. It was only then that the cold theories and dead statistics came alive. Before that, they were like the valley of dry bones in the family Bible. By the way, Victor Hugo called the Book of Job the world's greatest tragedy. The aristocratic conception of tragedy comes alive under the black and white magic of Marcel Proust's *Remembrance of Things Past*.

INTERVIEWER: It seems to me, however, that in the seven books that make up this masterpiece, Proust is in large part autobiographical and used models from his fashionable circle as characters.

TOLSON: But a flesh-and-blood model is still a model—not a character in a work of art. An artist is not a photographer, a case-historian. A da Vinci spends several years in the painting of Mona Lisa, constantly trying to capture "the fleeting manifestation of the secret soul of his attractive and winsome subject." A Hollywood cameraman would have done his job in seconds! That great Negro artist Aaron Douglass did a sketch of me. I wanted to use it on the cover of a book, *Harlem Gallery*, but Mrs. Tolson threw up her hands in horror! In a calmer moment, she said it did not look like me. Not at all! That was the very reason I liked it. It did not look like the Tolson that all his friends know when he is wearing one of his masks in society.

INTERVIEWER: I have seen the Douglass sketch, and I agree.

TOLSON: In the *Harlem Gallery* there is a certain Dr. Nkomo: he is an aged African and Africanist who works with The Curator. One day he commented on the difference between a character in life and a character in art.

His *idée fixe* ebbed and flowed across the dinner table:
"Absurd life shakes its ass's ears
in Cendrars'—not Nkomo's—stable.
If,
anchored like hooks of a hag-fish to sea weeds
and patient as a weaver in haute-lisse tapestry,
a Rivera or a Picasso,
with camel-hair alchemy,
paints in *fresco-buono*
the seven panels of a man's tridimensionality
in variforms and varicolors—
since virtue has no Kelvin scale,
since a mother breeds
no twins alike,
since no man is an escape running wild from
self-sown seeds—
then, no man
judged by his biosocial identity
in toto
can be
a Kiefekil or a Tartufe,
an Iscariot or an Iago."

INTERVIEWER: In other words, Dr. Nkomo contends that only in art can one, through the selectivity of the artist, know a character in the round.

TOLSON: Exactly. Socrates' "Know thyself" stated an impossibility. The Old Gadfly meant that one must know one's culture in order to know oneself. Of course, this complicates things, makes it more difficult to know oneself or any other self *in toto*. The artist is the only total *knower*. And yet, even his omniscience concerning a character he himself created may be questioned. Not even Shakespeare escapes this dilemma. Observe the centuries-old, many-angled interpretation of Hamlet, and the sound of fury of controversy through the ages.

INTERVIEWER: You said somewhere that a writer does not write in a vacuum, nor out of a vacuum.

TOLSON: "No man is an escape (that is, a plant) running wild from self-sown seeds." Those words are Dr. Nkomo's.

INTERVIEWER: This seems to make you an environmentalist instead of a hereditist.

TOLSON: How can a Negro be anything else, unless he becomes an "Uncle Tom" or an Iscariot? I repeat: A man is a jack-in-the-box. In International Law, the State is a personality. In the United Nations Assembly there are one hundred and fourteen personalities from every nationality, class, and creed. Every State, therefore, says to its fellow State, "What *manner* of man is this?"

INTERVIEWER: This is quite an intriguing observation. Then, you mean to say that the cause of so much misunderstanding in the United Nations is the fact that the States are in reality ethnic and national persons, with all their diversities?

TOLSON: Certainly. The personalities in the United Nations Assembly need a galaxy of novelists, poets and dramatists to help the diplomats interpret the motivations and actions of all these alien characters.

INTERVIEWER: You disagree with Plato, then, who would banish poets from his Republic.

TOLSON: Yes—although Plato was himself a poet and, therefore, would have banished himself from his own Republic. Perhaps poets are not Shelley's unacknowledged legislators; but,

anytime poets are persecuted and even exiled from their society,
a ruler has placed a seal on his own oblivion. Do you ask for
examples? Well, consider Hitler and Khrushchev. The poet is
not only the purifier of language, as Eliot insists, but the poet is
a sort of barometer in his society. The Latin word for *poet* is
"seer," a "prophet." The Hebrews seemed to have the same idea
in the Old Testament, as we see in the Psalms of David and the
Songs of Solomon. Through the eyes of Jouve's protagonist in
The Resurrection of the Dead, the poet foresaw "The White
Horse, the Red Horse, the Black Horse, and the fourth Horse,
which was the worst." Through the eyes of Markham's protagonist in "The Man with the Hoe," the poet foresaw the earth-
shaking revolutions that followed the First World War and the
Second. Walt Whitman was a seer; Hart Crane, also.

INTERVIEWER: Your name has been bracketed with both. In
the Second Section of the *Libretto*, you have The Good Gray
Bard in Timbuktu foresee the destruction of those great African
empires on the West Coast. Why not read that passage for us?

TOLSON:

The Good Gray Bard in Timbuktu chanted:
"Europe is an empty python in hiding grass!"

Lia! Lia! The river Wagadu, the river Bagana,
Became dusty metaphors where white ants ate canoes,
And the locust Portuguese raped the maiden crops,
And the sirocco Spaniard razed the city-states,
And the leopard Saracen bolted his scimitar into
The jugular vein of Timbuktu. *Dieu seul est grand!*

And now the hyenas whine among the barren bones
Of the seventeen sun sultans of Songhai,
And hooded cobras, hoodless mambas, hiss
In the gold caverns of Falémé and Bambuk,
And puff adders, hook scorpions, whisper
In the weedy corridors of Sankoré. *Lia! Lia!*

The Good Gray Bard chants no longer in Timbuktu:
"The maggots fat on yeas and nays of nut empires!"

INTERVIEWER: I think the two lines,

> And now the hyenas whine among the barren bones
> Of the seventeen sun sultans of Songhai . . .

are magnificent! We seldom see such alliteration and assonance combined. They are symphonic.

TOLSON: I like the synchronization of sight, sound and sense in poetry. I believe I have turned the trick in *Harlem Gallery*. I call these the S-Trinity of Parnassus.

INTERVIEWER: Let us return to the idea of the seer. In the last section of the *Libretto*, you predicted the rise of African republics. You foresaw, as Tennyson before you, a Parliament of Man.

TOLSON: That has been by-passed by many a critic. In 1947, when I was elected Poet Laureate of Liberia, there were only two independent black countries in Africa. Today there are thirty-three. It is a vision, right out of the Apocalypse.

INTERVIEWER: The *New York Times Book Review* said that your *Libretto* pictured not only the historic destiny of the Negro but that of the human race as a whole. A while ago we spoke of the musicality of your poetry. But there is another art that your work suggests to me.

TOLSON: Did you say, "Another art"?

INTERVIEWER: Yes, the art of painting. You have few rivals as a poet in imagistic ability—pictorial power.

TOLSON: You arouse painful memories of my salad days in Missouri. I started out as a boy artist. My father was a minister, poor as the proverbial church mouse in everything but books. Our table suffered because of this insatiable hunger. I was painting pictures when I was three or four years old—to the amazement of the elders. I guess I was pretty good at landscapes and seascapes, street scenes and faces. By the time I was ten, I was framing and peddling my pictures and making big money for a little black boy. I parted my hair in the middle, wore a flowing Windsor tie, and puzzled the elders with words. At twelve,

Claude, a lad who was a mulatto prodigy, and I had our own tent show. He could versify anything and invent mechanical toys. I painted the scenery in the tent show and played Caesar to Claude's Macduff. The kids paid their pennies to Claude, the business manager. Sometimes he came up short, because of his interest in girls. When I came across the word "satyr" in my reading, I knew Claude was a prodigy in another sense. Then one day in my twelfth year, at Slater, Missouri, fate entered my life, in strikingly Hardyesque fashion. The church and the parsonage were across from the old Chicago & Alton tracks. I remember that there was a big roundhouse in Slater at that time. One afternoon, a crack train had a "hot-box" across the road and down the embankment from our house. I was in the yard painting a picture. I don't know whether it was Coleridge's "Inspiration" or Cocteau's "Expiration." Anyway, I forgot about the stalled express train and was in the middle of my artwork when I felt, yes, sensed something behind me. I turned suddenly and there stood, leaning on the fence, the very artist I had seen in my art books. He had bushy hair and a magnificent beard. He wore a Byronic collar, an artist's jacket, and an artist's beret. His eyes fixed on mine, he said in Frenchified English, with a grandiloquent florish: "Marvelous! Marvelous! You must go to Paris with me! Where is your father?"

At last my dream had come true! As I ran to the house, I could see in my mind's eye the studios and cafés on the Left Bank of the Seine. I blurted out the good news. My mother stood aghast for a moment. Then she parted the curtains and took an angry look at the bizarre figure leaning on the fence. Suddenly she began to lock every door in the house. As she raced from room to room, she said not a word. That was just like my mother —part Negro and part Indian. After that boyhood tragedy, I never painted another picture. For days and days and days, I brooded. Now, my mother was always making up verses in her head. She was highly intelligent and imaginative, but had little formal education. Like my father, I was a bookworm. Later, much later, I began scribbling verses on tablets and scraps of paper. I repeated, over and over and over, Shakespeare's immortal words in Sonnet 50:

> Not marble, nor the gilded monuments
> Of princes, shall outlive this powerful rhyme.

So, at twelve, I decided to join the immortal poets in a future Paradise.

INTERVIEWER: Is your frustration as a painter the reason for the existence of the *Harlem Gallery*, with its verbal pictures?

TOLSON: A psychiatrist would have to answer that question. I do know that a picture gallery magnetizes me with a potent fascination. Sometimes I have a strange urge to seize a brush, but I have never succumbed to this inner pull of the ego.

INTERVIEWER: Then, what was the genesis of the *Harlem Gallery*—this human comedy with its Balzacian range of characters?

TOLSON: In 1930 I was a student, on a Rockefeller Fellowship, at Columbia University. I met there a dreamer from the University of Iowa, who was trying to put together a Proustian novel. The thesis for my degree was called "The Harlem Group of Negro Writers." As you know, the Twenties gave birth not only to the Lost Generation but to the Harlem Renaissance and the New Negro. Jazz became a fad—ancient African art, a novelty of the intelligentsia. I was in the middle of this literary revolution before the panic of 1929. One day I showed my young white friend a sonnet that I had written. It was titled "Harlem." He read it two or three times, and then said fretfully, "Melvin, Harlem is too big for a sonnet." That was the genesis of the *Harlem Gallery*.

INTERVIEWER: But that was in 1930—thirty-five years ago.

TOLSON: I know it seems like an age. The first finished manuscript of the *Harlem Gallery* was written in free verse. That was the fashion introduced by the Imagists. It contained 340 pages. The *Spoon River Anthology* of Edgar Lee Masters was my model. Browning's psychology in characterization stimulated me. I had deserted the great Romantics and Victorians. Walt Whitman's exuberance was in the marrow of my bones. I peddled the manuscript in the New York market. Nobody wanted it. The publishers and critics said for commercial reasons. A few of the poems appeared in V. F. Calverton's *Modern Quarterly*. Then I stashed the manuscript in my trunk for twenty years. At the end of that time I had read and absorbed the techniques of Eliot, Pound, Yeats, Baudelaire, Pasternak and, I believe, all the great Moderns. God only knows how many "little magazines" I studied, and how much textual analysis of the New Critics. To make a long story short, the new *Harlem Gallery* was completed, and now it is published.

INTERVIEWER: Who are some of the characters in this latest work of art?

TOLSON: To me they are living people, elbowing their varied ways through the chambers of my memory and imagination— lowbrows, middlebrows and highbrows like Dr. Nkomo, the Bantu expatriate and Africanist; Hideho Heights, the Redskin beatnik bard of Lenox Avenue in Harlem; Mr. Guy Delaporte III, the "big shot" of Bola Boa Enterprises, Inc.; Black Orchid, his blues-singing, striptease mistress of the Bamboo Kraal; Dr. Igor Shears, the stoic West Indian patron of the Harlem Symphony Orchestra; Snakehips Briskie, the forefather of the twisters; John Laugart, the half-blind artist from the Harlem catacombs; Kilroy, the president of Afro-American Freedom, Inc.; Black Diamond the kingpin of the Harlem rackets; the Zulu Club Wits, the Bohemian eggheads of the twilight zone of Afro-American culture.

INTERVIEWER: The *Harlem Gallery* is indeed a cosmopolitan gallery in the human comedy. What character is your favorite?

TOLSON: This is like asking a loving mother to name her favorite child, after she has suffered the doubts and fears of bringing her progeny into the world.

12.

Reflections on Richard Wright:
A Symposium on an Exiled Native Son*

MODERATOR: Herbert Hill
PARTICIPANTS: Horace Cayton, Arna Bontemps, Saunders Redding

HILL: I shall begin by asking Horace Cayton, who knew Richard Wright quite early in his career, to open the discussion. Mr. Cayton first met Dick Wright when Wright came up from the South to Chicago in the 1930's.

CAYTON: It is with great pleasure that I talk about Richard Wright. I think he had more influence on me than anyone else except Dr. Robert Park, who was a great sociologist and a ghost writer for Booker T. Washington. When Dick first came up from Mississippi, he was with his mother.

I was research assistant to the brilliant sociologist, Louis Wirth, at the University of Chicago, and one day there came a tapping on the door of his office. I opened the door and there was a short brown-skinned Negro, and I said, "Hello. What do you want?" He looked like an undergraduate, so I was perhaps

* This symposium took place August 8, 1964, during the seminar "The Negro Writer in the United States" at the Asilomar Conference Center, Monterey Peninsula, California. The seminar was held under the auspices of the University of California (Berkeley).

condescending in a polite fashion, and, of course, he *was* also colored. He said, "My name is Richard Wright. Mrs. Wirth made an appointment for me to see Dr. Wirth." That made me a little more respectful. I told him to come in. "Mrs. Wirth said that her husband might help me. I want to be a writer."

Well, I thought that was a little pretentious, a brown-skinned boy coming in to the University and saying he wanted to be a writer. Who didn't want to be a writer? But who could write? I began showing him the files in the office—I would not say that we were totally statistically oriented at the University at the time, but we were very empirical. We were going out studying every facet of the city. We were discovering the Italian district, the Polish district, the Irish district, the Negro community. We were studying the vast complex of human beings who make up that monster of Chicago, and Dick said, "You've got all of your facts pointed, pinned to the wall like a collector would pin butterflies." I looked at him. He was a poetic little Negro. I did not see Dick again for some years.

Later, I was running the Community Center on Chicago's South Side, and I got a wire from Dick asking me to meet his plane at the Chicago airport. *Life* magazine was doing a background story on Dick's *Native Son*, which was by then a bestseller, and Dick was coming out to Chicago to help them. Excited at the prospect of knowing and working with him, I was waiting at the airport long before the plane got in. The first thing Dick said when he got off the plane was, "Do you know of any Negro who has lost his job because of *Native Son*?"

For a week Dick was my guest. I found him one of the most interesting and fascinating people I had ever known. Born of poor parents in Mississippi, he had gone to a Seventh-day Adventist school where he had received something less than a high school education. When his mother brought the family to Chicago they went on relief (Mary Wirth was their social worker), and Dick joined the Communist party. While working on the Federal Writers' Project of the WPA, he wrote his first book,

Uncle Tom's Children. Then he moved to New York, where,
under incredibly difficult circumstances, he produced *Native
Son.* The book was an instantaneous success. It was chosen by
the Book-of-the-Month Club, and no other novel by a Negro
had ever received such widespread acclaim.

Dick was then in the process of breaking with the party and
was as bitter toward them as they were to him. He told me about
the party's reaction to *Native Son.* Since the book did not follow
the orthodox Marxist line on the Negro question, the Communists were quite hostile. Earl Browder, head of the American
Communist party, stated that he saw nothing wrong with *Native
Son,* but Dick did not accept this implied invitation to resume
his activities in the party. Instead, he published his famous re-
pudiation of the Communist party in the *Atlantic Monthly.**
From then on he devoted (and wasted) much of his creative
energy in fighting the Communists.

From this first visit on, Dick and I saw each other frequently
throughout the years. He would be my guest when he came to
Chicago, and I would stay with him, and his wife Ellen, on my
trips to New York.

Some years later Dick came to me and said, "I've come to
write a picture book" (which was later *12 Million Black
Voices*). "I want to get into your files. I want your sociological
concepts." I explained to him the idea of urban versus rural, of
culture versus civilization, or a sacred versus a secular society.
I talked about the differences between societies in which folkways determine the way of life and those which are governed by
contracts rather than promises, and from those two concepts
Dick came up with this lovely, poetic formulation: "The Lords
of the Land," who characterized the rural, sacred society in the
South, and "The Bosses of the Buildings," describing the forces
of the cold, impersonal cities of the North.

BONTEMPS: I knew Dick during the same period. I went to

* Richard Wright, "I Tried to Be a Communist." *Atlantic Monthly,* August,
1944.

Chicago in 1934. At that time Langston Hughes, who had returned from a year abroad in Russia, was living in Carmel, California. In his letters to me he wanted to know who the new writers were after things broke up in Harlem just two or three years earlier. I didn't know any, but Langston had heard about Richard Wright. When he came to Chicago, he said to me, "About this Richard Wright who's writing for *The Masses*, haven't you met him yet? Let's go out and find him." So we went to the phone book to see if there was any Wright in the neighborhood. We telephoned the only Wright we found in the vicinity of Thirty-fifth and State, and said, "Do you know anybody by the name of Richard Wright. He is a young fellow who is apparently a writer." And the voice replied, "Oh, you mean the numbers man."

Finally, we met up with Dick Wright at a party. The interesting thing I remember is that Dick was such a flaming young Communist at the time. He didn't have time to dance or anything like that, though he liked girls and was just at the dancing age, but he had great zeal only for his politics and his writing.

The next time I saw him he was in the Loop. I was standing on the corner waiting for a Cottage Grove streetcar, and he ran across the street and said, "Look here, I have just three cents. I need a nickel to get uptown." This was the Depression and such things were not unusual. I tried to give him a nickel, but he said, "No, I just want two cents." I gave him the two cents, and he said, "I'll bring it to you Friday night."

I thought he was joking, but sure enough, Friday night he came. He walked about two miles to our house and brought the two pennies. After that, every Friday night he used to come over. We'd have dinner and visit together and he'd begin reading us some of the stories he had written which later went into *Uncle Tom's Children*. This was his project then. I was closely associated with him through that book and through the writing of *Native Son* later on, when he moved to New York. Well, that's just a little sidelight out of the past.

REDDING: I remember Dick from the fall of '43. We met at the McCarter Theatre in Princeton, where Paul Robeson was doing *Othello*. During the course of the performance it was noticeable that Robeson was drooling, spitting really, in the faces of the other actors. At intermission we were standing in a group, Dick, his wife, my wife and several friends, and one of the men criticized Robeson for losing his saliva. Dick got very mad about this and said, "Don't you know that Othello was an epileptic, and that this is a conscious, a purposeful thing; this is part of the role." I don't think his anger had anything to do with the fact that he and Robeson were both Communists at the time.

CAYTON: That reminds me of another story about Dick and acting. When *Native Son* was produced on Broadway with Orson Wells, the show went broke and Dick, although he was tight with a buck, bought up fifty-one percent of that show and put it on the road. Canada Lee played Bigger Thomas, and Dick hated Canada's guts. God, he hated Canada. The reason he did was that he wanted to play Bigger Thomas himself. Hollywood offered him $75,000 and they were going to turn the characters white! As I say, Dick didn't throw away a buck, but he turned this down. He waited for years and went to the Argentine and he had some little blonde white girl play Mary Dalton, the girl Bigger Thomas kills. Ralph Ellison and I went to a preview in New York and there was Dick in the role. He must have been at least thirty-five years old, and what is Bigger, eighteen, nineteen? It was the damnedest thing you've ever seen.

REDDING: I once had an agent named Ann Watkins, and Dick didn't have an agent for his first book, but someone told him that he ought to have an agent and recommended Ann Watkins. Her office was then, and still is—though she herself has retired— at Park Avenue and about Thirty-eighth Street. People always entered her suite of offices from the side street, not from Park Avenue, a fact which Dick did not know. He was taking the manuscript of *Native Son* to her. He went into the Park Avenue entrance, which was the entrance to the plush apartments, and the elevator operator told him, "Boy, if you want to get up-stairs, you go to the freight elevator," and of course Dick left there in high dudgeon, and got another agent. Ann Watkins was so mad about it when she heard the story that she had the elevator operator fired. That stupid elevator operator's rudeness cost Ann Watkins in the neighborhood of $25,000.

I have just one more story. Dick owned a farm just outside Paris, and he bought that farm for one reason. He wanted to grow collard greens. He was quite frank about this. Raise some pigs and grow collard greens, because he had been brought up in the South on hog jowl and collard greens and he missed them in Paris. When his farm didn't do right and the greens wouldn't come up, he used to go to LeRoy's, a restaurant catering principally to homesick Negroes in Paris.

BONTEMPS: When I was in Paris, I was anxious to go to French restaurants, but Dick kept taking me over to LeRoy's. He thought I was just as anxious for hog maws as he was. I wasn't.

HILL: I think we should explain that LeRoy's is a little piece of Harlem's Lenox Avenue in Paris. Many of us who go to Paris find it, and Dick took me there, too. LeRoy was a Negro GI who decided he would never come back to the United States and he opened up this little place, on the Right Bank in the Montmartre section, and somehow he managed to get the collard greens, the chitterlings and the ribs and everything else. He was a gentleman whom one might describe as having a high visibility content. It was a kind of joke—you sat at the bar with LeRoy, who presided over the entire enterprise, and you said, "LeRoy, when are you going back?" And LeRoy would turn to the mirror and he'd say, pointing to his face, "When this turns white."

REDDING: I recall asking him when he was coming home, and he said, "Have they built a bridge?"

HILL: I think it would be appropriate here for Arna Bontemps to review, briefly, Richard Wright's work and influence, and perhaps to compare his early books with the ones he wrote later, in Paris.

BONTEMPS: Well, the Depression had sent the Harlem writers scurrying. But I think it more than compensated for this damage by the opportunities it provided for the next wave of literary expression by Negroes. Many old and defeated writers, like the poet Fenton Johnson, wandered into the Writers' Project of the WPA. But the Project also drew the likes of Richard Wright, Ralph Ellison, Frank Yerby, Roi Ottley, Willard Motley and several others, and began to create an environment in which the Negro writer could at last stretch himself to full length.

Wright ascended rapidly to a major rank among American writers, without respect to race. Here was a novelist, powerful enough to break out of the narrow compartment previously occupied by Negro writers. For one thing, he was acutely aware of his prison, and it did not take him long to conclude, as some critics have done, that the novel, as he knew it, was and had been, for generations, a projection of the value system of the dominant class in the society. He took advantage of the panic into which that society had been dumped by the Depression and allied himself with the critics of the basic assumptions of that society and demanded that it hear him out. The consensus of intelligent readers was that he made sense, that he handled his theme with authority, expressed himself with power and eloquence and was entitled to the place he had won in the literary life of the Depression years.

Uncle Tom's Children, the first of his major works, was a collection of four short novels, written while Dick was employed by the Illinois Writers' Project. It was drawn from memories of his Mississippi boyhood. The stories were almost unbearable evocations of cruel realities which the nation and the world had, in the past, been unable or unwilling to face. His purpose, his determination as a prose writer, was to force open closed eyes, to compel America to look at what it had done to the black peasantry in which he was born. Then, in a competition offered by a publisher for the best fiction book submitted by a writer on WPA in 1938, *Uncle Tom's Children*, later published by Harper's, was judged the winner. The critical reception was enthusiastic, and its author was launched. The same critics were more than surprised when *Native Son* appeared two years later and actually, as one of them said, "dwarfed its powerful predecessor." Wright had moved his setting to Chicago, and the narrative vigor, which had impressed readers of the four novellas, had been intensified by a deeper probing into the society that produced the characters. Dick had confirmed his own insight by a new acquaintance with sociology, thanks largely to Horace Cayton. It was seldom disputed, at the time, that Wright's was the most impressive literary talent yet produced by a Negro American. In the next ten years there were nearly fifty translations and foreign editions of his books. His writings became known around the world. His name was bracketed with America's foremost writers and interest in him as a personality began to spread.

Then came *Black Boy*, in 1945. Certainly *Black Boy* gave evidence that the range of its author, like his standing among his contemporaries, was still expanding.

At this point, Dick moved his family to Paris and promptly became one of the most celebrated American expatriates in Europe. He didn't publish another book for eight years, and when he did, *The Outsider*, which appeared in 1953, showed him bringing to bear on his writing the attitudes of French existentialism in the post-World War II era. But *The Outsider* was not quite up to Wright's earlier books. Something was missing. Perhaps it was anger. His new French friends had made the suffering, alienated author feel at home. He had given them his love in return. The anguish and outrage that made his early books memorable faded in the fiction he wrote in the remaining years of his life. *The Long Dream*, 1956, was a dim echo of the Mississippi stories he had written while he was still bleeding. *Savage Holiday*, 1954, was a paperback potboiler. Some of the stories collected in the volume *Eight Men*, in 1961, had been written years earlier and properly belong beside the novellas.

The Paris years, though they added nothing to Richard Wright's stature as a novelist, stimulated considerable writing of another kind, however. In 1941, between *Native Son* and *Black Boy*, Wright had written a deeply felt text for *12 Million Black Voices*, described as both a folk history of the Negro in the United States and a broad picture of the processes of Negro life. *Black Power*, in 1954, was also nonfiction, but in another vein. Wright's account of his sojourn in West Africa was effective personal journalism. The formula was repeated in *The Color Curtain*, 1956, based on the author's attendance at the Bandung Conference of 1955 on the Island of Java, and again, in *Pagan Spain*, in 1957. *White Man, Listen*, 1957, brought together a series of lectures delivered in Europe under impressive auspices between 1950 and 1956, years when any statement by Richard Wright was likely to be regarded as important in France, Italy, Germany, Scandinavia and elsewhere in the world.

REDDING: But about his going to Africa—I think his reaction was not a strange one, because I have heard others say the same thing. He went there seeking again a place, a home, and came away from there knowing that he had not found it.

One of the things that disturb me about James Baldwin is that, though someone has said that he has acknowledged his debt to Richard Wright, he has repudiated that debt, and this bothers me a great deal, because I think that there is no present writer, that is, no Negro writer now at work, who has not felt the tremendous influence of Dick Wright. Certainly, if we are in a renaissance, as it were, more or less similar, though very, very different from the renaissance of the Twenties, it is because of Richard Wright. Baldwin has never been fair to Dick Wright, or maybe to himself either.

HILL: In addition to the works that Arna Bontemps mentions, there is a very important essay by Wright on his own political development. Dick Wright evaluated his experiences in the Communist party and his decisive break with the Communists in a brilliant contribution to the volume entitled *The God That Failed.** In this essay Wright describes what it meant for him to be in the Communist party, and why it became absolutely necessary for his continued existence as an artist and also in terms of his personal integrity to completely break with the Communists. I think it is a moving and evocative work that tells much about Wright's development. It is also valuable for what it reveals about the internal life of the Communist party during that period, and I hope it is not going to be forgotten.

REDDING: And Dick did not, as so many did, lean in that direction simply because it was a fad. He was committed in a way that few Negroes of comparable stature were. It was an emotional, intellectual commitment of great force.

CAYTON: About the Paris years, I remember Saunders Redding's review of *The Outsider* in the *New York Times*. The review ended with the sentence, "Come back to us, Richard."

REDDING: Yes. Dick's first three books were far and away his best. Then he moved to Paris. His decision to go to France grew out of an experience he had in New York. He lived for a time in Brooklyn, 9 Lefferts Place. He wanted to get out, and he made several unsuccessful excursions into New York on an apartment hunt. Then he sent his wife to look. His wife was white, and she was successful. When they got ready to move in, and the landlord discovered who Dick was, the apartment was refused them. In the meantime, Dick had been invited to go to France, and he did.

Well, I think going to France, for Dick, was a mistake. I think it began that process of unraveling that showed up very early in *The Outsider*. He had been seduced by existentialism, and I am not at all sure he understood this. I think that this unraveling, this abandonment of the place where he lived, showed itself also when he began reaching out for other experiences—the whole business of going to Spain, of going to Ghana, the sudden new

* Edited by Richard Crossman (New York: Harper & Brothers, 1949).

ambition to become a jazz critic. I remember he had a most expensive phonograph in his Paris apartment, and he'd listen to jazz an awful lot. My feeling is that his abandonment of America did things to him, weakened him emotionally—he no longer had anything to write about. *Eight Men*, the book of short stories published after his death, seems to me to prove this conclusively. The stories that were written in France after he had left America do not begin to compare with the stories in that volume, which he wrote here in the States. You can see the difference, the emotional difference; the loss, too, of a kind of skill, particularly a skill in the handling of the language. He had forgotten the American idiom. I think France liberated him as a person, and this was good for him, but I don't think France was good for him as an artist.

As a matter of fact, I said this to Dick, because he was considerably disturbed by my review. When I saw him just six months before his death, I said to Dick and to his wife, "Dick, you ought to come back to the States. You've got no business in France." By this time, of course, he understood that.

HILL: I know that Dick was very disturbed by your review, Saunders. I saw him in the summer of 1959 in Paris and then again in the summer of 1960, and both times he spoke about your review. He said, "Well, I think that Redding is probably right. He might be right. On the other hand, so many other writers, white writers, have come to Paris—William Faulkner, James Joyce, Hemingway, Djuna Barnes, Morley Callaghan— they all came here for a time. They all worked here and studied. This enriched them. Why am I different? Is it because I'm a black writer? Am I not to be given the same opportunity as other writers to come to Paris, to come to Europe, to have the experience. Why is this denied me?"

Could we have a response to this point? Why was it all right for Joyce, an Irishman, or Hemingway, an American, to go to Paris, and why, as Dick asked, couldn't he go there also?

BONTEMPS: Well, I've thought about that a good bit, too. I

think he sort of hints at it in the Introduction that he wrote to his collection of short stories, *Eight Men*. There is a story there, and Dick tried to tell it in some detail. Dick did his best writing when he was unhappy, when he was angry, when he was under tremendous tension. And Paris relaxed his tension. It gave him a happy life, but he couldn't write when he was happy.

REDDING: Well, I think that he was alienated from the French culture in ways in which James Joyce and Morley Callaghan and the rest of them were not alienated. I think it had to do with the constant awareness of, well, here I am in Paris, and I can go any darned place I choose to go.

I don't think he ever understood this, really. He was very thoroughly American. James Joyce, Fitzgerald, the others—they were true cosmopolites, and Dick never was. Dick was a small-town boy—a small-town *Mississippi* boy—all of his days. The hog maw and the collard greens. He was fascinated by the existentialist group for a while, but he didn't really understand them.

BONTEMPS: He came to reject them later on, but certainly *The Outsider* was written under their influence; the plot of *The Outsider*, in fact, is almost identical with the plot of Sartre's *The Chips Are Down [Les Jeux sont faits]*.

Essentially, of course, Wright was and remained not only an American but a Southerner. Negroes have a special fondness for that old saw, "You can take the boy out of the country, but you can't take the country out of the boy." The saying could be paraphrased and pointed up in Dick's case. His deepest roots were in the folk culture of the bottom—not *deep* but *bottom*—South. The lore of that milieu was such an intimate part of his background he sometimes treated it as if it had all originated in his own family.

Take the story of the preacher who came to dinner, which he tells in *Black Boy*. This most familiar of Negro folk tales has stayed alive partly because it helped rural folk, one step removed from slavery, to laugh in the face of their own hunger pains and partly because minstrels and vaudeville comics have used it for laughs ever since. But to Dick the suffering expression of the child who saw the well-fed visiting preacher smacking his lips on the last of the chicken while the parents kept up their show of hospitality, the youngster knowing there was nothing more left for him, seemed so real, he apparently began to imagine himself the primary victim. I have occasionally asked others if they noticed this while reading *Black Boy*. Some had. None indicated having mentioned it to Dick, however, and I certainly had not.

As a product of the South, Wright represented that rare thing we sometimes call a clear case. I recall—thinking of clear cases —the story of John Chavis, of North Carolina, who came along early in the nineteenth century. Two planters in the Oxford area had argued over the question of whether or not Negroes were capable of being educated. The argument was a stand-off until they decided to back their opinions with cash. After the bet was made, there was the problem of finding a suitable case in point. It had to be a boy who was free, otherwise his master might not consent to this rather playful use of his time. It had to be a full-blooded Negro or the issue would remain clouded, no matter what the outcome. One party or the other might claim that blood-mixture altered the case. So it took them a bit of time before they eventually settled on John Chavis. They sent him to Princeton to see what he could do with the curriculum there, and I have often wondered who paid off after he wrote his dissertation in Latin and got his license as a Presbyterian minister.

In the sense of his being a product of the Southern environment and of the Negro's situation, Dick's case is equally clear. He was untouched by the redeeming influences sometimes present on campuses of colleges for Negroes in the region or even in the high schools. His was a total exposure to the callousness and cruelty of the closed society. Despite these odds, however, a delicate sensitivity survived. A major talent began to grow. There is a rumor that he wrote and published a story in a local

Negro newspaper before he left Mississippi. He had completed no more than eight grades—such as they were down there at that time. He was so much an American with very deep roots in Southern Negro life that the effort of the Sartre crowd to take Dick over was bound to fail. Although he was definitely influenced by them over a period of two or three years it was not lasting, it really didn't take.

REDDING: I quite agree. Existentialism is no philosophy that can be made to accommodate the reality of Negro life, and especially—as Dick Wright comprehended it—of Southern Negro life, which was Dick's major theme. Indeed, his only true theme. Involved Dick certainly was, but not as the existentialist is. Dick's involvement engaged his rational faculties rather more than the existentialist philosophy recommends or permits. The instinct to survive in a hostile world is always there, but Dick knew that the Negro's will to survive was sometimes weak, and he knew, moreover—because the reality of Southern Negro life had taught him well—that survival for the Negro depended upon his not making choices, upon his ability to adapt to choices (the will of others) made for him. He hated this, and it certainly had much to do with his expatriating himself; but it had something to do, too, with his early commitment to Communism, and it had everything to do with his later breaking with it—a break which represented at the time an important choice he could make without greatly threatening his existence.

CAYTON: Let me mention another aspect of Dick that I think may be of interest to young writers. Dick, you know, did not have a college education. He didn't have a high school education. In some respects, the first drafts of his manuscripts looked almost illiterate. He had to rewrite his books many times. He rewrote *Native Son*, to my knowledge, at least four or five times. This was his method, and I trace it directly to his lack of formal education.

HILL: But this is true of many writers. There are many who have to write and rewrite—despite a college education.

CAYTON: But Dick's problem was rather elementary, a problem of grammar and the like. He was a genuine self-made man.

The only person I ever met who was a better conversationalist —no, as good a conversationalist—was Sinclair Lewis. Dick read constantly and in many fields. I remember one time I had a tooth pulled in Brooklyn. I was in great pain. Dick and I were riding on the subway, and he was describing the nerve endings. I was quite angry. "How did you learn all this stuff?" I asked. And he said, "Well, there's nothing to it. I just picked up a book on dentistry." Then he went on to describe the functions of the body, and I said, "What are you, a doctor?" He said, "Anybody can be a doctor. You just sit down and read." And I said, "Please shut up, you son of a bitch."

Dick talked to me over a period of five years about a story he was working on. It was about a Negro woman who was just about light enough to pass, but she had bleaching cream, which was supposed to lighten her. This bleaching cream had arsenic in it, so that while she was committing sociological suicide, she was also committing biological suicide. And this is no exaggeration, because Dick actually bought up any number of bleaching creams and had chemical analyses made of them.

But more directly, Dick could move with any group. I remember the time I took him to Marshall Field III, at that time the fifth most wealthy man in the world. He'd just come into a vast sum of money and Dick and I were going to start a magazine. We entered Field's office, and I must say I was a little intimidated. The man had about $500 million. I looked for Dick to be a little intimidated, too, but here was this little Mississippi Negro sitting up, talking to this white gentleman, and he wasn't intimidated at all.

REDDING: No, I suppose he never was intimidated by people, but certain attitudes could intimidate him. Or maybe that's not the right word. The word is probably daunt, or dismay.

A little while back, Arna, in describing the Wright of the 1930's, used the expression "flaming," I believe it was, and said that he—Dick—was "burning with zeal and enthusiasm"; and this touches upon something I'd like to say, something pertinent. I'll be brief.

Dick did burn with zeal, but it was always zeal for a cause, and he tended to be chary and a little suspicious of people who didn't. He never seemed to believe that an attitude toward life that was lighted by the faintest ray of hedonism could be quite real and legitimate. The gods within him were saturnine, gloomy, of tragic bent. It was not that Dick wanted people to be enthusiastic over his cause of the moment, but he could only just tolerate the indifferent and dispassionate, the come-day, go-day people one is likely to meet in any sizable company, and the people to whom life is a joke, and not an ironic joke. Look at the groups toward which he gravitated in Paris: the existentialist; the black nationalist of *Présence Africaine* (which, incidentally, he helped to found); African exiles; Algerian expatriates, and the like— people with causes which he could embrace with whatever enthusiasm was left over from his own cause. A cause he never realized he abandoned—or did it abandon him?—the moment he took up residence in France.

I think it was this quality of his zeal that accounts for the almost total absence of humor in his books. Dick did not recognize the truly comic. The closest he could come to it was irony. But look at his irony, for heaven's sake! It seldom causes laughter. It is grim, sardonic, and never mirthful. It is the irony of the discovery that the rat-infested, vermin-ridden flat in which Bigger Thomas lives is the property of the "helpful," "generous," "sympathetic" Mr. Dalton. It is the irony of the young Negro who must disguise himself (unman himself!) as a woman in order to get a job, and of his being so completely mistaken for what he is *not* that the consequences, which might have been merely comical, are inevitable. There is instance after instance in Dick's work.

This humorlessness was Dick's greatest flaw, both as an artist and as a man. His best books, like those of Dostoevski and

Tolstoi, who were also writers without humor, compensate for it with their moral integrity, their social force, their truth; and I would like to think that *Native Son*, *Black Boy* and a half dozen of Dick's short stories will stand the test of time. But I also think that we're all agreed that less than ten years after the death of the man is too soon for final judgments of the still-living artist.

Biographical Notes

HERBERT HILL

Herbert Hill is labor secretary of the National Association for the Advancement of Colored People and a member of the faculty of the New School for Social Research. He is editor of *Soon, One Morning: New Writing by American Negroes*, author of *The Citizen's Guide to De-segregation: A Study of Social and Legal Change in American Society* (with Jack Greenberg); and assistant editor of *Employment, Race and Poverty* (with Arthur M. Ross). His essays on Negro history, literature and civil rights have been included in several studies, and he is the author of *No Harvest for the Reaper: The Story of the Migratory Agricultural Worker in the United States*. His articles have appeared in *Commentary, Buffalo Law Review, Annals of the American Academy of Political and Social Science, New Statesman, Phylon, The New Leader, Midstream, Journal of Negro Education, African Forum* and other publications. He has lectured extensively on race and culture at schools and universities in the United States, England and Europe. He has frequently presented testimony before congressional committees and was director of the seminar on the Negro Writer in the United States at the University of California (Berkeley).

ROBERT BONE

Robert Bone, a native of New Haven, Connecticut, received his bachelor's and master's degrees from Yale University and did extensive research in Negro writing at Howard University before receiving his doctorate in American Studies from Yale. He is the author of *The Negro Novel in America* (1958), and his articles have appeared in the *Bulletin of the College Language Association, Dissent, Tri-Quarterly* and other

213

publications. He has taught at Yale and at the University of California at Los Angeles, and is now a member of the faculty of Teachers College, Columbia University.

ARNA BONTEMPS

Arna Bontemps is a poet, playwright, novelist, and editor, and has served for twenty-one years as director of the Fisk University Library. His first novel, *God Sends Sunday*, was published in 1931. Among his numerous other books are *Story of the Negro, Black Thunder, Drums at Dusk, Lonesome Boy, 100 Years of Negro Freedom, Frederick Douglass: Slave Fighter and Freeman*. He collaborated with Langston Hughes as editor on *The Poetry of the Negro: 1746 to 1946* and *The Book of Negro Folklore* and with Jack Conroy on *They Seek a City*. His plays have been performed in New York, Cleveland and Amsterdam. He is also the editor of the recently published anthology, *American Negro Poetry*. He is a popular lecturer at schools, colleges and library conferences across the country and his poetry and prose have been frequently anthologized in England, Europe and in the United States. His work appears in *The Book of American Negro Poetry* (edited by James Weldon Johnson, 1931), *The Negro Caravan* (edited by Brown, Davis and Lee, 1941), *The Anthology of American Negro Literature* (edited by Sylvester C. Watkins, 1944), and *Beyond the Blues* (edited by Rosey E. Poole, 1962).

HORACE CAYTON

Horace R. Cayton was born in Seattle, Washington. He is co-author, with George S. Mitchell, of *Black Workers and the New Unions*, published in 1935, and collaborated with St. Clair Drake on the sociological study *Black Metropolis*, which won the Anisfield-Wolf Award in 1945. His autobiography, *Long Old Road*, was published in 1965. After graduation from the University of Washington, Mr. Cayton pursued graduate studies at the University of Chicago and New York University, and took special training at the Institute for Psychoanalysis in psychiatry and the social sciences. He has held teaching positions at Fisk University, the College of the City of New York, the University of Chicago, and the University of California (Berkeley). He has been a Fellow of the Julius Rosenwald Fund; research assistant in Studies in Geriatric Mental Illness at the Langley Porter Clinic, San Francisco; special assistant to the Commissioner of Welfare, New York City; and director of the Parkway Community House, Chicago. His essays on mental illness, race relations, and religion have been included in several important studies and his articles have appeared in *The New Republic, The Nation, Holiday*, and *The American Journal of Sociology*. For more than twenty years his weekly column appeared in the Pittsburgh *Courier*.

OSSIE DAVIS

Ossie Davis is the author of the successful Broadway stage play *Purlie Victorious*, in which he played the lead. He has performed in several major motion pictures as well as in the theatre and television, and writes plays, short stories and poetry. He was born in a small town near Waycross, Georgia, and attended Howard University in Washington, D.C. He is a frequent lecturer at universities and schools where he is well known for his readings and dramatic presentations. His poetry has appeared in the anthology *Soon, One Morning: New Writing by American Negroes.*

NAT HENTOFF

Nat Hentoff, a former editor of *Downbeat* magazine, is well-known as a leading authority on jazz and folk music. He is a staff writer for *The New Yorker* magazine. Mr. Hentoff has written extensively on civil rights conflicts, and is the author of *Peace Agitator: The Story of A. J. Muste* and *The Jazz Life*, and co-editor of *Hear Me Talkin' to Ya* (1955), *The Jazz Makers* (1957) and *Jazz* (1959). His study of the Negro protest movement, *The New Equality*, was published in 1964, and his articles on a wide range of subjects have appeared in *The Reporter, The Village Voice* and other publications. He is a member of the faculty of the New School for Social Research.

M. CARL HOLMAN

M. Carl Holman, formerly professor of English at Clark College, Atlanta, Georgia, and editor of a weekly newspaper, the Atlanta *Inquirer*, is now an official of the United States Commission on Civil Rights in Washington, D.C. He holds graduate degrees from the University of Chicago and Yale University. In 1944 he received the University of Chicago's John Billings Fiske Poetry Prize. His prose and poetry have appeared in *Phylon, Verse*, and other publications, and in several collections including *Poetry of the Negro* (edited by Langston Hughes and Arna Bontemps, 1949) and *Soon, One Morning: New Writing by American Negroes.*

LEROI JONES

LeRoi Jones spent his early years in Newark, New Jersey, studied at Howard University and did graduate work at Columbia University and the New School for Social Research. His published works include two volumes of poetry, *Preface to a Twenty Volume Suicide Note* (1961) and *The Dead Lecturer* (1964) and a nonfiction work, *Blues People: Negro Music in White America* (1963). He is also the author of several controversial plays that have been produced in New York and Los Angeles. These include *The Dutchman, The Toilet* and *The Slave.* Mr. Jones lectures frequently and teaches modern poetry and creative writing at the New School for Social Research. His fiction and essays have appeared in the *Saturday Review*, *The Nation*, *Downbeat*, *Yugen*, *Metronome*, *Poetry* and the *Evergreen Review*. His poetry and prose were included in the anthology *Soon, One Morning: New Writing by American Negroes*.

ALBERT MURRAY

Albert Murray was born in Nokomis, Alabama, and spent his early youth in Mobile. A major in the United States Air Force (retired), he was associate professor of air science in the Air Force ROTC. He has studied at Tuskegee Institute, the University of Michigan, the University of Chicago, University of Paris, Northwestern University and New York University. He has taught literature at Tuskegee Institute, and his essays, criticism and short stories have appeared in *New World Writing*, *Life*, *The New Leader*, and other publications. He has also served as a consultant on cultural history to The National Education Television and the United States Information Agency.

SAUNDERS REDDING

Saunders Redding, whose early youth was spent in Wilmington, Delaware, was graduated from Brown University and holds the Ph.B, M.A. and Litt.D. He is currently Johnson Professor of Literature and Creative Writing at Hampton Institute, Hampton, Virginia. He was a visiting professor of English at Brown University (1949–1950), where he conducted a graduate course on the Negro in American Literature, and during the academic year of 1964 was a Fellow in the Humanities Program at Duke University and the University of North Carolina. Professor Redding was a Rosenfeld Lecturer at Grinnell College, Iowa, and a visiting lecturer at Bowdoin College, Maine; Hamilton College, New York; Lake Forest College, Illinois. His first book, *To Make a Poet Black*, was published in 1939 and was followed by *No Day of Triumph*, which won the Mayflower Award for distinguished writing in 1944. His other books are a novel, *Stranger and Alone* (1950), *They Came in Chains* (1950), *On Being Negro in America* (1951), *An American in India* (1955) and *The Lonesome Road* (1958). His articles, reviews and essays have appeared in many publications and his critical study of Richard Wright was published in *Soon, One Morning: New Writing by American Negroes*.

HARVEY SWADOS

Harvey Swados, a member of the faculty of Sarah Lawrence College, is the author of many novels, essays and short stories. Among his books are *Out Went the Candle*, *On the Line*, *False Coin*, *Nights in the Garden of Brooklyn*, *A Radical's America* and *The Will*. Six of his stories have appeared in *Best American Short Story* annuals. He has received fellowships from the *Hudson Review* and the Guggenheim Foundation. His essay "The Myth of the Happy Worker" received the Sidney Hillman award in 1958. He has written for *Esquire, Atlantic Monthly, Partisan Review, New World Writing* and many other publications.

M. B. TOLSON

Melvin Beaunorus Tolson was born February 6, 1900, in Moberly, Missouri, and was educated at Fisk, Lincoln and Columbia Universities. He was granted fellowships in literature by the Omega Psi Phi fraternity and the Rockefeller Foundation. His long poem "Dark Symphony" won the National Poetry Contest conducted by the American Negro Exposition in Chicago, and in 1952, *Poetry* magazine gave him the Bess Hokin Award. He is the author of several plays including *The Moses of Beale Street, Southern Front* and dramatizations of George Schuyler's novel *Black No More* and Walter White's *Fire in the Flint*. Of his verse drama, *Libretto for the Republic of Liberia*, published in 1953, Allen Tate stated in his Preface: "For the first time, it seems to me, a Negro poet has assimilated completely the full poetic language of his time and, by implication, the language of the Anglo-American poetic tradition." Mr. Tolson's volume of poetry *Harlem Gallery* was published in 1965. An Introduction by Karl Shapiro said: "A great poet has been living in our midst for decades and is almost totally unknown, even by the literati, even by poets. Can this be possible in the age of criticism and of publication unlimited? It is not only possible but highly probable." His poetry has appeared in the *Atlantic Monthly, Poetry, The Prairie Schooner*, and in several collections, including *The Negro Caravan* (edited by Brown, Davis, Lee, 1941). His long epic poem "Abraham Lincoln of Rock Spring Farm" appeared in *Soon, One Morning: New Writing by American Negroes*. He is presently Avalon Professor of the Humanities, Tuskegee Institute, Tuskegee, Alabama.

Index

Format by Sidney Feinberg
Set in Linotype Times Roman
Composed, printed and bound by The Haddon Craftsmen, Inc.
HARPER & ROW, PUBLISHERS, INCORPORATED